DO YOU KNOW . . .

- The gay decade of greatest financial opportunity?
- The worst gay-specific investment traps?
- The best way to get cash from life insurance—while alive?
- How to turn your 30s into a wealth-building decade?
- The financially sane way to give to gay causes?
- How gay couples can legally save big tax dollars?
- Why gay consumer activism doesn't pay?
- How art, artifacts, and other collectibles let gays "spend to save"?
- The financial argument for safe sex?
- The best financial timing for children?
- Ways to ward off the financial fallout from AIDS?
- The one jointly held asset that causes the most trouble when a gay couple splits up?
- The nine essential insurance actions gays must take?
- The worst financial decade in gay life?
- Two gay health hazards as costly as AIDS?

The answers are here,
in this readable guide to financial success
that no gay or lesbian can afford to overlook. . . .

Gay Money

Gay Money

▼ ▼ ▼ ▼ ▼

Your Personal Guide to Same-Sex Strategies for Financial Security, Strength, and Success

▲ ▲ ▲ ▲ ▲

Per Larson

A DELL TRADE PAPERBACK

A DELL TRADE PAPERBACK

Published by
Dell Publishing
a division of
Bantam Doubleday Dell Publishing Group, Inc.
1540 Broadway
New York, New York 10036

Library of Congress Cataloging in Publication Data
Larson, Per.
   Gay money : your personal guide to same-sex strategies for financial
security, strength, and success / Per Larson.
      p.   cm.
   ISBN 0-440-50799-5
   1. Gay men—Finance, Personal. 2. Lesbians—Finance, Personal.
   I. Title.
   HG179.L268   1997
   332.024'0664—dc21   97-570
                                                            CIP

Printed in the United States of America

Published simultaneously in Canada

June 1997

10 9 8 7 6 5 4 3 2 1

BVG

Dedication

To celebrate and commemorate ten years
of growth, commitment, and love
with Colin Daniel Patrick O'Connell

▼▼▼▼▼

Contents

▲▲▲▲▲

PART II ▶ Gay Issues

▼▼▼▼▼▼▼

The Gay Balance Sheet: Same Sex, Different Dollars

▲▲▲▲▲▲▲

Being gay all begins when it dawns on us that we're different. Likewise, our money issues become gay when it dawns on us that we're different financially. In both cases it was there all the time—but once activated there's no turning back.

Being gay is both an asset and a liability. Since most of us don't have children, for example, we're immediately hundreds of thousands of dollars ahead; yet by not being able to marry, the Hawaiian courts tell us, we're penalized in over 450 ways. At the workplace being gay is a plus in some jobs, and gets us fired in others; some of us may survive vile workplace situations in the closet, while others miss golden opportunities.

So the picture is mixed—and varies from person to person because we're so different from each other. What's clear for all of us is that our money matters differ from the 90% majority. The bottom-line question is how they differ—and how we can tailor the general and straight field of personal finance to our gay needs and wants.

Consider me a translator. For five years I've worked with over five hundred gay individuals and couples to figure out what parts of personal financial advice apply to us—and what parts are mostly for the marrieds with children.

I started because one year—as for many of us—it seemed like all my friends died. I'd stopped my own venture-capital-backed business and started problem-solving the financial fallout we face when we're sick.

After fifteen years of consulting with corporations, this consulting with individuals gradually taught me how our personal finances differ from the 90%. There's nothing like life-threatening illness to reveal the bottom line.

The common thread in all this is that our financial circumstances can be strikingly different from the mainstream. We have access to assets that few marrieds dream possible. But we are also hampered by economic obstacles that no one else in society faces—obstacles deliberately placed in our path.

Sometimes our ways of dealing with those obstacles result in liabilities that add financial injury to society's insult. That many of us survive this gauntlet and go on to thrive is nothing less than an economic miracle.

This is not a book about who we are. That part's self-defined—if we think we're gay, we're gay. This is about what we do financially, and how well we do economically. The financial part is personal, the economic part is communal. To be successful as gays we need to make both parts work—so this is a book of personal agendas and agendas for us as groups.

We're everywhere. We draw from every group conceivable. We're largely invisible, but it's not who we are that makes us money as much as what we do with what we have. Our behavior and our circumstances count in finance, not our characteristics.

As you read ahead, keep in mind that whether or not any one thing applies to you today isn't as important as whether it tends to be true about us—and thus could be true for you tomorrow. In gay finance, expectations and possibilities can be as important as realities. Because of how we might respond to them, for example, some potential threats can actually cost us more unexpressed than they would if their actual damage were carried out—such as unseen costs of closet living, which can be far higher than the most threatening results of coming out.

As we identify the differences that are unique to us, we'll explore how they can result in profits or losses to us as gay people. We'll focus on how to either capitalize on our assets or compensate for our liabilities. We'll identify the best times to act—and what to do if we've missed our windows of opportunity.

My job is to plant ideas and nurture understanding. Your job is to take the best and chuck the rest.

► Assets: the Gay Economic Advantage

Overall, being gay can be an economic plus.

Gay assets can produce the best results when combined. I call this combination our "gay advantage."

The assets below are possible for all of us. Because they'll appear in all chapters, we'll pay some detailed attention here as to how they work.

- *High discretionary income,* early in life.
- *Entrepreneurial characteristics,* with few children to compete with career.
- *Networking,* offering access to all levels of society.
- *Mobility, adaptability, and portability* that the nineties seem to require.

Here's how these assets can be put to work:

High Discretionary Income

With few kids or dependent spouses to support, a higher proportion of our incomes is left over after necessities as a surplus. And with no expensive weddings or ruinous divorces to worry about, the continuity of these regular surpluses is further protected.

I call this discretionary income advantage our "gay money." The problem is that many gays treat this money the same way as they do "mad money"—and spend it on consumer wants, rather than save it to invest toward future needs. Gay money gives us a choice. We can use our discretionary dollars as ballots for consumer servitude, or apply them toward a form of financial self-government that guarantees that our unique needs, wants, values, and purposes will be well served throughout our lives.

This is no call for simple living: this is an invitation to self-sufficiency. Often our ideas of what we want out of life can be pretty complex and very unique. The question is: Do we buy into the American dream as advertised for the 90%, or do we make our gay fantasies concrete realities?

What obscures this choice day-to-day is that the 90% tends to spend what they earn. Our discretionary income gives us the luxury of creating a different pattern of spending. Saving is a form of spending—on future needs. Some of us buy present value, others buy future value; some value immediate comfort, others value future comfort. No matter how little you think you make, you can convert today's discretionary dollars into tomorrow's wealth. Spending whose value depreciates quickly over time gradually impoverishes us; investment that increases our discretionary dollars enriches us. Our choice is that simple.

Pouring gay money into aggressive investment, with the benefit of compounded and often tax-deferred returns, increases our future freedom. Here are some other examples of investment action:

- Spending on skills to increase our career potential can multiply our wealth-making capability.

- Having a financial cushion can permit us to dare ask for that raise, to make that suggestion at work, to change jobs more frequently, to hold out for a better offer, and to deal better with discrimination.

- Hiring professional help to unravel our hang-ups, to deal with unknown situations, and to tap into expert knowledge can increase our potential.

These investments all take cash to start. But for the most part they're a one-time investment. They then can take over and generate returns year after year.

The key is choice. Even if we choose to have children, and incur those expenses that reduce our discretionary advantages, we can choose to have them later when our investment base is in place. By saving for future comforts and toys we can sustain higher levels of satisfaction. By disconnecting from consumer society we can have control over our time through financial independence much sooner. By recycling ourselves through retraining, career changes, and personal growth we also keep ourselves more active, current, connected, and challenged.

Entrepreneurial Characteristics

Without the distractions faced by the family-tracked 90% we have the option of making career a priority. If we're abused for who we *are,* it somehow makes sense for us to focus on what we *do.*

Many of the skills we cultivate for survival work well at the workplace—where, when we produce, we earn respect. Our loyalty to employers, peers, and clients is proverbial, if we're rewarded and appreciated. From the playground to the classroom to the workplace we're used to having to prove ourselves. Even when we do this to excess, and many do, we can still be ideal employees and star performers.

We don't need to be assigned high-profile supervisory positions; our street smarts and outsider perspective make us excellent corporate intrapreneurs. In history we have a long tradition of being the Merlins, Richelieus, Leonardos, working well behind the scenes in staff or consulting positions. Today, we often have the attitudes required of successful entrepreneurs simply because we're used to being out on our own, not expecting much support, thinking on our feet, adapting to what we encounter, monitoring our environment carefully.

Consider the good that can come out of what we once felt to be bad. Knocked around, we often acquire a wise wariness. Not segregated, we gain valuable breadth of experience. We're skilled at selling ourselves and overcoming buyer resistance. Years of walking a social tightrope often give us experience in modern getting-to-yes (rather than confrontational) negotiating techniques. We have an outsider's perspective; we're good trend spotters; we can be less prone to rely on assumptions, and more likely to question dominant views. In the 1990s these are personal survival skills of high professional value.

Networking

We are oriented toward the larger world, not the closed family.

- Because we're freed of the tradition of pressure-cooker families, we base our lives on friendship and extended families instead.

- Because of our limited numbers and our invisibility we become skilled at searching each other out.

- Because we draw our members from across the social spectrum, we have access to virtually everywhere.

- Because we tend to prefer partners who are different from us in a wide variety of ways—age, income, ethnic background, social class, style, personality—we regularly cross all kinds of social barriers, gaining an intimate knowledge of society's various sectors.

- Because we're used to frequently monitoring our environment for friend and foe alike, we spot new developments, handle complex information, and make good forecasts.

All of this gives us a wide array of contacts, and the skills to put them to our professional use. True, we do have some strikes against us—closed old-boy networks, the liability of lacking a spouse for professional functions, the suspicion that sometimes greets our silence about gay issues. Even with the risk of being labeled and treated as oddballs in a society that ultimately values mainstream behavior, we can turn our social skills and circles into professional networks of considerable promise.

Mobility, Portability, and Adaptability

Few kids and no marital ties encourage a mobility that suits the project-oriented 1990s corporate nomads required today. Being judged by skills and results already is a safe haven for us; being able to go where the company wants is a further plus.

Some overall circumstances tend to support this role for us.

- The married 90% with kids increasingly want secure jobs and minimal family moves.

- The practice of awarding jobs, promotions, and raises to workers because they're raising a family is less common.

- Fewer companies are stressing nonportable pensions; most have shifted over to tax-deferred savings plans where at least our contributions can move with us.

- Companies that take the lead in benefits have started introducing even portable disability policies.

- Cafeteria-style benefit plans that enable individuals to choose benefits specific to their needs are increasingly common.

- Companies are converting more and more employees to independent contractor status, offering packages generous enough to pay for individual coverage.

When exercised appropriately, our mobility can bring us independence—from America's increasingly standardized society, from stereotypical values and official pronouncements, from circumstances too rigid to be tailored to our own needs. We are already experienced at reinventing ourselves. Under the best of circumstances, we can create our own lifestyle, can evolve from gay-proud to gay-natural, and come to value the freedom to be ourselves as an ultimate goal in gay life. I know it—because I've helped gay and lesbian clients achieve that goal every day.

These four assets can also make us super planners—a key to financial success. We've got surpluses to plan with as well as an uninterrupted time horizon to plan in. We can be our own bosses if that suits us—giving us many more options. We're so connected that implementing our plans is that much more assured. And we're mobile, adaptable, and free to pick among those options.

But first we must address the roadblocks in our way.

▶ Circumstance Counts: External Liabilities

We face formidable public enemies. The rocks on our road were deliberately put there. These are not barriers that can be overcome by simply education or hard work. We may now have characters on sitcoms, but these harsh realities remain. They're our not-so-gay context:

- Illegality
- Marriage barriers
- Discrimination
- Violence

These are no mere personal inconveniences. They are true financial leg-irons—manacles that constantly change their form and application. Their very existence costs us dearly, every day of our lives, causing regular damage even if they flare up only now and then. They are simply always there—as are the fear, anxiety, and anger that they cause. As a result we overcompensate, overmonitor, and overreact—and become our own jailers through self-doubt, self-hate, and self-destruction.

It's not all bad news; these challenges can prompt great inner strength, ingenuity, and skill. Experience acquired in fighting one challenge gives clues in how to resolve the rest. But whatever our reaction, their financial impact is profound.

▶ Public Enemy #1: *Illegality*

Little need be said here; the facts are all too eloquent. The 1996 legislation against gay marriage testifies that hate against us is alive and kicking—and that we are considered expendable. In twenty-four states and the District of Columbia our lovemaking is still a crime. In forty-one states we face legal job discrimination. Only two hundred out of tens of thousands of local governments have adopted gay rights laws. That employers should afford us equal rights was never seriously considered prior to the 1990s. The U.S. military has spent close to one half billion dollars in the past ten years in their effort to root us out. Bills are continually presented to Congress and state legislatures to take rights away from us. Our elected officials refuse even to pass legislation that would but tally the crimes against us. The bottom line in politics is grim.

Short-Term Costs and Savings

In principle the solution is clear: activism. In practice we need to first untangle the twisted financial tactics we've built around these rocks in our road. Before we finally blast that rock to nothingness, we've got to first undo many economic work-around arrangements that we put into place.

The short-term effects of illegality are all related to notions of what we can and cannot do—and what others can or cannot do to us, including denying us our basic rights. Whatever our enemies may actually do to us, our own reactions to this lack of legal existence can end up damaging our finances far more. Those reactions can range from false bravado to very real self-betrayal.

Some in our community have embraced the status of outlaw, believing it confers special rights on them because the law itself is unjust. This outlaw status can be simply a rich source of sexual excitement, it can be taken as an excuse to reject the other laws of society, and it can give rise to fantasies of escaping the laws of economics. Being outside the law can easily translate into being above the law. And that can mean disconnecting from the economic system through a willingness to evade taxes, declare bankruptcy, barter, work off the books, and play welfare systems for what they're worth. These strategies rarely work in the long term and those who follow them can be economically sidelined in ways that even society's antigay laws could not achieve. We need to beware of the seduction of this financially dark side of gay life.

Far more in our community suffer from varying degrees of taking their illegal status to heart—and viewing their homosexuality as an indication of an immoral condition or handicap to be overcome. Those who have inherited this mind-set tend to follow two basic economic strategies: the closet and the good little gay. The closet strategy is one of minimization—shutting down, holding back, and hiding among the average—hardly the mentality that's going to win jobs, earn raises, get promotions, or launch new ventures.

The good-little-gay approach is one of maximization—overreacting, pushing too hard, overmonitoring. No wonder we wear ourselves out and become our own tough act to follow.

Long-Term Assets and Liabilities

The economics of the industrial age created us as a people—giving us time, money, and a place to be ourselves. It also translated preindustrial notions of our immorality into contemporary notions of our illness and illegality. One result: The law must define who we are before it can define what we can and cannot do. This suggests that our best economic strategies are those through which we define our own different identities.

There are different ways to do this:

- Defining who we are not—no longer buying into the system; stepping off the treadmill, getting out of the heterosexual hamster cage, unhooking ourselves from family-oriented consumer society, shedding mass-marketed identities.

- Defining who we are as individuals—recognizing that we'll always be the spice in humanity's life, that we'll always be a minority within minorities, and that this outsider position gives us not only a freedom to be who we wish but also a leverage point for taking best advantage of the economic system.

- Defining who we are as a community—translating our anger into financial independence, networking, and fighting first at the workplace.

Simply put, our best interim response to illegality is to work outside and inside the system as it best suits us—never assuming that the system on its own will take care of us or automatically meet our needs.

► Public Enemy #2: *Marriage Barriers*

Our most glaring legal barrier is lack of marriage. The economic issues of marriage have been all but lost in political discussion. One point worth remembering is that the only marriage that counts is the one done by the state—the same one that is dissolved by divorce courts. We would do well to weigh whether we want to embrace marriage as a package deal; it simply may not suit the many different kinds of relationships we've invented without it.

Short-Term Costs and Savings

At first glance, this "loss" actually generates major short-term savings: the obvious costs of church weddings and divorce.

Wedding extravaganzas often carry five- to six-figure price tags. It's almost as if straight society were saying, "You'd better stay together and have kids—see how much money we're spending!?" Even if we could have a full-scale church production, our outsider status and same-sex mentality perhaps immunize us from this economic insanity of straight culture. Most of our commitment ceremonies seem more like inexpensive Quaker rituals than society's gala affairs—even though some in our ranks would probably jump at the chance to show the 90% what a Real Wedding looks like.

The true poison pill in the marriage cup is the likelihood of divorce. Let's face it: divorce is designed to protect the formerly weaker sex—and children—and we rarely have either of those. We don't have to offset the income inequities of a man compared to a woman—nor those of a nonworking spouse. Divorce also *seems* designed more than a little for revenge. We have little basis economically to participate in the straight custom of tearing each other apart financially just because they've broken up. When marriage does come, let's pray it doesn't offer us the dubious legacy of divorce case-law—since it's based on experience that is rarely comparable to our own. If that's part of our marriage gain, will our divorces be in fact *more* expensive? We will then truly have got the booby prize.

Taxwise, be glad we are not able to take advantage of joint filing tax rates: to be advantageous they require having a non-working spouse—and who among us wants *that*? Otherwise they penalize married straights more than $1000 per year.

We have one other immediate tax advantage over marrieds. As a couple we can *each* take the once-in-a-lifetime exclusion of $125,000 after age fifty-five on any capital gains we generate when selling a house—while marrieds can take only one. Although this looks great in principle, it can become a problem when we want to buy real estate jointly—especially if we each have a previous home.

Finally, we do have a small tax advantage in IRAs, since we can count only our own incomes in determining eligibility; marrieds may earn too much as a couple. Still, marrieds are able to make spousal contributions, and we aren't.

It's good to remember that it's not wise to build a life around tax advantages, since they can be changed with the stroke of a pen. Any pluses from joint filing, IRAs, and capital gains could soon be taken from us with proposed federal legislation.

Long-Term Assets and Liabilities

The long-term costs of marriage exclusion turn out to be much higher than these short-term savings. Consider that the 1995 report of the Hawaiian Commission on Sexual Orientation and the Law identified more than 450 rights and benefits denied gay people when it recommended that the state legislature grant full marriage rights.

At the top of the list are estate taxes. Since these are all tied up not only with matrimony but with patrimony—inheritance by blood relations—it is not likely that we'll see much change here no matter what marriages we arrange. Gays can now shelter only $.6 million from federal estate tax (versus $1.2 million for marrieds). And, unlike marrieds, we face limits on how much tax-free money we can give our partners under protection of that shelter—only $10,000 a year.

Sharing real estate without a legally sanctioned union brings its own challenges, often requiring awkward and risky measures that still leave room for unexpected and disastrous tax penalties. For example, we have to pay the costs of new mortgages if we transfer ownership of a house to our partner. And we may be prevented from naming partners as beneficiaries on our life insurance policies unless we can show an "insurable interest" such as owning real estate or a business together.

Our surviving partners are not entitled to a spouse's Social Security benefits. Often we can't inherit a partner's pension. As a result we have to save and invest more than marrieds, as if single, even when both have retirement plans.

Even when retirement benefits can be inherited, we're forced to liquidate them within five years—and pay the whopping tax bill. But a married spouse can defer distribution until retirement.

Our wills are often contested. Even if the basis is spurious, the very act of contesting itself triggers a compromise settlement because of the legal costs to defend it. Our lawyers need to be experienced to overcome these and other challenges created by our partnerships' outside-the-law status. That can mean that they—and our wills—are usually more expensive. If we're short on funds, or if we're penny-wise/pound-foolish, we may end up with poor legal documents that require much greater expense to administer in probate and court fees. If we resort to software packages written for marrieds-with-children, watch out!

We have few automatic legal protections for spouses in case of disease, death, disability, or divorce. Few come to me with contractual safeguards in place for these big *D*'s.

Gays need a battery of powers and proxies if they do not wish their biological families or the state to run their lives in time of crisis. Marrieds can always fall back on their legal status as husband and wife. Every day you can be sure that at least one of us is turned away and banned from caring for a loved one because documents are missing or poorly executed. These documents are financial powers—and their lack can result in heavy financial loss.

Even if this patchwork approach is complete, it never quite equals the seamless status of legal marriage. Gays always seem to suffer the all-too-common situations where hateful birth families seize power, empty bank accounts, steal furnishings, throw away personal effects, and steal or damage or destroy a partner's belongings—all with the blessing of the law.

Our psychological, social, and political costs as couples are real too. We have few formal, widespread, time-honored, legal, or automatic supports for our relationships. Social stereotypes within and without our community undermine our coupleships. Our relationships take time and work—and money. And our money issues, undefined by tradition or laws, are tinderboxes waiting for an incident.

Few companies recognize our partners in genuine, everyday ways. And having social pariahs as partners hurts networking, where spouses count. The fact that we get almost no spousal discounts and are often challenged in hotel arrangements is just the tip of the iceberg that is the daily assault on the integrity of our relationships—requiring us to divert time, energy, attention, and often money, from some other need.

When we seek counseling we find there are few therapists qualified and experienced with our inventive relationships. Our professional advisors often leave our partners out of their considerations unless we carefully educate, structure, and monitor their work.

We often don't let our advisors know the specifics of how our relationships work financially—and we ourselves often plan only as individuals, without reference to our companions. Over one third of my callers are amazed at my suggestion that their partner be part of our planning meeting. Our flexible relationships may change more—and more often—and we forget to tell our therapists, CPAs, lawyers, brokers, and financial advisors that this important facet of our financial lives is different.

Because of all these complications, we are a people for whom it is written, "An ounce of planning is worth a pound of problem solving."

► Public Enemy #3: *Discrimination*

Discrimination is a financial fact of gay life. It's *everywhere:* in public places, in families, in housing, and at work. According to one corporate diversity report, one quarter of America's workers are still afraid of catching AIDS from a homosexual at the workplace, and two thirds of CEOs are afraid to put a gay or lesbian on a management committee. The problem is real; between 16% and 44% of gay men and lesbians in twenty major cities have experienced some form of workplace harassment or discrimination related to their sexual orientation, according to a National Gay and Lesbian Task Force study.

Unlike other minorities we face *legalized* discrimination. Apart from a few municipalities and exceptional employers, gays have virtually no protection under the law against discrimination. We can be refused rentals, bounced from clubs, denied access or facilities while traveling—all for no apparent reason, thanks to our invisibility. We're regularly and with open righteousness refused spousal discounts in commerce and in travel—even in the case of the death of a partner. Even the Vatican describes us as physically and mentally ill and endorses discrimination in housing, the military, teaching, and adoption.

The same discrimination against blacks, Hispanics, Asians, disabled, Native Americans, and women would bring thousands into the streets. With us that kind of support is hardly conceivable—that's how deep the discrimination against us runs.

When we do get legislation passed, counterlegislation often quickly arises to publicly and proudly question whether we deserve protection. That comes pretty close to our being declared fair game. Rarely are we seen as human beings who deserve equal rights.

Short-Term Costs and Savings

We would do well to remember that the childhood rhyme—
"Sticks and stones may break my bones but words will never hurt
me . . ."—left something out: ". . . unless I set my life up to
escape them." Time and again, the avoidance tactics we set up so
as not to trigger discrimination in the first place can bring their
own costs. Begun in our youth, when discriminatory pressures are
at their greatest, the trek to the closet can lead to long-term lost-
opportunity costs, greater than its promised short-term safety.

The economic irony about discrimination is that incidents of
it can help us—if we use the incidents to address their economic
root causes and to mobilize help in doing so. Action to fight
discrimination is empowering economically. And liberating these
incidents from the silence of the closet can help us prove that our
obstacles are real—something few of the other minority groups,
or the majority, are willing to admit. One of the biggest problems
in getting corporations to act is lack of a smoking gun. Incidents
give us the evidence we need to plead and process our case.

Long-Term Assets and Liabilities

An economic rule of discrimination is that subtle, small doses
are even more damaging than isolated incidents. This is its Chi-
nese water-torture nature—to which many of us succumb over
time. The sad truth is that many of us expire as full persons not
with a bang but a whimper.

Incidents can hide a more faceless enemy—lavender ceilings.
Lesbians face double ceilings—as women and as gays. What's
pernicious about this is that we often invest ourselves 110% in
corporations who give us little encouragement, only to find out
we're the first to go just at the point when we have the most to
lose. This is a real problem that highlights the limits of ever being
able to forge our careers totally as employees.

Publicized incidents of employment discrimination can be a
blessing in disguise—waking us up and rallying allies around us.
Our best workplace argument thus far in gay liberation has been

that discrimination is bad for business—that it creates labor unrest and poor public relations. In business we're often the canary in the mine; if companies treat us well, they'll treat any minority well.

Incidents can serve as reminders that we'll always be underdogs economically, with all the advantages and disadvantages that this entails. As a small percentage dispersed over all the small groupings of society, we need guerrilla tactics coupled with "I'm #2" strategies. They make us alert and skilled—they make us planners whether we want to be or not.

▶ Public Enemy #4: *Violence*

Gays generate such strong feelings in society that we are still hunted, beaten, and killed for sport. This is a deep financial issue because it influences our economic willingness to take risks and to be assertive—qualities that are rewarded in our economy. Therefore we need to know facts. Consider these findings of a recent survey of Vancouver gays and lesbians: one third of the respondents reported incidents of physical assault; another third reported repeated threats of assault; 90% reported verbal abuse; a majority revealed that they believe they will face discrimination on the job; and almost 20% fear murder itself.

Clearly, the economic havoc of this mind-set extends beyond the direct repercussions of each act of violence. The constant threat, and the broader culture's apparent indifference to our plight, can breed negative attitudes that define the way we see the world—whether or not we are victims of violence ourselves.

Short-Term Costs and Savings

Violence terrifies. Its outbreaks disrupt the continuity our financial strategies require. And our fear disconnects us from our focus, corrupts our financial thinking, and threatens the stability and continuity that are our financial assets. What truly matters is that we realize the repercussions of violence on our economic stability and readiness. What we need are control measures such as more extensive hate-crime reporting. The enemies we fear loom far greater in our imagination than the weak bigots who magnify their power by hiding in the dark. Far better to smoke them out so that we can get on with our financial lives. As Abraham Maslow pointed out, we must assure our security before we can aspire to actualize our potential.

Long-Term Assets and Liabilities

The most prevalent cost of violence lies in our reaction to it. With the future uncertain, we can justify spending on today's comfort now at the expense of our ability to finance tomorrow's needs later. In the face of violence gay life has always discounted the future. But planning for the future is central to our economic success. Only by saving and investing those early surpluses of discretionary dollars can we compensate for our lack of economic advantage in later years. If we're overwhelmed by feelings that we need creature comfort now—because we fear there may be no later years—the violence done to our quality of life will be far more widespread and thorough than anything our enemies can do.

▶ Liabilities II: Our Private Pitfalls

Our public enemies would be enough to tax any financial plan; recognizing that is a major first step in securing our gay money. If our enemies were purely external, our job would be much easier. The true threat to our personal finances, however, lies within—in how we cope with the circumstances of being gay. Often the by-products of short-term thinking, overreactions, or misunderstandings of how gay life works financially, our private traps can be as economically dangerous. Unmanaged, they can undo any advantage our assets might have given us. Understood, worked around, and transformed, these same liabilities can add to—not detract from—our balance sheets.

Here are those pitfalls with references to the chapters in which we'll explore them fully:

- Health risks, especially those that we refuse to acknowledge—see "Financial Health and Illness."
- Closeted living—see "Gay Careers"
- Ignorance about the tax system—see "Gays and Taxes"
- Passive financial relationships—see "Gay Coupleship"
- Ghetto living—see "The 20s"
- Spending too much of our discretionary income—see "The 20s"
- Hoarding and hyperliquidity—see "The 30s"
- Working for others, especially in later years—see "The 40s"
- Underinsurance—see "The 50s"
- Underfunding retirement—see "The 60s"
- Leaving this life without a trace—see "The 70s"

These private pitfalls can derail us economically more directly and more dramatically than any external force. Only by walking through the minefield they represent, neutralizing them, and in some cases mobilizing their power for our good, can we experience the full benefits of the gay economic advantage. It can be done; think of it as your opportunity to see what kind of job you can do within. Maximizing our assets, minimizing our liabilities, and harnessing both to create the financial base from which we can then realize our personal and professional goals—this is what *Gay Money* is all about.

► Financial Success: Our Differing Bottom Lines

Financial success, like sex, is in the mind of the beholder. You can, and *must*, define it for yourself. If we measure gay lives by the short-term rulers issued to the 90%, we're failures—with no marriages or kids to show for our lives. Let them have their rulers. We can measure our lives by the longer time horizons possible with the gay lifestyle, and see the great opportunities to achieve and appreciate what we need and want out of life. Some of these achievements may even turn out to be useful to other gays, and even the community at large.

We can grow extended families and friendship circles of enduring value.

We can nurture corporate families that will live long after we pass away.

We can create products, services, systems, inventions, organizations, public and private works, simply because we have the resources, the independence, the networking, the mobility, and the time to do so.

These achievements describe the much broader landscape of gay personal finance—a field of action bounded not by family but embracing an entire community. What's the difference? One summertime *New York Times* Op-Ed-page editorial commenting on a surge of grasshoppers said, "Somehow, out in the West, the grasshopper seems more sympathetic than he does in the old fable. The difference between an ant and a grasshopper is that a grasshopper believes in posterity while an ant prefers immediate family. What is so improvident about grazing all summer, waiting for wings, and then laying eggs that will hatch when winter has come and gone and you have come and gone with it?" It's not such a bad life to leave to posterity what we create rather than only pass on our genetic legacy.

The time is right to pursue the goal of gay financial freedom. "Now" is always the right time for action when you've been waiting centuries. Still, several factors make the 90s perhaps the best opportunity so far in history to improve the economic lot of gays. Decades of gay activism are bearing fruit. Legal actions are beginning to have the effect of a siege machine, ranging from the

Supreme Court defeat of Colorado's antigay agenda to the Hawaiian court's endorsement of gay marriage. Efforts at the workplace are sweeping geographic locales, industries, and the *Fortune* 1,000. And we've broken most media barriers.

As you'll see, my experience with my clients points toward a very distinct gay money map. The aim is to survive our teen years, escape our 20s temptations, use our 30s to build careers, investments, and relationships, launch our own interests in our 40s, lay up our harvest in our 50s, provide for our not-so-advantaged later years by our 60s, and be able to make a contribution to our community by our 70s. However closely you decide to follow this route, it pays to keep in mind these fundamental principles:

- Our money matters can be drastically different from the 90%, presenting both unique advantages and handicaps;
- Our advantages can be capitalized on and made into assets;
- Our handicaps can be hedged by preventive action and often turned to our advantage;
- Our differences can be orchestrated into a financial foundation for success.

Because we are often so different from the mainstream, only some of the traditional tools of personal finance may apply. We need to tailor any assessment, analysis, and advice we get about our finances. Our real opportunities will be tapped only if we write our own scripts, mark our own maps, and define wealth our own way. By the time we're through, we'll have an action list of ways to harness those advantages and a map with which to avoid those handicaps—and find the route by which an increasing number of men and women are forging a financially successful gay life.

▶ A Gay Economics Crib Sheet ◀

Since so much is at stake, let's look at a quick summary of what makes or breaks us financially in gay life—a sort of gay economics crib sheet.

Windows of Opportunity

Gay money is best leveraged earlier than later. The gay advantage is best honed in the 20s and applied in the 30s; it's under attack in the 40s and disappears in the 50s. Our youngest gays are in the most danger from uncontrollable external forces; as we get older our personal pitfalls should have our focus.

Hot Spots

The corporation can be our protector and launching board—but may downsize us as we get older. Corporations value what we gays have—mobility, networking, an outsider perspective, independence. Yet problems of being a gay peg in a straight hole can develop from the 40s onward unless we choose our corporate allies wisely. It pays to choose companies that encourage coming out—and to come out as soon as possible. It may pay better to be the boss than to be the employee.

Money Machines

Intrapreneurship and entrepreneurship may offer the best protection against eventual invisible discrimination. They may also break the limit that hours places on wages. Even work with corporations may be best structured through independent arrangements and priced on value rather than hours. Many by-products of gay experience are useful at the workplace.

Leaks and Drains

We are a people, not a market. There is little gay pride in purchasing power—and our extra spendable income can be used against us. We can't buy gay identity by buying gay. Our greatest danger instead is spending our discretionary income advantage on current psychological needs. The ghetto can socialize us but it can also be an economic tomb.

Shaky Ground

We should always remember our lack of legal protections. We can never have enough agreements covering assets, sharing arrangements, acquisitions, delegated powers, and our final wishes.

Alligators

Add to our obvious enemies the boss who just loves the closeted workaholic who's out to prove gays aren't wimps at the workplace. Also less than lovely is the salesman who plays the gay affinity card to the hilt. Find out if the workplace practices of the gay-friendly corporation match their marketplace advertising.

Coming Out

Invisibility is a two-edged sword useful only as a defense, not to advance a career. An essential, eventual element in any gay financial strategy is coming out—on one's own terms. What does this mean financially? It means being well defended externally instead of internally—through networks, multiple skills, sabbaticals, job hopping, career switching, early retirement, and entrepreneurship. It means opening oneself up rather than shutting down, financial assertiveness vs. passivity.

Community versus Common Cause

Personal finance is personal. In early years giving is personal, and usually not measured in money. Our first duty is to save and invest so as to not be a burden to the community. Beware national gay organizations without grassroots, 900 numbers that profess to support gay causes, and credit cards that attempt to equate community responsibility with using gay cards. Contribute at first to gay groups—such as work-related groups or personal interest groups—that combine both personal and community needs. As you grow older and more secure financially, endow causes and people that will have a lasting impact on life.

PART I

The Gay Decades

▼ ▼ ▼ ▼ ▼ ▼ ▼

The Gay Timelines:
How Personal Life-Stages
and Social History
Make Us Different

▲ ▲ ▲ ▲ ▲ ▲ ▲

We started with a snapshot, taken from many angles, to see how differences derived from sexual orientation can count financially as assets or liabilities. Let's now make that snapshot a moving picture and move it through time in two ways. What does that reveal?

- As we become more experienced, our priorities change.
- Each gay generation is marked by strikingly different events of its particular epoch.

Financial actions work best when tailored to our financial facts, especially if those facts change dramatically over time. If we fail to take into account the stage of life we're at and the history we come from, our financial picture will be inaccurate and possibly misleading. Let's find those missing facts and see first how age itself impacts us. Then we'll assess how our history marks us financially.

Financial Life-Stages

When we're in the midst of our detailed days it's easy to lose sight of how we change over the years. Perhaps we don't want to remember how naive we were, or face the fact that each of us will one day fall sick and die. The present, for all its inconveniences, may by comparison look like a pleasant place after all.

Common sense reminds us that our needs and wants change as we age. For years philosophers and psychologists such as Jung and Erikson have speculated that definite stages of life mold those needs and wants—an idea developed by sociologists such as Daniel Levinson in his *Seasons of a Man's Life* and popularized by Gail Sheehy in her *Passages*.

Straight Stages

The problem is that all this theorizing and writing is about the 90%—about being married with children. This becomes glaringly clear when we read between the lines of books and magazines about personal finance, or review a supposedly personalized printout from a financial software package. They all assume we're straight. Do the straight stages apply to us? Not to my gay and lesbian clients, they don't. See for yourself how you compare to the following:

• Straight teens get a chance to sort out their identities as young men and women with family and peer support.

• The 20s are largely motivated by the possibility of marriage and kids, no matter what immediate options are chosen.

• Most straights marry and begin planning for or having children by the 30s. From then on their lives are largely about paying and providing for the kids. Straight relationships are still mostly based on legal marriage.

• The 40s start the emptying of nests. Changes in relationships between wife and husband often explode in divorce.

• The 50s see wives passing through their change of life, often gathering steam while many men simmer or fade, especially if those men tied their careers to corporations—and didn't make it to the top.

• The 60s can be a blossoming period where family finances recover, with the family again being centered on children and grandchildren, and men and women freed from their specialization as wives and husbands.

These characterizations are deliberately stereotyped to dramatize the strong focus among the 90% on family and children; where, when, how, and whether they exist in a specific person is beside the point. Moreover, straight life-stages are changing more rapidly than even mainstream media may reflect.

Gay Data

What's clear is that we differ from the straight scenarios dramatically. If we build our financial lives with their blueprints, we're in for many expensive surprises.

Gays see life "at an angle." Our perspective is shaped by that fire dance called gay life: living closeted lives, fending off pervasive prejudice, fearing violence, and having no credited parts to play in the American dream.

Gay life-stages are hard to document, and at times even hard to imagine. What little data has been published has created widely varying—and perhaps grossly distorted—pictures of our community. Luckily, to tailor our financial actions to our circumstances and character, we need only identify benchmark financial facts of relevance to us personally. Our task here is not to describe our entire community, but to highlight those life-stage definitions that work for us. Just think of the seemingly endless variety of forms of relationships we invent. With so many opportunities and detours before us, our financial maps need gay-specific landmarks.

Gay Decades

Let's now look at the economically relevant stages of our lives:

• Gay teens feel isolated and often suffer the kind of discrimination that only kids unsure of their sexuality can inflict. No wonder gay teens commit three times as many suicides as their straight peers. Gay teen years are about survival—and delayed experience.

• Many gay 20s feel they have emerged from hell into heaven. Discrimination is lower in this decade than later—a sharp contrast to the teens. At this age we're prized by the community. We're largely unburdened by notions of marriage or kids. We're often attracted to urban centers. The 20s are all about coming out—and this euphoria can literally intoxicate.

Liberated from the "straightjackets" of our teens, our 20s can pass with few reminders that this is our crucial window of opportunity to start saving for the future.

• The age-thirty transition period is often simply missed. Without any wakeup call to economic reality like marriage or kids, we can drift financially throughout the 30s—as long as we have our looks and our health.

Our discretionary income surpluses camouflage the fact that gay men by now are paid less than straight men. Lesbians may be paid much the same as straight women, but this is of little comfort against society's overall financial discrimination against women. The real blow comes not in lower raises but in being sidelined into service, technical, and support jobs, as our investment window starts to close.

Under the best circumstances we can use the 30s as the Productive Years, building careers, investments, relationships, and real estate, in stark contrast to straights creating families with children. This is a great dividing decade.

• By the time the 40s hit, when it's clear that we won't be marrying, many of us may be regularly harassed, excluded from networking, denied training, passed over for promotion, and often downsized. By careful selection and through entrepreneurial ventures we can escape all this. The 40s remain peaks that are tough to climb and perilous to descend—offering a view both of past preparation and the results of our actions. The 40s are Reality Time for us.

This is also the period when missing out on nearly all spousal benefits hits home. While we escape the tax code's marriage penalty, many financial supports for relationships now come up missing when we need them. This seems to be a decade of being under attack from AIDS and breast cancer.

• In the 50s we can lose the advantage that extra discretionary income gave earlier, just as the eroding effect of discrimination begins to take its toll. Now age discrimination occurs—particularly harmful, since our community discriminates against its own seniors. Lavender ceilings come into play precisely when we need peak income the most. Many of us are in fact picked off just at the time that we expected to have harvested the fruit of our careers.

• The 60s and 70s are the bottom line for us. Hopefully we chose wisely and have:

> sufficient investment income to offset lack of spousal pensions,
>
> extended friendship circles, and families of choice to offset fewer children,
>
> a legacy of having created something that will tie us to generations to come.

Gay History

Personal life-stages describe only part of our economic context. We also need to take into account how the decades that we grew up in marked us financially, especially as gays. Our unique historical experience forms our financial assumptions, shared expectations, and survival mechanisms, and we need to allow for this in our financial problem solving.

In walking through the financial issues that emerge and change as we grow older, let's take into account, and benefit from, the rapidly changing historical life experience in our community:

• Gays now in their 70s, born in the 1920s, tasted the last years of a public gay presence that then vanished for fifty years. With careers launched by World War II, this generation rode postwar prosperity. Yet many of this generation married, most were closeted, and few are out in today's gay community.

• Gays now in their 60s, born in the 1930s, knew only the backlash against the open early years of those first decades of the century. Disciplined by the rigors of depression and war, they have few spending problems; they were the pioneers of the great gay retreat resorts and the so-called "gay professions."

• Gays in their 50s were the first to taste the early fruits of gay liberation in the 1960s and have ridden the crest of the baby boom ever since. This is the generation to whom Stonewall—like much else financially in their lives—was a gift. It's a generation of opportunity, but it has seen many of its early leaders die.

• Gays in their 40s flourished without restraint in the liberated 1970s, only to be mowed down in the 80s. This generation had high financial expectations too. Their personal dreams and financial fantasies often then became nightmares. The prime focus among those fortunate enough to have survived seems now to be security; their careers and relationships have often been delayed or damaged, and they're in personal and financial shock from AIDS.

• Gays in their 30s saw the promise of gay liberation and postwar prosperity dissolve just before they could grab it. A crowded generation with high expectations, they've been scrambling economically ever since—holding our economic bag in many ways.

• Gays in their 20s, born in the 1970s, are the great unknown. With little in the cupboard due to AIDS and the aging of America, Generation X may turn tragedy into challenge or may turn off. In many ways they're all about coming out—and climbing out—of economic and medical hard times.

• Gays now in their teens have known only liberation, AIDS publicity, backlash, and a community decimated of elders. They are the troops upon whose shoulders the burdens of the boomers may fall. Theirs is the Millennium with all its terrors and promise.

As we proceed to explore the challenges and opportunities of each decade, let these profiles function as markers on our personal financial maps. While our specific path may fall near or far from them, they create a context in which to do our planning. They offer no complete picture of the gay community, but combine salient characteristics encountered often enough—as confirmed by the experience of my clientele—to both influence our behavior and reference our decisions. Hopefully marking their presence and impact helps us understand and navigate our financial lives.

▼▼▼▼▼▼▼

The Twenties—
Our Extended Financial
Adolescence

▲▲▲▲▲▲▲

▼ ▼ ▼

Jay has just come to Denver, having graduated from a college near home in Kansas. He's got a place to stay with a high school friend who turns out to be gay—who shows him the bars. Jay had been offered a trainee position in a Denver bank, but a weekend job he got bartending could turn into a full-time job with good pay in Denver's top bar, allowing him, even encouraging him, to spend some daytime hours at the gym. The drinks are free and he's in the limelight every night now—a far cry from hiding out in his hometown. By his mid-20s Jay's life has really moved into fast gear. No Denver bash is complete without him—but the alcohol and drugs take over at times and Jay wonders how far he can push the envelope. He's afraid to test for HIV at this point, and is even starting to worry about having become a fixture of gay Denver life and about the new bartenders who are pushing their way in.

His friend, John, has taken a management trainee position at Coors and just doesn't have the time Jay does for Denver's active gay life. John's met some gays and lesbians at the Coors gay group and his social life is pretty much centered on them. He's also decided to take his MBA at night school, since Coors has a tuition reimbursement program—and promises to move him into marketing management while he completes the program. He's a cross-country skier and later in his 20s meets a gay entrepreneur, Jud,

*in ski country, with whom he settles into a comfortable relation-
ship. John decides to leave Coors as he nears thirty and to take
four months hosteling in Europe (one with Jud) before starting
work with Denver's second largest retailer in marketing.*

▲ ▲ ▲

The gay 20s are all about moving from Adolescence to Adulthood. The 20s problem is that some of us never entirely get there.
The 20s opportunity is that this decade presents us our greatest
window of economic advantage.

Given the terror of our teens, the seductive splendor of our
20s is hard to beat. We burst from isolation into independence,
from furtive sex to sexual freedom, from their money to our
money. No wonder many of us are hellbent to have that missed
adolescence.

Many of us enter our 20s lacking socialization in areas that
our straight contemporaries gained in their teen years. Money is
often one of those areas. For as long as gays continue to have to
grow up in secret, the meaning of money gets mangled. Given
this, it's easy to see spending as the opposite of oppression. Expressing our gayness often starts with spending. It's a universal
salve for all those childhood hurts and teen wounds—and it's
common in America to solve problems and satisfy needs by
spending.

The understandable yearning to recapture lost teen years can
really set 20-year-old *adult-adolescents* back economically. Real adolescents have their families to fall back on when they make financial mistakes; gay adult-adolescents fall back on their own
discretionary incomes at a time when the question of how those
suddenly plentiful discretionary dollars are applied is crucial.

Not only is there spending to indulge; the 20s can also offer a
possible feast of sex. After feeling unaccepted as teens, we're seduced by our contemporaries' photos plastered all over the gay
media. As sexual adolescents we make expensive dating—or cruis-
ing—a permanent lifestyle rather than the transitory training
ground it really is. When earning and saving compete with spending and indulging in the gay 20s, gay money often loses ground.

In contrast the 90% are applying the lessons they learned

from the playing fields and dating games of their long-past adolescence. With the notches of their teen years already in place, they're busy thinking of achievement in work and family. While we test ourselves against our own, they're testing themselves against the world. Not that they're good and we're bad. They simply had the chance to date, make their mistakes, and learn their lessons—early. In the 20s tug of war between reality and fantasy, they're opting for money.

The recently liberated gay adolescent-adult may enter the 20s starved for fantasy and headed for economic disaster. Very likely we still labor under a basic mistrust; we may also still be working through our teen shame and doubt. It's no wonder that seizing our economic advantage and trying out career initiatives are often the last thoughts in our minds.

Without the wake-up call of marriage and kids on the horizon our opportunities can drift silently away. If we don't set our own wake-up call, we may become addicted, expose ourselves to AIDS, get lost in the ghetto, spend without any view of tomorrow—and suddenly wake up one morning ill, hungover, and not having provided for being older. Moving up the hour of that wake-up call in time to catch the economic express train sums up our financial task of the gay 20s.

► The Gay Journey—the Strategies of Segregation, Assimilation, and Immigration

The 20s set life's economics in motion. It is a time for choices, one of the first of which has to do with how we move as gay adults into the larger world. Financially we've developed three ways of dealing with the 90%:

segregation as a ghettoized group;

assimilation, which can mean anything from silence to camouflage to living a life of tacit understanding;

immigration, or negotiating admittance, acceptance, and participation.

Segregation

Having experienced childhood's doubt and fear in isolation, it's natural for us to want to group. A gay group can help us work out our mistrust and shame issues, at the same time that the high hormone levels of our 20s drive us into each other's arms. These combined forces impel many of us into the gay ghetto.

When the Ghetto Works

The ghetto is bigger than geography; as a community it can now export gay culture to everywhere we are. No longer is the trek to the gay neighborhoods of the big cities essential. We get socialized on the Internet, through our media, via mail order— and for better or worse we're now front-page news.

Sometimes the ghetto parents us in a way we all would like parents to be: encouraging and permissive, supplying a keen sense of family that may have been missing in our teen years. It can help us replace shame, doubt, and isolation with pride. Its sense of community provides shared traditions, rituals, a language, and a common agenda. It helps us repair damage from childhood. Through its traditions and training it helps us make up for experience we never got to have. In this sense the ghetto is an engine of economic development. It gives us practice in developing powerful networking tools. It helps us understand what's possible, what we need and want, when to do it, where to get it, and how to do it—whatever it is.

Under the best of conditions, time spent in the ghetto gives us a highly structured rite of passage few other groups have, giving birth to a larger sense of community. That's when it's at its best— as a financial multiplier, not a subtractor; when it builds confidence, not dependence; when it acts as a base for departure, not a world apart; when it reminds us we're everywhere, not just within its walls.

When the Ghetto as a Solution Becomes a Problem: Separatism

The problems come when we overstay our need—when our short-term wants override our long-term needs. The ghetto is a school without graduation ceremonies, a rehab with no defined length of stay, and a waiting room with no set departure time. As an extension of our teen years it can go on literally as long as our health and money last.

Setting itself off against society, the ghetto can encourage a polar-opposite perspective on life: personal versus professional, gay versus straight, freedom versus money. Within it we can extend teen freedoms and fantasies, at the cost of neglecting the future. It can easily become the place to spend all our money, in addition to spending all our time. Its one-stop shopping can provide identity, interests, ideas, skills, support, and style, but often it exacts a steep price, delivering group think, narrowness, routine, dependency, and a lot of F-words: fads, fancies, fashions, and fantasies.

The ghetto spells financial trouble when it starts to limit us:

We curtail the experimentation and growth of the 20s in return for gay rituals and routines.

We give our careers second shrift, get sidelined, shirk responsibility, and fall off the sharply rising 20s earning and learning curves.

We spend, rather than save, and thereby lose this one chance to ride long-term investment returns and compounding.

We develop dependency as a lifestyle, whether it's on chemicals, people, sex, distraction, or the ghetto itself.

We use gay life as a narrow focus rather than as a point of departure in life.

Assimilation

If the ghetto ultimately goes nowhere, is assimilation our economic expressway into adult work life? Assimilation used to mean going into the closet—pretending to be married or actually having America's 2.5 children. What new meanings does it have now?

This may be the most practiced and least talked-about strategy in our community. Let's face it: many of us are simply not able or inclined to make gayness a very big part of our life.

In these situations we may not have to worry about the over-socialization of the ghetto or about spending our 20s in fantasy-land. We might do well, however, to ponder whether we might be undersocialized as gays. Perhaps we also need a little more gay fantasy—and financial dynamics—in our lives. We have to become gay before we can mobilize all our gay advantages. Only gay awareness can alert us to gay liabilities, which don't go away if we simply don't call ourselves gay.

If assimilation means shelving, burying, or changing our gayness, we're more derailed than we are lost in the ghetto. Why? Because gayness always comes out, whether we want it to or not. And we may find that it does at a time when it's hardest or most expensive to deal with. The sooner we take up our gay identity, the better equipped we are to protect it economically.

To thrive financially, to experience the gay financial advantage, we must exist socially. Somehow we have to be gay in a social group. If that group is too small, our opportunities are that much less.

Immigration

While segregation and assimilation are the typical ways in which our relationship to society at large is couched, they are social, not economic, strategies, and may be at cross-purposes with our economic goals. One economic strategy for dealing with the 90% is modeled on a time-honored way of gaining one's place at the American table: immigration.

When we follow that path, we neither buy our way in as assimilationists nor buy our way out as ghetto separatists. We simply work harder and manage smarter our financial lives. We search for niches where we're protected or are at an advantage.

Life becomes for us an economic rock climb where we value financial handholds over promises of rights, and lock in our gains as we go.

The financial facts of life are that it's tough for us to survive economically. We can flourish—but it's hard work, requires skill, takes patience, demands sacrifice, and is no party. The immigration approach starts with recognition of our economic realities: that earlier is not just better, but may be our only time to salt away savings, to thunder ahead in career, to multiply skills, to gain exposure, to perform mightily, and to go off on our own.

Immigration is all about moving ahead economically inch by inch. It means safeguarding our privacy, lining up allies, avoiding battles we can't win, balancing our famed loyalty with realism, and saving, saving, saving—and investing, investing, investing— for financial strength.

▶ The Health Hurdles: *Addiction and AIDS*

In the 20s, gay life is not always gay. If we've emerged from teen discrimination, hatred, and violence, we may not be in great shape psychologically.

As battle-worn gays it's easy to retreat into the temporary solace of alcohol, drugs, and sex. As teens, studies show that two thirds of us were in danger of chemical addiction by the age of seventeen. If our socialization in the ghetto is bar based, or if we're using our 20s to catch up on teen experimentation we never had, drugs and alcohol may seem like just the ticket. And as many young gay men still discover each day, the rush to trade in teen memories of loneliness for the promise of sexual connection can be fatal when we refuse to let a piece of rubber get in our way.

Why this emphasis on the dangers right up front? Because these are the core financial issues of the gay 20s. Far more than budgeting or money management, each of these economically all-or-nothing propositions can produce financial fallout that may never be overcome in a lifetime—losses that may also cost us our lives.

We'll discuss spending and saving—the other 20s issues—below. But first things first. This is our immediate hurdle. If we can't get over it we might as well close the book on our lives, financially or otherwise. It's as final as that.

If you've already got a problem here, the next step is to immediately turn to the chapter on our health for detail on damage control. If there's doubt on these matters, or the possibility of a problem, read on.

The Financial Argument for a Sex Strategy and Sex Tactics

Much has been written, and needs to be written, about why we continue to have unsafe sex. Perhaps what's been missing is a focus on the financial consequences—which may be more frightening than the abstract concept of dying. New drugs may in fact save more lives but may also make life a financial living hell.

▼ ▼ ▼

Joe, 22, mentions he's having unsafe sex. As a financial advisor, I search for analogous situations. We discuss how it's like going to Atlantic City with not only what he's got in the bank, but all the money he's likely to earn in his lifetime—about $1.5 million—then putting 25 to 50% of it on the roulette table where the odds are two to one against him, in favor of the house.

I describe how Mark, 25, just found out he seroconverted by landing in the hospital with PCP. Mark had to take short-term disability after his hospitalization; during those five months his income fell from $3,500 to $1,000 a month. I mention Mark's out-of-pocket costs are running about $9,000 for the year for nonreimbursed alternative treatments for pain and loss of feeling, extra cleaning for his soiled clothes, therapy, and costly food supplements (that taste like hell). This reduces his 60% disability income of $25,000 down to $16,000. Even if new drugs stabilize him, the physical and mental side effects of the medications

*and the HIV probably mean Mark will not regain the work—
and level of income—he had.*

▲ ▲ ▲

The insult of dying a slow or lifelong financial death can be
worse than the physical injuries inflicted by HIV. This is the case
with Mark.

It's truly tough that we had to postpone the pleasures of teen
living. But teen experimentation is automatically limited by family and financial restraints. Acting out teen fantasies in the gay 20s
is playing with a loaded economic gun. The prices are all too real.

The Economics of Addiction

Alcoholism and drug addiction have a much *greater incidence*
and *higher cost* in the gay community than does AIDS. People in
bars may end up drinking and drugging more than scoring sex.
The booby prize of addiction, on top of its own costs, is that it
easily leads to HIV.

The direct costs of addiction are different from those of HIV.
With HIV there's not much cost at the outset, and when costs
happen their unpredictability is almost as terrifying as their magnitude. With addiction the costs just accumulate inexorably, one
drink or drug at a time. The unpredictability with addiction is
expressed in the questions: When do the catastrophic events happen, and When does recovery require outside intervention?

▼ ▼ ▼

*Anne's finances don't add up. She's got a $72,000 annual
income, doesn't travel much, has an average rental, has no car—
but there are no savings. Her initial focus when she comes in is on
investments—but there's little to invest.*

*She's reluctant but together we succeed in tallying up what she
probably spends in the bars during the week and in the clubs on
weekends. She tells me about a few incidents. One time $3,500
worth of cameras were stolen after she'd passed out. She fell on the
way home one night and ended up losing three weeks of freelance*

work. She was mugged in the club district, causing $4,000 dental work. She's lost keys, burned fancy furniture, ripped clothes. Increasingly she's looking forward more to her evenings than her days—and her high-income trade as a graphics designer. Last month she inexplicably lost two clients. Anne has no interest in stopping her nightlife, but faced with these costs she agrees to an outpatient treatment program.

▲ ▲ ▲

People numbed out on alcohol or drugs have amazingly high tolerance for physical and emotional pain. Sometimes a tally of the financial pain and a linking of the tally to all that self-medication provides the needed wake-up call.

The Payoff in Restoring a Long-Term Perspective

The impact of addiction on the gay personal bottom line is the greatest threat facing any gay starting out in life. Any gay financial plan must be able to detect financial fallout from addiction.

The deepest damage done to our balance sheet by health problems is that we become obsessed with the present and lose sight of our futures. We not only miss the overall patterns of unsafe sex, addiction, and mental illness, we forget the link between our actions now and our results later.

The key preventive measure we can take is to fantasize about our future life through planning—and stop living our fantasies. Take time to cultivate an overall awareness of the economic dynamics of your specific life. Think through the landmark events that would not just make your day, but make your life a life worth living. The longer the time frames we can imagine, the stronger will be the economic safety net we weave—and the more spring we'll get from using that net as an economic trampoline. Planned right, we have a clear shot at success, with the head start of extra discretionary income and the advantage of few obstacles along the way.

This may well be our greatest achievement in the 20s. It certainly takes plenty of work. Our childhoods were likely to have been either disrupted by harassment or paralyzed by deep fears and doubts. Rushing into the postponed pleasures of the 20s, we're easily captivated by slogans to be present, here and now. If we fall into addiction of one sort or another our vision will certainly be here and now, for the future will be utterly clouded. If we acquire HIV, we'll definitely be living day-to-day—but it won't be pleasant.

Banking those dollars and building that career may be hard, but it's not impossible. Think of the 90%, think of other successful immigrant groups. If undertaken early enough, our long-term vision will not only keep us connected with what we need but will accelerate the time when we can truly have what we want. It's truly possible to achieve financial independence at age 40 via savings and investment. That vision has to be as concrete and as immediately appealing as any invite to set it aside for short-term pleasure. For it is the long-term perspective that holds the key to all forms of wealth. Wealth is the wine we lay down, the collections we build, the dollars that compound, the investments that grow, the mortgages paid down, the exponential jumps in the value of what we create, the capital of growing career experience.

Only the poor delight in baubles, seize the day, settle for raw brew, spend current change, numb out the moment, and live in the present. Perhaps it's time to confront the fascination and love affair many gays have had with the poor—when being gay meant being without prospects. Those days when the only places we could be public was in lower-class saloons and at slum street corners are long over. There's nothing sexy any more in being poor.

► The Gay 20s—Spend or Save?

If health isn't an issue, a young gay's focus can be quite simple: Spend or save.

Without marriage and children to plan for or spend on, we

face a different financial picture than our straight contemporaries. While most of the 90% may not have large amounts of spendable income until after child rearing, we frequently find ourselves with a spendable surplus, even when we start with the same salary.

We have two basic choices to balance out: Spend the money for present pleasure or save the money for future pleasure. There are few financial techniques other than the mastery of this balance that a gay in the 20s must acquire.

Our challenge is that high spendable income in the 20s only gives us *apparent* wealth, an illusion made worse by the contrast with cash-poor teen years. Because we seem to have so much more cash than others, it's easy to fall into the belief that it won't stop. But it does—when the children of the 90% grow up. Then, in our 50s and 60s, it can seem like there's been a run on the bank:

- We may no longer have more discretionary income than marrieds.

- We may have lower absolute incomes.

- We may hit significant job discrimination.

- We may hit the lavender ceiling.

- We may have no close biological family to support us.

- We may have by then acquired a spending habit we can't kick.

Society doesn't help us think long term in the 20s at all. We're at an age where we almost desperately want to be loved (especially after the terrible teens), and we may be particularly vulnerable to ad-based fantasies, especially in our own media. Their message? Everyone loves the Big Spender. Little reference is made to the fork in the road that we face: to accept the immediate illusion that our surplus spendable income is unending, or to pursue the vision of lifetime financial success made possible by saving this temporary surplus now. One way to compare the two is to tally up how much money is at stake if we save. Another is to see how much disappears if we spend.

► **Gay Private Dilemma #1:** *Gay Spending—*
The Gay Dividend or the Gay Disease?

What do most of us actually do in our 20s? Spend, spend, spend, often in an indirect attempt to defend against discrimination.

> Ghettoists may pay to join special interest groups that offer strong identity—and high maintenance costs.

> Sensualists may search comfort at any price—whether it's in sexy clothing, segregated vacation packages, or gay bars, baths, clubs, and restaurants.

> Assimilationists may try to purchase acceptance by buying, buying, buying into mainstream consumer society.

> Isolationists may prize security in things—furnishing their homes as fortresses.

> Gays may invest in fantasy lifestyles decorated with symbols of superiority purchased at a great and irredeemable cost.

These are some of the core spending styles of gay life. They are survival tactics, not success strategies. Each of these lifestyles is fueled by the surplus spendable incomes in early gay life. Each may dull present pain but is a drain on the future. Unchecked, they'll assure gay wealth remains but a vague promise.

▼ ▼ ▼

• *John is an opera queen in the making. His annual box, magazine subscriptions, books and scores, restaurant dinners and club outings, fancy duds, and rounds of increasingly elegant private dining are running him about $4,000 to $5,000 per year. Over twenty years this will have become a six-figure lifestyle.*

• *Tammy is the wild woman from Miami. Her club clothing, bar bill, home liquor bill, drug bill, party boat, house parties, and restaurant tabs are running her about $7,500 per year. After ten years of this she'll have aged ten years more than normal—and she could have bought herself real estate or a career for the same $100,000 compounded amount.*

- *Tim and Tom opted for suburban life. Their four-bedroom rambler is mostly empty but cost about $10,000 extra to furnish and $5,000 more to maintain than their city condo. They now have a $30,000 Suburban four-by-four whose maintenance and gas costs are twice those of their old gas-efficient Honda; it also depreciated an extra $5,000 the first year they bought it. Their mortgage is mostly interest during its first fifteen years—the point at which they break up. All told this suburban fantasy costs them about $150,000 more than city life would have, plus the greater isolation they felt after having pursued this "normal" lifestyle.*

- *Alice and Allyson have a home. Their house is full of toys—the cost of which has run about $55,000. They've put in a pool, whirlpool, new kitchen, entertainment center, and custom lighting system for another $65,000; but these types of improvements rarely add more than half their cost to the value of the house. The pool actually decreased the home's value. The toys aren't used much, take up space, and get out of date fairly fast. All told they have sunk about $75,000 into this money pit that they'll never see again.*

- *John's apartment is twice the average cost in his city, but it has a fabulous view. It also required a fabulous decor at a cost of $40,000. John's wardrobe runs about $5,000 a year more than need be. His good taste totals about $25,000 per year—more than enough to have made him a millionaire by age fifty—but by then he won't have anything to show for it that isn't long out of fashion.*

▲ ▲ ▲

What's wrong with these scenarios? Not the spending, per se—it's the *timing*. There's nothing wrong with opera, pools, parties, toys, or high living—later on in life, when we can not only afford but appreciate them. There's a great deal wrong in spending the capital that would finance that future.

That's what we're talking about in the 20s. Those discretionary dollars are our capital. In economics the purpose of capital is to beget income—to be a kind of financial fountain. For anyone, the 20s are laying-away years; for us, with our less-than-fabulous futures, this laying down is crucial.

Those of us who take this spending fork in the road—who opt to buy the future today—will have the economic engines of compounding and tax deferment working for them. They are powerful engines indeed. Compounding allows us to make money on the money we've made, reinvesting our returns at such a rate that it is realistic to expect to double our money in as little as seven years, only to double the doubling in future years. And tax deferment permits those returns to compound with no tax bite while it's happening. Taxes only are due when we withdraw the money in later years, when our tax rates may be lower as well.

Let's say we wanted to have $100,000 in twenty years. To keep things simple let's make sure these figures take inflation totally into account, so those future $100,000 dollars are exactly the same value as the dollars we put in today. If well-wishers give us $10,000 on graduation, or if we put $100 a month away during just our 20s, we'll have that $100,000 waiting for us in our forties.

Here's another way of looking at how this works: It's like getting future benefits at a discount. We get to have $100,000 worth of benefit twenty years hence from an affordable, small investment now. The future's on sale! And we gays with our discretionary dollars are in a position to buy a lot of it—now.

Here's one last way to weigh our needs and wants—present and future. Financial success can be pictured as a four-square table.

	Needs	Wants
Present	1	2
Future	3	4

- Most people in the world are in square 1, barely meeting present needs.
- The first step out of poverty lands people in square 2, where

pent-up wants burst forth. This happened with consumer spending after World War II. This happens after the gay teens.

- Most straights are in square 3 meeting the future needs of their children.

- We are in the incredible position of living most of our lives in square 4, where we ensure that our future wants are satisfied. The irony is that doing this can be satisfying as well.

► Gay Spending Dilemmas—*External Pressures to Spend*

What blocks us along the way? Nothing but ourselves, the sirens of straight and gay society, and greed of those who would like to suck us dry along the way. Unless these drags, digressions, and distractions are disposed of early, many of us may blow this unique chance at future wealth in favor of paying for pleasant present pastimes. If we safeguard our savings, we have an incredible chance at financial strength, security, and success—for life.

► Spending Dilemma #1: *Early Gay Catastrophes Make Money Matters Seem Unreal*

Teen suicide, AIDS, bias-based violence, and the lesbian breast-cancer epidemic, can plunge us into intense present despair in which the future seems not even to exist, much less to be something to save for. We may witness promise and fortune disappear with a diagnosis, in an incident, through a senseless act. Friends get fabulous sums from selling life insurance, yet may die in months. As treatments improve with AIDS, the financial quality of life can get worse. Psychologically it's as if the Roaring 20s, the Depression, and the war years were all combined.

In these times our first task is to focus on what's economically real for us; that's why they call it *personal* financial planning.

Faced with chaos, our first goal should be financial security and stability.

▶ Spending Dilemma #2:
The Gay Market Trap

Gays in their 20s are under marketing assault as easy pickings for gay and mainstream merchants alike. Gay media confound gay pride with being a gay market, when the prideful thing to do is to save, not spend. Gay power is only power when it's saved—not when it's spent.

Financial realism is key to personal planning. Studies show that gay men earn somewhat less than straight men, and gay women earn as little as women in general. Period. What the gay media do is survey their upscale subscribers and then portray *all* gays as wealthy. In truth, *most* magazine subscribers are upscale.

The financial fallout is that many gays commit to keeping up with these mythical gay Joneses and spend, spend, spend. The political fallout is that the religious right quotes these readership surveys to defeat us, as it tried to do in Colorado. Even the minority opinion of the Supreme Court quoted those figures and characterized us as too rich to need political protection.

These marketing messages promote a common economic pitfall for minorities: buying the symbols of success when thwarted in actually getting it. It's a poor use of funds, and puts us even further behind the economic eight ball. Proving our worth as consumers instead of as people is paltry politics. The politicizing of spending carries a stiff price for us. The only ones to benefit from a gay market are those who would exploit it by these deceptions.

Is it prideful that investment firms use gay employees to get us to lower our guard while they try to steer us into high-commission products? Does identity come from advertised brands of jeans, beer, and water? Very often those corporations who promise gay-friendliness hide the harsh reality that the word *gay* is absent from equal-opportunity policies, that no gay employee groups exist, that the word *gay* isn't mentioned in employee or customer service training, and that gays never make it into executive ranks except as spokespeople.

The harsh reality is that we need saving, not spending, from us—and performance, not promises, from them. This substitution of gay purchasing for gay power ignores our need, similar to that of any other group wanting a place at the table, to make money work for us. Simply look at what successful immigrants are doing—what any group knocking at the American gates has done. They save, they develop skills, they care for their own, they persevere, and they succeed as individuals and as a group. They recognize that economic strength counts far more than buying power.

Yes, we are banging on corporate doors—as employees and as shareholders, not consumers—demanding adoption of Equality Principles that anti-discrimination policies include sexual orientation, that our employee groups be recognized or encouraged if other employee groups exist, that diversity training include our issues, that our spousal benefits equal those of married employees, that advertising avoid the use of negative stereotypes, that gay vendors be treated equally, that accommodation be made for employees facing disabling illness, and that merchants practice these principles and not just promise to be gay friendly.

► Spending Dilemma #3: *Politicized Spending*

Not only are we seduced by straight advertising to spend our way to immediate gratification, we're being assured by gay merchants and by some gay leaders that we can achieve our political and social agendas as well by simply buying gay symbols, using gay credit cards, and using gay phone services.

This mixing of messages weakens our savings resolve. Spending is spending. Credit cards are debt, period. Phone services should be judged by cost, service, and convenience. End of discussion.

Beware of promises to contribute a percentage of the take to worthy causes. You usually have no say over what they are. Lots of expenses can be deducted along the way, including high representation fees for the spokespeople. If a charity looks like a business and acts like a business, you can be sure it is a business—except for its charitylike sheep's clothing.

In our 20s we have more time and energy to give than money. Philanthropy is for later life. To be able to give later, we're better off saving now. Tithe for then.

Lastly, avoid buycotts and boycotts. Spending is too vital. Its purposes must remain pure and free of secondary agendas. We are usually too small and dispersed a minority to make much of a difference in the marketplace. Direct political action as shareholders or employees is far more productive.

► Gay Spending Solutions

Spending can be such a loaded issue for us that the best approach is often to be eclectic and practical—to do whatever works. In fact, oversystematizing can be a symptom of how desperate the situation is without being a solution for it. Here you'll find a simple list of actions, only a few of which need to work to lead out of the spending trap.

► Spending Solution #1: *Me, Inc.*

We gays are like a very unusual business that has very low start-up costs but high costs as it matures. In many ways we're like the summer resort business. Our discretionary dollars are our profits as Me, Inc. Saving and investing those dollars so they can carry us over our uniquely harsh winter is the secret to our success. Since the outside world has made it pretty clear that being gay means you're on your own—even when you're in a couple—this is a good time to start thinking about yourself as Me, Inc.

▶ Spending Solution #2: Form a Family

A crucial realization is to see that over the span of our lives we provide for a number of financial selves, or financial stages. It can be helpful to see this as your own private family: yourself in your 20s, 30s, 40s, 50s, 60s, and 70s, on your stages of exploration, building, changing, harvesting, celebrating, and teaching. Define your own stages; decide what decades are worth saving for.

▼ ▼ ▼

Angel is 26 and confused. He moved to Los Angeles five years ago. He's working at a studio in accounting. And he feels pulled in a dozen different directions. One weekend, he decides that if he's really a Me, Inc., he'll put together an imaginary board to represent all the influences trying to run his life. He's got a chair at the board table for these groups: Parents, the Latino Community, his Straight Sisters, the Accounting Profession, the Gay Caballero, his Future Partner, his Angel in Midlife Revolt, his Angel as a 50ish Adult, his Angel returns to San Diego at 60, and his Angel in Retirement. On important decisions he polls these different perspectives—and to his surprise he has a growing sense of who the person is who's moderating all these discussions—his inner self. When that inner self is truly in command of Me, Inc., he'll be ready for his major financial decisions—but not until that moment comes.

▲ ▲ ▲

▶ Spending Solution #3: Plan for Tomorrow—Don't Budget for Today

Marrieds with children must budget monthly for today's needs; we have the luxury of planning annually for tomorrow's wants. We can plan over longer, more natural periods of time, time frames that are tailored to our goals and style, not just the annual calendar. We can plan for a lifetime.

► Spending Solution #4: *Tailor Planning Time Frames*

Choosing our own time horizons for our plans gives us control and predictability. School calendars condemn many of the 90% to plan by the year. Without children we can design our planning to fit what's most likely to happen, improving our accuracy in both predicting and reviewing results. Some time-frame options that may work better than the 90%'s month or year include:

- quarterly (e.g., for salespeople or during periods of great change)
- twice yearly (e.g., where income varies greatly during the year)
- nine months/three months (e.g., for teachers)
- yearly (e.g., for those with stable, long-term finances)
- two, three, or five years (e.g., for a specific goal)

▼ ▼ ▼

Donna is 22 and just starting out in greeting card sales. Their big year ends with the end of the summer—so she plans September 1 to September 1. Her girl friend, Val, is 26 and in teaching. She plans in the same time frame. Because Donna is busiest in the summer—when Val isn't teaching—Val takes care of the household then while Donna takes over in the fall when Val's school year starts. They plan their vacations over winter and spring break.

▲ ▲ ▲

► Spending Solution #5: *Plan by Purposes, Not by Categories*

Because we benefit by planning our spending and income over long time frames, we have the option of planning our future according to our purposes—not just accounting our past by categories. This enables us to see our financial forest and not get lost in its trees.

Rather than using monthly budgets that focus on immediate needs and fixed expenses, as embraced by families tight on money, we best apply our surplus spendable income by focusing on long-term needs and variable expenses with long-term spending plans, not short-term budgets. With a spending plan we can apply our discretionary income to our purposes, programs, and projects, over our entire lives, grouping expenses by what they do for us, not by their expense type.

Purposes for spending aren't always noble. Some purposes may seem psychological—and that in turn may give clues to alternative courses of action that may not involve spending at all. Keep planning private, so that this reflection can be frank. Financial stuff can be intensely personal; many of my clients tell me things they won't tell their therapists.

Grouping by goal gives us information for managing our lives. This is planning, not accounting. The bonus to this approach is having a more deliberate life. We can replace lethargy, habit, and impulse with *choice* in our spending, and literally get more for our gay money. Knowing why we're spending, instead of just on what, may encourage us to dream more, to envision better, and to reflect honestly on what's truly given us great value over time.

▼ ▼ ▼

Tina pulls all her fixed expenses—the typical budget stuff—into one glop she calls her "nut." After making her $3,000 monthly nut, she plans and tracks spending for her dreams:

Relationship	*$6,000 over the next two years (commitment party, two-week second honeymoon trip, quarterly four-day retreats, monthly weekend outings, ten book-on-tape rentals to listen to together, weekly video rental)*
Financial investment	*$1,000 a month ($350 of which is tax-deferred and matched by her employer)*

Computer graphics skills	*$12,000 over a four-year cycle (equipment, three courses, subscriptions, tutoring, supplies)*
Friendship	*$4,000 a year (entertaining, dinners, parties)*
Keeping current	*$1,200 a year (cable, newspapers, subscriptions, one conference, two workshops, a dozen books)*
Style/image	*$3,000 over a two-year cycle (to develop a core wardrobe)*
Comfort	*$3,600 this year only (furniture, lamps)*
Creativity	*$2,000 most this year; remainder next year (including $600 a year for art books, subscriptions, a workshop, museums, one membership)*

▲ ▲ ▲

► Spending Solution #6: *Generate Alternatives—The Case of Travel*

Spending is all about purposes. The basic spending decision is whether this action serves our purpose better than alternative actions. Let's take a look at perhaps the most popular big-ticket item for gays: gay travel.

Travel is a traditional way to change the weather. But what additional purposes does travel provide for us? That should be our first action: sorting out our expectations and weighing our alternatives. Whether or not you travel, the following questions can give you an idea of how to define the purposes that inform your spending.

Is travel an exit from the pressures of minority living? Have we considered the value of an exercise program?

Do we seek a visit to a gay mecca? If travel is a way to be openly gay, this might be a good time to consider coming out in more direct ways.

Are there implied promises of sex? What about the other weeks of the year?

Is it letting loose, going wild—going gay? Perhaps all-gay events will fulfill this.

Are we buying status? Would label clothing, or community leadership, do the trick better?

Are we seeking the freedom of invisibility? Or might we simply change our customary haunts?

Are we fed up with routine? Are there other ways to reshuffle our cards and mix up our lives?

Do we need to recharge our batteries? Would a personal day do?

Do we want to meet someone new? How about an assertiveness-training workshop?

Do we want elegance? What if we went out in tuxes to new or customary haunts?

Do we seek being catered to? How about a series of special evenings out?

Are we tired of discrimination? How about fighting back by writing letters through GLAAD?

Do we want pampering? Can services be traded with others?

Do we search for a total all-enveloping experience? What about a spa-day?

Two valuable things happen through this perspective: alternatives are generated, and if travel truly is the winning ticket, we can pour ourselves into it wholeheartedly.

▶ Spending Solution #7:
Generate a Baseline

All plans, all measurements, need a starting point. Because our discretionary incomes are potentially so large, a key concept for gays is that of the "needs nut"—an overall yearly figure for needs, organized by purpose, program, or project, not by payee or type of expense.

Our needs should be predictably simple: rent/mortgage, insurances, utilities. The needs of the 90% are often unpredictable because of children. This is the fixed part. Any expense that must be made goes here—all spending that keeps the basic ship afloat, including annual expenses like insurance premiums. Most of this information can be put together from reviewing your checkbook; since the payee is regular, little additional notation is needed.

You can facilitate future planning by choosing forms of payment that do not destroy the data you need for tracking. Here's how to prevent that and to make things easier:

Checks: Make sure checks are entered in the check register—not to balance the account but to capture the data. Add on the second line the check's purpose, program, or project name in addition to the payee on the first line—a good way to see if your spending is on purpose! Photocopy old registers for your planning folder—the original register is a tax record. (Photocopying registers is a good security measure in any case.)

Credit slips: Write the purpose, program, or project name on the credit slip; treat the credit slip like a check. It's a financial document with valuable information for review later. Even better, in addition to this keep a credit register to capture what the expense is for—not just who it's paid to. This is especially important, since many merchants have credit-card names that are meaningless when the bill comes around.

Cash: Use as little cash as possible; this makes good security and great information catching. To generate a baseline on cash expenses, get or make a receipt for each expense, no matter how small, for a "measuring period." Write the date, purpose, and amount on the slip. At the end of the period sort the slips into piles by purpose. After several tries at this you'll soon identify where most of the cash is going—and you'll immediately have second thoughts about some of the purposes served. How long a period? For those who use little cash, a few days will suffice; the more cash that's spent, the more value will be mined from this painless exercise.

The estimate for the nut, these registers, and the cash tracking will help plan and track whether you're applying your money where you think it's going. The greater the discrepancies, the tighter the tracking should be. It's vital that these reviews be flexible and frequent. Their usefulness is in generating information and ideas.

Planning and tracking are not accounting. Some may like entering these figures into a software money program, but it's far better to use successive approximation over long periods of time. Only if our reviews are quick, painless, interesting, and productive will we continue them. If they become a pain, step back and simplify—otherwise you'll soon have no planning or tracking at all.

► Spending Solution #8: *Make It Real*

In our 20s our luxury dilemma is choosing between the short and long terms. One quick way to resolve that is to make the long term concrete—as tantalizing, promising, and seductive as ice cream waiting in the freezer.

Certainly one technique that works in this direction is creative visualization. Many books and tapes on using visualization exist.

We need something more immediate. Shell shocked from the teens, we may require a lot to offset the call of the ghetto and gay media. We may need to explore.

Exploring is a powerful career technique that can be geared to life planning. It means finding real live people to talk to about the future. In careers, for example, we explore by calling on leaders in the field we're starting out in to see where the field's going, what it's all about, what we can do to succeed in the long run. Big shots invariably are flattered by such calls once they realize they're not for a short-term purpose such as a job search. These are calls for mentoring—and being a mentor is a time-honored role for a field's shakers and makers. Like a job or a lover, we only need one.

Exploring often means literally travel. Our dreams may involve a geographic shift. Nothing can replace being there, personalizing it. Subscribing to a paper from our dream place can make it concrete.

If our dreams are in the arts, commit with the feet.

▼ ▼ ▼

Gail loves graphic art. Her first small purchases have put her on buyers' mailing lists. She gets invited to most openings now. She's contacted professors in the area, has visited personally with specialists at the auction houses, and knows by name some of the curators in the area.

▲ ▲ ▲

Halfway house solutions are a good way to get serious about a life goal. If it's real estate, it's wise to rent before buying. If money's tight, a working vacation during a holiday peak period in a resort area gives frank views behind the scenes.

▼ ▼ ▼

Jim has a deep love of the outdoors. In high school he worked at summer camps. During college he got jobs in the national parks. His stint in the Peace Corps didn't hurt his résumé at all. He made sure his insurance job has flex time—which enables him to work compressed weeks. Now he's seeking to be a working member on an archaeological dig by postponing his start on his next job.

▲ ▲ ▲

The goal? Being able to answer without hesitation "What are you saving for—and why?" Dreams are living things. They need to be nurtured, in small doses, regularly—then they will soon grow of their own accord.

▸ Spending Solution #9: *Work from the Top Down, from the End Back*

Start by writing your own obituary, the article that would appear in the hometown paper, the testimonials recited by your loved ones—and don't forget the newsreel of life that's supposed to zap before our mind's eye in our final moments.

Again the solution's economic, not just financial. Let's start with the overall likely financial outlines of life. The fact is that most of us are millionaires over our lifetimes, and that gays have the chance to be millionaires just in terms of discretionary incomes alone.

How? Let's say that the average American man earns $1,500,000 in his lifetime, while the average woman earns $1,200,000 (we'll keep everything in current dollars to keep things comparable). Assume that fixed expenses average $500,000 for most people plus another $400,000 each for 2.5 children or $1,000,000 in child support. Because we don't have that last expense, we can end up with an extra $1,000,000 in personal disposable income. That can make for quite a party or a lot of financial freedom.

Now customize it. Is your family long lived? Is there a threat to your health? Make a guess as to when you *might* die. Remember: do everything in pencil!

Using books like this helps you decide what kind of work transitions you might make. One way or another, decide on the number of years you'll probably work full-time.

Take your present salary, rounded off to $1,000. Using rough tax rates (e.g., 15, 25, and 35%), estimate how much in taxes you probably pay. Subtract that from your salary to give you your net income figure. (You'll also see how much motivation you have to cut your taxes over the long haul.)

Now estimate your yearly "needs nut": rent/mortgage, insurances, utilities. Subtract that from your net income figure—and you now know your approximate discretionary, spendable income.

Multiply that figure by your number of earning years and you have your lifetime spending plan.

You can now ask yourself some very real questions.

• In the kinds of work you envision, how much would your real income go up over the decades—just because of age and performance?

• Would your "needs nut" necessarily go up if income went up? If so, why? Keeping your nut small is the simplest way to expand lifetime spendable income.

When expenses are tallied over a lifetime, their value is often put into high relief. Habits that cost a little multiplied by several hundred times a year multiplied by thirty to fifty years may reveal a high ultimate cost that has little value. This kind of tally can also spotlight later expenses whose cost can be largely borne by investment returns—if savings are begun now. Measuring value over a lifetime puts most expenses on a common ground. Spending lacks comparability when micromeasured—especially by that misleading straight tool, the monthly budget.

Looking at a lifetime of making and spending money may reveal areas where spending should take place, where it's now absent. Retirement may not be the only goal missing; often the finer values of life get shortchanged when our attention is glued to the ground and we shuffle from day to day, with little meaning to our spending. In Debtor's Anonymous they have a saying when overhauling a spending plan: Don't forget the flowers.

▼ ▼ ▼ ▼ ▼ ▼ ▼

The Thirties—
Coast or Build?
Personal, Career, and
Financial Investments

▲ ▲ ▲ ▲ ▲ ▲ ▲

▼ ▼ ▼

Tam's been a flight attendant for Southwest now for eight years. She's got good pay, great style, and is the talk of the town in several major cities. Lately she's been seeing Pam, who's working in creative graphics for a major ad agency in Austin, who wants a house—and who wants to settle down. Tam's intrigued with Pam, who's a saver and has started investing in a major way. She can't figure out how Pam does it on a salary less than hers. She likes Pam, she likes Austin, but the party beckons.

Pam likes Tam, but she's got her heart set on having a home. She's happy in her work and knows that in the long run it offers her great creative outlets and financial opportunities. She's built a good network of friendships, and her family's here. She wonders if she could ever get Tammy out of the sky—in so many ways. Tammy's tantalizing, but Pam's love is for a home, for a career, and for a life—not a lifestyle.

▲ ▲ ▲

If we graduate from the twenties with sound health, self-knowledge, and savings habits, those are the tools we now need to build three key assets: relationship, career, and investment. Since career and couples are discussed in their own chapters, we'll focus on investment in exploring the potential of the 30s.

One reason the 30s are so good for investment is that they're one of the two "smooth" epochs of our lives when we can get a lot of financial groundwork done—the other being the 50s. With enough money coming in to make a difference, we can now have an unbroken line of sight on our future goals, and can bring them closer with time, reflection, and effort well spent here. Psychologically our lives are humming. We're fine tuned to our tasks, such as career building and understanding investment.

One reason for our lack of disruption is lack of children and their $400,000 price tags. If we want children, it's best to leave these production years as intact as possible. In this decade everything can seem to come all together: experience, training, contacts, funds, energy, health, motivation, support, and direction. Don't break the focus!

That's also why it's so important for gays in the thirties not to have a hangover from the twenties. Yet many gays are not only hungover but still addicted—and not just to the alcohol or the drugs. Many of us want to hang on to the apparent freedom of our lately won adolescence even if it jeopardizes financial freedom later. It's not hard to understand why. An extended adult-adolescence offers immediacy—not the long term—desirability, recognition, pleasure, living in the *now*. Plus, adult-youths are virtually all we see in gay publications and gay culture. All this makes leaving the 20s tough.

The Age 30 Transition

The traditional wake-up call to the 30s is the Age 30 Transition. This is highly predictable for heterosexuals, perhaps because for them it's linked to the child-rearing cycle.

Like the later midlife transition, though, it has a basis in personal development as well—a shift highly relevant to us. The party of the 20s is over, the innocence is gone, and it's time to settle down. This transition is to be welcomed; it gives us maturity and offers depth and dependability.

The idea of the Age 30 Transition comes from Daniel Levinson in his classic work *The Seasons of a Man's Life*. Although Levinson's work covered only straight men and, like so much research of this time, omitted women, the trends I've noticed with my clients confirm that the concept is workable for us. It's best to start this transition on time in order to hit the 30s running, I've found—especially since, without the wake-up call of marriage and parenthood and with possible hangovers of delayed adolescence, many of us miss the call. Some gays just roll over to enjoy the dreamy 20s some more, pretending the thirties just aren't there.

This transition is an invitation to move from the jungles of the 20s to come out as seasoned adults onto the rich, high plateau of the 30s: a perfect place to build. Yet gay culture doesn't always support this trek. Our stereotypes of the future can be downright dreary, defined simplistically as opposites of the 20s. The irony is that if we remain in the 20s mind-set we create a self-fulfilling prophecy for a truly dismal financial picture. The full thrust of our discretionary-income advantage comes onstream in our 30s. Missing out on this chance to leverage our advantages is like being late to work, except it's our own life-work we're missing out on, and there can be serious consequences. Whether you're building a career or a relationship, the gay advantages start to recede after the thirties, as the hurdles grow higher.

▼ ▼ ▼

Jack sees his future as a painter. He used his 20s to explore the art world and study abroad—and getting his teaching certificate. He now has a fairly solid body of work and a vision that may support an arts career. He plans to use the 30s to live and teach in Europe at an American school there. This will permit him the time and money to build contacts for opening a gallery in Atlanta in his 40s to showcase not only his own work but to act as an agent for European artists in America. He feels the teaching credentials will enable him to possibly tap grant money—and that the European experience will ensure that his connections with the international art world are sustained.

▲ ▲ ▲

Our 30s opportunity? We have more to build with *and* the building is easier than during any other decade—if we understand the pattern and if we plan accordingly. For this is the decade when plans have the most power. If leverage depends on the length of time we have available, the 30s offer us the greatest leverage on the future.

► The Thirties Straightaway

Welcome to your second adult act, the one where your audience either gets into it—or they leave because nothing is going on. How can you tell if you're ready to make your life a smash hit and not just a one-act play?

- You're not only saving, you have the savings habit.

- You have clear visions of your dreams and goals—and what they require.

- Your focus is on how to realize your dreams—in great detail.

- You genuinely like working out beyond the gym, building financial muscle, toning career skills, exercising flexibility in your relationships.

- You've learned how to have a ball during the day, and not just in the shadow-world of night's seeming protections and fantasies.

Ready or not, the thirties are the working years, when whatever work that gets done is capital that produces dividends for life. If you're not ready, it's not too late—but it's getting there. If you're not sure, it's time to ask yourself some questions on fundamental issues: It's time to put those 20s dreams and discoveries into action:

Dreams: Do you have a clear vision in the large-scale areas of career, skills, savings, investment, relationship, housing, and location?

Coming out: Are you out about being gay in a way that makes you comfortable? Do you treat it the same way you'd treat other intensely personal, valuable information about yourself?

Work: Do you have a job or a career? If your work folded next month, do you have concrete half-steps you could take to capitalize your experience into greater advancement?

Income: Does your work satisfy as much for its opportunity as for its income?

Skills: In what ways will you outgrow your skills, experience, and knowledge, and how might you compensate for this? What money and time are you willing to put aside per year for improving your skills?

Independence: To what degree do you want self-sufficiency? Does your work match that?

Location: What are the criteria you'd use to judge the attractiveness of a place to play and work? How does your present location measure up by those criteria? How could you best explore adjustments and alternatives to make your reality match your dream?

Housing: How important is having a home to you? What proportion of your spending is associated with home? Is that what you want—now? In ten years? Later?

Insurance: Do you have comprehensive medical insurance? If you were to lose your income-earning capability, are you covered for at least 60% of your present income tax-free? Do you have life insurance that allows payout of all the death benefit if you have less than one year to live?

Savings: What percentage of gross income do you save per year? Is it at least 15% (minimum)? 20% (good)? or 25% (best)? Do you know how much you'd need at age sixty-five to produce an income satisfactory to you? Do you know how much that translates into in terms of monthly put-asides?

Investment: Do you have virtually all of your savings in stocks? Are your investments diversified like a layer cake? If the market went down 10% or 20%, do you have a fire drill for what you'd do? Do you have enough access to cash that you could pay your monthly "nut" of needs for three to six months?

Relationship: How many acquaintances do you know whose name you'd remember at a party? How many friends do you know whom you've called up in the last month? Do you have a friend in whom you could confide nearly everything? Do you have a friend whom you'd trust to handle your affairs if you were unconscious for more than a week? Do you have a lover with whom you discuss your personal finances? your mutual finances? who would help in a pinch? who would help you financially through an illness lasting three months?

There's no getting around it—the 30s ask us to work hard today for a better tomorrow.

Understandably, many report frustration with the 30's focus on the future. The lucky ones are so exhausted from this work they don't mind putting off the pleasures of the fruits of their labors. You may do well to think of the 30s as the financial gym—the time to pile on more weights, to hit and go through walls that limit performance, to continue the run—to build, build, build.

Another way to think of the 30s work is to approach it as two careers: one where we work for others, one where we work for ourselves. Even when we get the work-for-others part down pat, I've noticed, our work for ourselves is frequently neglected. So much of my work with clients is helping them learn to just show up for themselves. Perhaps the decades of messages that we're lower than the lowest makes it hard to give our higher needs priority. Often our finances reveal if we've let ourselves down—by carrying balances forward on credit cards, forgetting to save, raiding savings, or simply not investing.

The stark truth encountered in the 30s is that it's not possible to care for ourselves, financially or otherwise, unless we've done our 20s work and resolved our childhood issues. It takes solid self-confidence, positive self-regard, and to-the-core self-acceptance to invest in ourselves. Why would we want to work hard for someone we think is no good?

In terms of personal finance, our sense of self-worth must be articulated in two vital ways: a career that suits us so well we can pour half our waking lives into it; and a commitment to the importance of our dreams by starting to save, envisioning the decades of our lives, and producing plans so real, they can compete with present pleasures. If something is missing, our first 30s task must be playing catch-up, because all this is sequential. If everything's in place, it's time to do the really challenging 30s work: investment.

▶ Lifestyles to Look Out For

We all react differently to the gay experience. In personal finance some lifestyles can sabotage our very ability to save, much less invest, while others make us millionaires. Before we see how investment can power our dreams, we'll first have to deal with our dragons, and identify those lifestyles common in the gay community that do not work well financially.

The common thread in all of them is compromised liquidity. Investment is all about liquidity. Cash is energy, potentiality, freedom; when it's simply stored, it loses power, and when it's applied, it gains power. Our financial success depends entirely on when we need and how much we want this power—and when it is most available.

You may have never considered your level of liquidity, but as you look over this familiar collection of lifestyles to avoid—or escape—you may see yourself in a new light.

► Gay Lifestyle Pitfall #1:
Anxious Negative Liquidity

The gay who has credit card debt in the 30s is mortgaging the future to pay for the present. As that debt mounts, we create the very situation that we fear, where our freedom of action is gradually diminished to nothing. This is a big-time red flag. For solutions we're talking therapy, twelve-step groups, and possibly bankruptcy. The goal is simple: each day we stop debting, there's progress. If you can't, it's time to ferret out the underlying dynamics of this self-defeating behavior.

▼ ▼ ▼

Renaldo is very striking—and had quite a party in his 20s. However, he's now $45,000 in debt, hasn't moved very far at work—and has disabling effects of HIV. We decide only a clean slate will give him the ability—and the will—to make financial headway at this point. He declares bankruptcy, changes jobs so he can convert his group life insurance to individual coverage, and gets a new job with better group benefits—and new group life insurance. As a bonus, he decides to sell the converted coverage when its suicide clause expires—after two years—to give himself an incentive to not only build security in his 30s but literally invest in his future.

▲ ▲ ▲

► Gay Lifestyle Pitfall #2: *Pseudoliquidity*

One possible sign of financial paralysis occurs when savings match debt—no matter what the level of each. Although cash seems to be available, in reality more is being paid in debt service than savings interest, creating a net outflow. The solution is psychological—it is probably no accident that the two balance out—but the situation can usually be more immediately solved by a "stand-down," where small amounts of savings are used to pay down the debt.

▼ ▼ ▼

Lynn earns $80,000 yearly but has no savings. She has a rolling $6,000 credit card balance—and $5,000 in savings. We decide to capture cash expenses for a month by grabbing receipts. The decisive moment comes when she pays off her credit balance. We then reorder her spending categories to highlight and reduce her "comfort" expenses—and we discover she spends little on "self-expression."

▲ ▲ ▲

► Gay Lifestyle Pitfall #3:
Angry Nonliquidity

Another path is that of dropping out of the system. Temporary disconnection from society can serve a purpose as long as alternative lifestyle communes don't end up as another gay separatist ghetto.

Cash isn't the enemy—or the savior; it's how we apply the cash.

▼ ▼ ▼

Lee is an entrepreneur at 30. His early success in business often makes him feel doubly robbed of the good times he sees all around him. So he takes advantage of his authority and has all the trademarks of an independent spirit—blue hair, earrings, boots, and black leather. Not until he attends a radical faerie gathering, though, does he come to peace with his business path—and realize he doesn't want any movement to socialize him any more. But he returns with determination to spend mornings at home, to take three-day weekends once a month—and falls into a relationship with an equally independent spirit, creating a social group of his own. He starts developing managers at work—and looks for-

ward now to the day when he can sell the business and move onto
something new when he's 40.

▲ ▲ ▲

► Gay Lifestyle Pitfall #4:
Panicked Unknown Liquidity

One reaction to the unpredictability of discrimination or AIDS is
a difficulty in envisioning the future. As under wartime conditions these gays tend to stay in the present—ever vigilant. This
paralysis in the present can prevent any serious investment considerations of any type.

► Gay Lifestyle Pitfall #5:
Reactive Aliquidity

We've mentioned the tendency to spend our way through our
20s. Sometimes the spending hangovers continue—to cause even
greater harm.

Spending may seem like freedom in the 20s and 30s, but
future spending will be determined by our declining incomes if
we don't save by our 40s or 50s. Why save? To be free.

► Gay Lifestyle Pitfall #6:
Fearful Hyperliquidity

The fear of violence and discrimination we all face inspires many
gays to live out of a financial suitcase. They keep assets highly
liquid, as in CDs and bank savings accounts, transforming
homophobia into investophobia. Even when they save abnormally
high percentages of discretionary incomes, they live lives on hold,
frozen by fear into inaction waiting for the worst. As inflation

erodes their earning power year after year, they simply don't grow; they shrivel and get left behind.

There is a counter-intuitive divergence between savings and investment that is striking. Even after ten years, one dollar is worth only $1.28 at 2.5% savings bank rates, $1.62 at typical bond rates, but $2.60 at 10% average stock market rates due to compounding. Saving is a *necessary* condition, not a *sufficient* condition, for financial success.

► Gay Lifestyle Pitfall #7: *Passive Liquidity*

By far the most common case is the person who's maxed out on the employer 401(k) plan but who lets it go at that. This is no time to be a passive player at the investment table. Even with the limited choices that most company savings plans offer, investments should be monitored carefully. Moreover, "I saved at the office" is an insufficient investment plan for any gay who has extra discretionary dollars. Most investment, after all, is with after-tax dollars. This is the decade to be a top investor, moving aggressively with every spare dollar available.

► Gay Lifestyle Pitfall #8: *Liquidity? What's Liquidity?*

For some of us the decision not to invest is linked to a general conclusion reached probably in childhood that financial stuff is straight stuff—and that business stuff isn't gay. As long as those discretionary dollars roll in, it's quite possible to lead our lives this way—for about twenty or thirty years. Then reality steps in.

Many of us grew up with straight parents with whom we never identified. Their talk of money was no easier to relate to than our straight peers' talk about the expenses of dating. And if we ended up in the ghetto, much of the money talk amounted to the blind leading the blind. The result is a discomfort with financial issues that prevents us from forming a strategy—without which we're just drifting, until our spendable surplus disappears and we hit the tough times of later gay life.

The Investor in Each of Us

The final lifestyle pitfall—the false claim that finances are for straight people—is my favorite to address with my clients, many of whom I've converted to the opposite point of view. Investment, I tell them, can be an especially gay practice, particularly in our 30s, not just because we need its eventual payoff but because it draws on many skills we've acquired through a gay life. Not only does investment fit well with our social and political agenda—securing financial freedom to go along with the social; adopting an alternative lifestyle distinct from the conservatist norm—it extends the psychological agenda that has brought us this far.

First and foremost is the obvious truth that investment is essentially gay neutral. The fact that we can't assume the same of the workplace—and must take into account the possibility of office homophobia or discrimination suddenly eliminating or simply limiting our income—is one of the most important financial reasons for building an investment portfolio. Investors face no discrimination, as long as they have money to invest. By rewarding the use of the discretionary dollars that we've seen we have in surplus amounts, in fact, investment can appear to be downright gay-friendly.

In fact, it rewards our gay perspective, drawing on the skills, knowledge, and training that we've received along the gay way. Consider your investor potential along the following familiar lines of hard-won life experience:

• *Running the gauntlet* may have toughened us. One of the biggest mistakes in the market can be running with the crowd; smart moves are often contrarian ones.

• *Living on the outside* may have freed us from America's homogenized thinking. The market demands this ability to face raw data with original thinking.

• *Monitoring our environment* may have taught us the skills we need to watch the markets, which take monitoring of all types at all times. The myth of the investment we can just let sit—is just a myth.

• *Having to act on our feet* in public can give us street smarts. Thinking on our feet and inventive problem-solving suit fast-moving markets.

• *Dealing with unpredictable people* and environments trains us in performing "what if" analyses. Spinning scenarios is the essence of what's needed to stay one step ahead in the market.

• *Living a bicultural life*—in the world of the 90% and the 10%—can give us an edge in critical thinking.

We've got what it takes. We might as well apply it, and be paid handsomely for it. But let's face it. This is not something we do naturally. Investment is a higher evolutionary skill, usually triggered by marriage and children, those eloquent reminders of the future. If those triggers aren't there, we need to invent replacements; that's where the plans and dreams you considered earlier come in. As powerful a motivator as those dreams may be, however, investment is a learned, not an intuitive, skill. Getting that lesson now will serve us well later when we're also tempted to bolt and fly by the seat of our pants.

Investment Is Empowerment

Still, investment is intensely psychological. It touches, and is touched by, issues of self-esteem, appropriateness, confidence, assertiveness, ambition, competitiveness, reflection, judgment, decision making, and risk taking. Investment is therapy when it comes to these issues—and it benefits from therapy.

Many of us emerge into adulthood with problems in some of these areas. We may simply lack experience, or we may identify these characteristics as the province of straight people. By the time we reach our thirties, we're running out of time to address these issues; investment is a gay-neutral arena in which to work them out.

Employment is not often empowering these days. Because many gays are often loyal, people-pleasing, workaholic, we may end up being used—and not adequately rewarded—in today's cost-cutting climate. Control is increasingly elusive in today's corporations. Investment can be an antidote to this. Investment puts us in the driver's seat. We may not feel comfortable at first but get used to it: it's highly rewarding, financially and psychologically. Diversified investment is like employing many companies to work for us. And we should manage them as fiercely as they manage us in the 90s.

Investment taps our entrepreneurial instincts even if we don't want to start a business. Entrepreneurship is investment in just one company. To have a stake in the dividends and capital growth of many companies is safe entrepreneurship, a good offset to work-for-pay.

Investment is income liberation. The number-one limitation to wealth is the link between time and money. It's possible to build a fortune by saving hourly, but it's long and it's hard. Since our potential may be limited by discrimination in paid employment, developing investment as a second career is not only a way out—it's a way to accelerate wealth.

Investment is empowerment. It's working for ourselves. It's freedom. It's our commitment to the power of our ideas in action.

► Pulling Together a Gay–Specific Investment Plan

We're ready. We've got the will. We've got the wherewithal. What are the actions, specific to our circumstances, that we might safely take?

At this point it makes little sense to focus on micromeasures such as optimizing money-market yields, balancing a portfolio, or deploying sophisticated tax measures. A basics-first philosophy may even spare us from distraction in overly sophisticated financial products that make only their designers rich. Our task is first to get simple answers as to what, when, where, and why—and only then as to how.

In the big picture we spend, one way or another, everything we earn. In each spending decision we choose between the present and the future. Each charge slip is a ballot. Do we want it now? Do we want it later?

All spending is investment; it has a goal, it has assumptions; it takes present action with the hope of future gain. All spending and investment has a payoff. And these payoffs can be profits—or losses.

If we invest in what the bars and discos offer, our dividend may be a hangover, cigarette burns, empty pockets, and somebody in bed whose name we can't remember. If it's tax-deferred growth stocks, our money is doubled in four to seven years. If it's in comfort foods, our payoff is a lean larder and a fat body. If it's in the stock market, the average return is 10.5% a year. That's investment 101.

Staying low tech in the 30s with investment is as simple and vital as our challenge in the 20s: stay healthy, explore work, and save. The 30s formula? Save regularly, defer income, invest widely, and go growth. With those four corners secured we've already got most of our gains locked in.

Like the 20s work, what's important is to just do it—we can fix mistakes later. Just make sure now you have something to improve later. It's so easy to delay investment especially if fear is in the picture. Do whatever it takes—small amounts, automatic withdrawals, an investment club, an investment buddy—to start and then stay the course: just like at the gym.

▶ Gay Investment Action #1:
Want Something

We start by lengthening the time line of our wants. This stage can benefit from our using some of the available self-help material that can be tailored to our tastes and can be taken in small doses.

The best books and workshops about money are the ones that give us assessment tools like the following, one of the most useful exercises I've seen to help us to focus on what we want. If other approaches than this come to mind, do them first. Nothing is sacred about these suggestions; their only purpose is to get you to start thinking.

A Be-Do-Have, Needs-Wants, Time-Money Exercise

Get out three sheets of paper. Get in a reflective mood. Spend very little time per step; *completing* this is the goal, not perfection.

We'll first do a data dump on three pages; then we'll dissect the data to help our understanding—just like taking apart a frog in biology.

1. Data Dump

• On one page, note on one side all the Things you *now* have in the approximate order of their importance to you; note on the other side all that you don't have, that others have, or that you might need or want to have in the near, mid-, or far future.

• On a second page, note on one side all the Activities you now do in the order of their importance to you; note on the other side all that you don't do, that others do, or that you might need or want to do in the near, mid-, or far future.

• On a third page, note on one side all the Characteristics that are You, in the order of their importance to you; note on the other side all the characteristics that aren't you, that you can see in others, or that you might need or want to be in the near, mid-, or far future.

2. Dissection

• Underline those Things, Activities, and Characteristics that are *necessary* to you—whatever the reason.

• Star those Things, Activities, and Characteristics that you want or might want—whatever the reason.

• Put a question mark on those Things, Activities, and Characteristics that may be good for others but which don't seem to fit you.

3. Comparison with the Measures of Dollars and Time

• Put an *annual* dollar cost estimate for all those Things, Activities, and Characteristics that can be dollarized—if this is easy to do. Put a question mark after the amount if it's especially hard to estimate.

• Go back over the lists and add any Things, Activities, and Characteristics that don't cost money that you might have missed. Mark these by "$0."

• Go back over the lists and add any Things, Activities, and Characteristics that don't directly cost money but which may require a definable and large amount of time—annually. Mark these with a "T" and note a rough estimate of the number of hours per year they might take in your life—if this is easy to do. If it's calculable but iffy, add a question mark.

• Go back over the lists and add any Things, Activities, and Characteristics that don't take much time that you might have missed. Mark these by "T=0."

4. What-If Planning

Now that you have the raw data for your annual spending plans you can look ahead, by going back through the data, perhaps with a different-colored pen, and jotting down alternative goals than the ones you seem to be following now.

This exercise may be a start. If it was worth the effort, you might want to investigate books on values clarification.

► Gay Investment Action #2: *Gradually Question Money-Losing Lifestyle Strategies*

Chances are, the above exercise taught you something about the dollars and sense of your lifestyle. Let's focus on just one gay lifestyle—home fortresses—that can turn out to be a money-losing proposition. Gearing up with too much gear doesn't make sense until after we've settled on our long-term life-choices. But I've seen countless clients who seem to be able to store savings only in unsalable things such as homes, furniture, and adult toys.

▼ ▼ ▼

Robert and Maurice often bought significant pieces of furniture after their major fights, perhaps a symbol of reinvestment in their relationship. When the going gets tough, Alice and Alecia get going—on yet one more credit card vacation. Joe has an incredible media room that seems to absorb more and more of his time and money—because it's so incredible. But Joe seems to have lost interest in those parts of the real world he can't control and increasingly lives in his fantasy worlds.

▲ ▲ ▲

This is a rough area to assess; we can easily move from simple style to obsession without realizing it. Asking yourself periodically how much you'd really lose if you had to sell your treasures may focus your spending. Another indicator may simply be the cumulative price tags, weighed against an assessment of whether overall finances are sound, and whether important safeguards are missing from economic life.

▼ ▼ ▼

Paul is the fixer-upper while Alan is the banker; Paul pours three months of labor each year into elaborate Christmas decorations. Both are pleased with the trade-offs now but are wary of what happens when Alan retires.

▲ ▲ ▲

These homebodies may see home as a fortress, where they finally get comfortable in a society that is distinctly discomfiting, but they are pouring their paychecks into home improvements that may never see a payback. Even in normal markets most home improvements add but a small percentage of their cost to the value of a house. The items that truly add value may be too prosaic for some of us—such as better roofs and *vinyl* siding. Our touches—marble baths, swimming pools—can actually make a home hard to sell. As for fixing up a rental, which many of us still do, forget it.

▼ ▼ ▼

Beth and Sue took inventory of their possessions and made a list (that's called "striking a balance sheet") showing first the value of their money accounts and then the money they'd paid for their major possessions (their liquid and illiquid resources). After some reflection they chose to rent out part of their home, sell their extra car, and give some furniture to Goodwill. They drew up a list of any big-ticket items they might need in the next five years (a "capital budget"). They listed furniture they might gradually replace with items of higher potential resale value. They began a savings plan with monthly contributions increased every three months—to be reviewed in a year. After a year's dialogue on where they're literally putting their money, they decided to sell the house, get a low-maintenance condo, use weekend trips to explore a new place to live, and pour the savings into financial investment. That's long-term planning.

▲ ▲ ▲

▶ Gay Investment Action #3: Build Investment Smarts

Investment is best learned through expert advice, applied with guidance, through experiment. It's a technical topic, not a touchy-feely issue. The key is to apply it a little bit at a time. We start by defining our needs and wants. We continue by questioning what the experts say. It's especially smart for gays to treat investment as a knowledge and skills challenge, not a motivational problem. Motivation by itself can lead to uninformed mistakes—and until our confidence is built, we're too susceptible to gurus. Guidance, meanwhile, can be found in all sorts of places, but only by the person who's truly looking for it.

▼ ▼ ▼

George realized he had no way of judging whether he needed advice from his CPA brother-in-law broker, his ex-lover's financial planner—or something else. He started spending Saturdays in his local library, scanning just the small, stand-alone, two-column articles on investment that appear in the "Money and Investment" section of The Wall Street Journal. *After that he looked at the investment sections of personal finance magazines. Then he took out one personal finance book and read just its chapter on investment. His initial focus was to get the hang of what his range of choices was. He's started a subscription to a personal finance magazine.*

Increasingly alert to both his need for some guidance and the gap between what the straight media were talking about and the things he was concerned with, he came across an older gay at a dinner party who seemed interested in the subject, fairly successful himself, and willing to spend time talking about it. Voilà! A mentor. Now he's taken home two personal finance books from the library simply to compare what they cover under investment. (His healthy skepticism is starting.)

He's considering taking a summer course on investment alternatives at his local college. In two months he's planning to take some time at a friend's beach house, off season, to walk the beach and think through what he himself really wants, what he might need. After that he feels he'll be able to use professional advice.

▲ ▲ ▲

▶ Gay Investment Action #4:
Consider Investment in the Present Tense

We're a very present-focused people. While this may bring many personal benefits, it's a problem in investment. One way to work around this is to make future priorities items on our present agenda and to spend on investment the same way we pay for our fixed expenses. Automatic monthly deductions from our current account reminds us that investment is as vital as our rent or mortgage. We're simply moving this category up the spending chain. It's a question of which check is the first out the door.

There also is a sound investment technique called "dollar cost averaging." That expression means that we invest a fixed amount each month—no matter what the market is doing. This averages our returns, minimizes the chance that we might put our money in at precisely the time that the market is at its lowest, and avoids that worst temptation to get in at the top of the market.

Why not try to buy in at the top? That happens to be the classic investing mistake—timing the market. With all the hurdles we face to investment, gays can be tempted to make up for lost time by trying to make a killing. This risk is compounded by our feeling we have less to lose than those with families to worry about. Just remember: data show that those who try to time the market get killed more often than they make a killing—and many of them may be much smarter than we amateurs coming from behind. We may be more tempted than the 90% to do this, but why do something that fails?

▼ ▼ ▼

Anne knew she would not invest unless she made it automatic. She opened an account with a mutual fund family requiring little initial investment and arranged for monthly transfers from her checking account just as she does for the rent. Now she feels she has to bone up on her investment options because money's going into the account; she's starting with the investment reports available through the fund. After this she'll start a second fund as a temporary way to get another perspective on these issues. She's

*also heard about a lesbian investment club where members invest
a steady amount each month.*

▲ ▲ ▲

► Gay Investment Action #5:
Start Slow, Start Small

If we have little experience and are starting from scratch, we face
many extra hurdles, and it makes sense to build up speed gradually. It's a little like gaining access to a thruway; we don't want to
suddenly plunk ourselves down, with our slow speed and minimal
skill, among those going 60 miles an hour.

In investment this calls for diversification. This technique
presents two advantages for those of us who are investment neo-
phytes. It first educates us better by exposing us to a wider variety
of investment vehicles. It also minimizes our risk, especially at the
outset, by encouraging us to explore just as we did with career
options in the 20s. It is from these explorations that we'll learn
what areas in investment appeal to us, perform well, and offer
opportunities for specialization.

▼ ▼ ▼

*John received a considerable inheritance from his lover. Shell
shocked by the death, he put the funds first into a savings account, then moved the funds into a money market account, getting experience with and studying the market. He then moved
some funds into short- and medium-term CDs to give himself a
total liquid cushion that would cover his fixed expense nut if he
were out of work for up to nine months. After this he began
moving the remainder of his funds into no-load highly rated
conservative mutual funds while he began an adult university
course in how to invest. After trying small companies, large mainstream companies, bonds, several industries, and the international market, he decided that, because his job involved a great*

deal of international travel, he would focus half of his investment in that area.

▲ ▲ ▲

► Gay Investment Action #6:
Find or Found an Investment Club

That virtually no gay investment clubs exist is testimony to our Great Gap in investment. Clubs fit virtually all our investment requirements: they're local; they're based on commonalities; they counterbalance reckless risk-taking. Gay special-interest groups are great alternatives to the bars and clubs. It's time to rally round the flag of economic equality and financial freedom.

Such clubs are good places to overcome inertia, admit weaknesses, learn from others, and make friendships among like-minded people while working investment issues. Investment clubs have excellent track records, often outperforming the market; their consensus approach gives the group endorsement many of us prefer.

Investment clubs can also be the safest way to do socially responsible investing. That's a sophisticated bet that the companies that put gay-friendly policies into practice ultimately perform better in the market.

► Gay Investment Action #7:
Consider Collectibles

Our long time frames make semiliquid assets such as some forms of collectibles good candidates for investment. Some collectibles offer good prospects for long-term appreciation. We also have the outsider perspective to spot collectibles on the rise—and the time to research them.

▼ ▼ ▼

Joan anticipated that her aunt would leave her about $75,000. She had few immediate needs but deep concerns about *her 50s and after. She decided to become very knowledgeable about a period of French painting in the late 1800s and about one artist in particular. This artist's paintings had steady value, were pleasing to her, were enough in number to foster a market, and had climbed gradually over the last twenty years. She went to auctions, studied catalogs, talked to curators of the auction houses, phoned authors of articles about him. When the inheritance did come she was ready to purchase a single high-quality piece. She'd researched how to insure and store it. In ten years it tripled in price; in twenty, it had gone up five times in value.*

▲ ▲ ▲

In some ways collectibles are the quintessential gay investment. They not only increase in value but they often recognize and reinforce personal values and interests. It's key for us to continually decide with collectibles how much they're an interest, and how viable they are as an investment. They can be the very opposite of investing—spending that burdens our lives with extra maintenance, that literally weighs us down. Yet even without financial value collectibles can add to life.

▼ ▼ ▼

Victor's town house was filled with everything about bears. Teddy bears everywhere, prints of bears, bear paper towels, a bear phone. But sprinkled among the toys were oil paintings with bear themes that had high enduring value. In contrast, Victor's lover, George, collected baseball memorabilia. He had bought heavily into baseball cards but ended up having made a poor selection of type and quality—and realized too late that he was subject to a market with wild swings.

▲ ▲ ▲

Without children the tangibility of collectibles can appeal to gays. They reflect our personalities. They can add to life's quality. They require deep what-if future thinking, since both our personal values and the value that the market puts on them can change.

Collections can also provide the present, concrete pleasure—

and attractive qualities—of evident wealth. Gays with collectibles tend to have well-defined interests and knowledge. They add to our attractiveness as we grow with our collections. Perhaps this is a Dolly Levi philosophy of money: cash itself offers cold comfort, but if it's put to use it can add doubly to life's pleasures.

▼ ▼ ▼

Larry decided to collect prints of a certain era. He now has a small one-bedroom-apartment picture gallery. This has become a lifelong passion, leading him into the social life of the city's galleries, museums, and artists. His home and personality have this distinction. And his collection steadily grows in value at a rate twice that of inflation.

▲ ▲ ▲

► Gay Investment Action #8: *Real Estate Lessons*

Real estate is loaded with straight mythology that can lead us astray. Most recommendations about real estate assume marriage with children. With growing families to house, straights tend to buy real estate too soon for their incomes to support easily; as a result it becomes their main investment. They may consider it a home, but if it's taking all the money they might otherwise invest, that home is by default their investment strategy. This is the basis for an important lesson in investment: those salt-of-the-earth homeowner types are often proud of not playing the markets, yet they may in fact be putting all their investment-dollar eggs in a single real-estate-market basket with poor prospects for the future.

If we do that we are not only foolishly overinvested but we also handicap an important gay advantage, our mobility. Without children we often can respond better to career opportunities that require mobility: new jobs, temporary assignments, new training, and changing companies. We're top candidates for overseas assignment. Tying up our assets in real estate can obviously make such flexibility difficult, if not impossible. This is why buying a vacation home that we can rent may be better than buying a primary home we can get stuck with.

Steering our lives by looking in the rearview mirror of our history can be a dangerous strategy, but I've seen plenty of real estate purchasing decisions made in just that way. The 1990s leveling-off in real estate values confirms a major lesson in investment: The future drives the market, not the past. Faced with the uncertainty and messiness of the future, many of us may seek solace in the fixed data of the past, only to learn that trends just get us to where we're at. They're our best explanation of what's happened up to now, a direction that will, and should, change tomorrow. Up to now, real estate was buoyed up by preferential tax-rules and the 90% baby boomers needing houses for all those kids. Now those houses are emptying—and tax rules are a political football.

Some gays go suburban. Yet suburban homes are geared to marrieds with 2.5 children. Is this trying for equality by imitating heterosexual nesting? If so, it is a costly strategy. If you find yourself looking at suburban houses with two to three bedrooms you don't need, it may be time to do some individual or couple's therapy. Houses are poor substitutes for identity, equality, or marriage.

Many gays may be better off forgoing full-scale picket fences during at least the start of their 30s. If we do succumb, we'd be wise to consider fifteen-year mortgages. Many of us have adopted the 90% excuse to buy houses they have to buy anyway: "I'm losing so much in taxes." In truth, this lets tax strategy drive investment strategy. A far better idea is to hire excellent tax counsel and consider other ways we can generate active, more substantial, tax savings.

We should be wary of buying real estate jointly with none of the implicit legal bonds of marriage. If a lover flies the coop, for example, we can get stuck for all mortgage and maintenance costs—only to have a hard time clearing the title if we can't find that errant love. No real estate should be jointly acquired unless there is a legal agreement about expense sharing, rental income, and property disposition—under varying circumstances. It's worth it to bring in a lawyer sooner rather than later.

On the other hand, joint property acquisition can—in certain circumstances, appropriately handled—maximize the unique characteristics of our relationships, such as age or income differences.

▼ ▼ ▼

Prosperous Pauline fell in love with hippy Helen. Helen's inexpensive apartment went coop, offering her an attractive insider price. In their agreement Pauline made the down payment and both split the low maintenance. The agreement gave Helen a much greater percentage of any profits from sale during the first ten years, gradually scaling down to a fifty-fifty split at around year fifteen—balancing out Pauline's money and Helen's insider price.

▲ ▲ ▲

The fact that the IRS doesn't recognize our relationships can be a financial advantage in real estate, though it's tricky enough territory to require expert input. If there's rental income, for example, it can be protected by shifting it to the partner with the lower tax rate. Sometimes, if partners can justify one owning the city home with the other owning the country home, renting out to each other can be mutually beneficial—if residency, deduction limits, and other IRS requirements are met. Any transactions such as these may have long-term impacts on capital gains and our ability to use our $125,000 lifetime capital-gain exclusion—another reminder that good ideas and intuitions are a good start but need competent professional testing to be viable.

The key in real estate is to start with the goal, not the solution. Real estate can seem like a solution to all our desires, a real package deal, when in truth it is more like a hammer looking for a nail: a narrow solution appropriate only under certain circumstances.

▼ ▼ ▼

This is certainly true of George and Gary. Both stood a chance of transfer, requiring that any real estate they bought remain easily salable. Both wanted more quality than local rentals provided. Gary could use the deduction. But neither had the time to devote to a home; both had put their primary focus on career. And Gary's savings and investing were negligible. Conclusion? An easily resalable condo—and putting their long-term focus in other investment vehicles.

▲ ▲ ▲

Renovation is a time-proven gay strategy for real estate success. New trends and opportunities start on the fringe as we do; they fight their way to center stage as well. Being on the fringe does help us spot renovation possibilities first, and bring them into being.

But their success has often been because they coincide with broader urban trends. We may be taste setters, but leaders succeed by staying at the head of the parade; and that depends on a good sense of where the parade is heading on its own accord. It takes two to tango, and with innovation we are wise to remember we'll always be dancing with an elephant.

Being innovators can in fact make us blind to financial realities. Sweat equity plus gay style is still a winning combination *if* the market five to ten years in the future is going to want renovated buildings in that area. Simply being innovative and having good taste doesn't excuse us from assessing the future needs and wants we're renovating for.

Real estate does offer opportunities to marry personal and financial interests. If we go to certain resort areas year after year, buying rental estate can be a doubly smart move. Socially, being an owner, as opposed to a renter, can make a great difference. Financially, what was a net outflow can become net income.

▼ ▼ ▼

Joe worked in Philadelphia but loved Fire Island and Puerto Rico. At forty he bought his house on Fire Island; at forty-five he renovated the lower level as a rental. At fifty he added a two-rental unit on the same land. At fifty-five he bought a beachfront condo in San Juan, renting it out at first. At sixty he retired and spent six months in San Juan, five months on the Island, and a month visiting friends. His rental income, on top of his tax-deferred payouts and Social Security, enable him to match his previous income, stay even with inflation, and have an attractive lifestyle.

▲ ▲ ▲

One gay-specific reason why rental real estate may be appealing to us is the independence it can bring. As corporate pyramids get narrower and we get tossed off, rentals are a fine safety net. Having wealth in tangible form confers social status at a time when corporately it may be eroding. And managing real estate can be a satisfying occupation in later years, offering deductions, appreciation, income, and prestige.

► Gay Investment Action #9: Keep the Focus on the Long Term

If our health remains good, we have one splendid advantage: a clear, unimpeded shot at our long-term goals. This means we can take advantage of the capital appreciation, higher security, and often tax-advantaged status of longer-term investments. The risk of such investments is largely in the *short term* if they have to be cashed out prematurely. If we're not cashing out for decades, these investments have greater *long-term* dependability.

This is our essential gay advantage in investment—one that literally can multiply our discretionary-dollar advantage in savings. The 90% cannot access that formula nearly as much, since their investment perspective during childbearing years is largely short term. We can more easily satisfy the general rule of investing that the investor be able to weather market swings before needing to liquidate.

If our highest gains and greatest security is in the long run, that may also give us a great economy of effort. Those condemned to live in the short term must monitor and change investment allocations more frequently; they can be overwhelmed by the sheer number of alternatives available. Longer-term possibilities can be more easily identified, more thoroughly researched, and more carefully considered.

This long-term reach makes it profitable for us to study specific companies, industries, and geographic areas in depth. After our safe educational period of diversification we're in a position to take full advantage of our research. This is in fact the approach advocated by Peter Lynch, who set records for returns in the mutual fund world. Lynch suggests working from our immediate experience and personal knowledge to identify and explore in depth what sectors to invest in—and which to stay away from.

► Gay Investment Pitfalls

Before we launch these careers as investors, there are some gay-specific pitfalls that should be dealt with. Ignored, these internal conflicts can delay, defer, and deter us from investment for years.

► Gay Investment Pitfall #1:
Security and Risk

Given what we face, many gays have a deep desire for security. That can be a fundamental flaw, since investing is all about taking risk. We can better understand financial risk by breaking it down into its smallest components: taxation, inflation, fluctuation, ignorance, and vulnerability.

• Taxation is best dealt with by hiring competent tax counsel, including a tax attorney, whose communications are protected by client-attorney privilege. We're talking tax advice here, not just tax-return preparation.

• Inflation is best dealt with by monitoring—whether through subscriptions or the Internet. In investment, staying current is a requirement. The advice of the money media is after the fact and geared to marrieds; but we only need the business media's reporting of trend data.

• Fluctuation can be offset first by diversifying our investments. As we gain experience, it can be better offset by going long term in our investment choices. Just as in bicycling, only being in the saddle—gaining the concrete experience of surviving fluctuations—can bring us to the point where it's a breeze.

• Ignorance is the easiest to compensate for, through the study of how markets operate. Beware the temptation to short-circuit learning through reliance on expert recommendations. Others' opinions will never offset investment queasiness as effectively as a solid understanding of market dynamics. Books and newsletters oriented toward education—not tips—are required.

• Vulnerability is best offset by other financial measures: career, tax, legal, and other safeguards. Only time can provide equanimity; but this can be accelerated by a growing awareness of the history of the market. Just make sure you aren't seduced by trend analysis alone along the way.

▶ Gay Investment Pitfall #2: *Closeted Investing*

Gays often do not self-disclose with doctors, lawyers—and investment advisors. Even when we come out we may remain silent on our total investment picture—about our lovers, our estranged families, or our health. This can result in advice that may be the total opposite of what we should do. Advisors presume marriage and kids, and are usually ignorant of the ways in which we're financially different.

▼ ▼ ▼

Jonas worked with me on the impact of HIV on his financial future. We covered his employee benefits, private insurance, and then his investments. When asked whether he'd told his broker about his status, he answered no. Yet his health was so much in peril, he might have to leave work within six months. He wasn't out at work either.

His broker had put him entirely into investment vehicles that were appropriate to his age but inappropriate to his health. He asked me to call his broker for him to break the news and discuss the implications. His broker was shocked at how the news totally threw the portfolio out of balance.

Over the next three months Jonas was able to speak more freely with his broker about possible events, such as going out on disability and needing these funds well before the time he'd originally anticipated. He also came out at work—getting the security of the protections of the Americans with Disabilities Act. With the support of management he stopped his old strategy of being the superstar and adopted two salespeople to mentor, on whose sales he was given a percentage override.

▲ ▲ ▲

► Gay Investment Pitfall #3: *Misplaced Loyalty—Displaced Decision-Making*

Mistreated, many of us come out of childhood with profound distrust. The dangerous flip side of that fact is that after so much discrimination some gays seem overly grateful when solicited and sought after—as consumers. When someone overcomes our distrust, we can swing too far the other way, and become entirely too loyal. This may be relatively harmless with clothing salespeople; it can be disastrous in investing, if it means surrendering investment decision-making to a broker. It gets especially dangerous when brokerages use gay employees to push products to the gay market. Broker commissions are not only high, they vary with incentives to unload securities. If we're loyal sheep when making financial purchases, we may be fleeced in the bargain.

▶ Gay Investment Pitfall #4:
Investing When Ill

Some people with life-threatening illness sell their life insurance in order to make a killing in the stock market. This motivation can cause them to sell too early and get too little. It can also expose these funds to the unpredictable swings of the market, and complicate the unpredictable needs for cash that serious illness can impose. That might mean taking money out of the market during one of its downswings.

▶ Gay Investment Pitfall #5:
The Straight Wave

The markets we invest in are often dominated by America's *straight* family demographics. As outsiders we may have enough distance from what's happening in markets to spot new developments early. This can also be a blind spot, if we project our perspective and values on the market. We need to be bicultural—to live both in their world and ours. Remember while investing that we are but a small percentage in this homogenized pot. We can ride waves and spot niche opportunities but can be flattened and left behind by the straight wave if we forget who really drives the markets.

▶ Until You're Ready—*Parking Funds While We Gear Up for Investment*

Given all these dangers, it may be much wiser to park money in no-load mutual funds while we get the education our second career as investors deserves. That at least will get us used to investing, and to the idea that "easy does it" works in investing too.

Why do we buy time? To educate ourselves. Investing is all about feeling our way, getting to know the lay of the land, and making gradual inroads while constantly evaluating how well we're doing. A year's subscription to *The Wall Street Journal* or two hours per weekend on the Internet's Motley Fool are worth far more than a seemingly free education from a gay-looking broker motivated to steer us into highly commissioned products.

We can use mutual funds to build good investing habits. We should watch fund expenses. Perhaps we'll choose "C-Shares" with their modest 0.5% commissions so we can have the benefit of some broker advice and responsibility. We'll watch out for "back-end loads" (commissions paid when we sell). As we become more knowledgeable, we'll look for funds focused in the areas we've begun to identify for our specialization.

Unfortunately, the mutual fund is at best a temporary solution. Why? We'll get no advice from a no-load fund. Often we'll have a tough time even getting through the 800 lines—especially at those times when the market is in chaos, when we need it most. Mutual funds go up and down, just like the stocks in them. They may seem like savings accounts, but remember they not only have no stated interest rate or insurance; they can go down. If you think them through, mutual funds are not much different from giving a broker our money, letting him move it around at will, not being able to talk to him, with no procedure for complaints or arbitration. We'd never tolerate that with a broker—but that's basically how mutual funds work.

By the end of our mutual-fund tutorial we may have come to the conclusion that true investing boils down to individual stocks and bonds, period. We may become aware that attempts by financial professionals to repackage stocks and bonds as financial "products" are made as much to maximize their income as to offer possibly better returns.

Those of us who discover we've no interest in investment may then make an educated decision that mutual funds will be our main tool of investment. But we still have to select the funds, tempering our risk, and our results, through diversification. Even with mutual funds, we must always remember that just as there are bad stocks, there are bad funds. We still have to show up with more than just our money.

If we discover we truly have no interest in this second career, we can focus on educating an investment manager paid .5–1.5% of our assets as to what our needs and wants are in detail. Managing our advisors is a job we can never abdicate.

Although it may make us uncomfortable, investing ultimately means understanding a part of the market so well, we can skillfully pick stocks and bonds directly—and stay with them long enough to prove or disprove why we bought them.

We do this in other areas of life; investment is no different from making hypotheses and educated guesses at home, in the office, on the road, or with our spouses, all the time. That's not gambling, which is another form of dependency: depending on chance, with odds loaded against us. Investing is applying what we know to a given situation, making the best decision we can, acting, monitoring how it's doing, and continuing to remake that decision if the amount at stake merits the time, effort, and money. It's nothing more than that. Voilà: our second career!

▼ ▼ ▼ ▼ ▼ ▼ ▼

The Fabulous Forties— Coming Out into Our Own

▲ ▲ ▲ ▲ ▲ ▲ ▲

▼ ▼ ▼

Mitch has been hard at it and he's near the top of his ad agency—but he's fantasizing more and more frequently about chucking it all. He just split up with his lover of eight years, Tim, and Atlanta seems awfully empty without him. Recently he's been tiring, and it looks like chronic fatigue syndrome is firmly entrenched. Mitch and his financial advisor look over his past life, his present quandary, and his unknown future. They decide to agree with his doctor's recommendation to take long-term disability to fend off the symptoms. In the past two years Mitch has stayed mostly at the country place and has pulled together a script that has stirred some interest, and possibly an option. Over the last year Mitch has met Matt, a lawyer who's just made partner—a good foil to Mitch's rapidly evolving future.

Tim's also at the start of his 40s and is a respiratory therapist in a managed care practice. He's going full tilt income-wise— and has been offered an ownership position in an entrepreneurial "doc-in-a-box" emergicare operation. Tim's always lived in the shadow of his lovers; without Mitch he feels funny thinking about going into his own practice. One of his concerns is that he's never come out as a gay man, and the practice would put him in a more public position than he's ever been before. He's got every bit as much of an itch to change—but the steady income has almost a hypnotizing power on him.

▲ ▲ ▲

The 40s are the home of the famous heterosexual midlife crisis. Do we have one? None? Several? Like so much of American culture what we are told about the midlife is both myth and metaphor born of child rearing. The only solid data about the midlife was published in the 1970s, and then only about a few straight males.

Yet the chronological and psychological reality of a transition at midlife cannot be denied. The ideas of the midlife—the recognition of mortality and the desire for a second chance at life—transcend gender or sexual orientation. It is here in the 40s when these ideas somehow become very real—and their financial effects can be dramatically concrete. As we get to face who we've become, and who we really are, we also get our final chance to launch ourselves as who we want to be.

What makes the midlife a crisis for marrieds but a transition for gays? The 40s can be all about moving beyond old structures into freedom and metamorphosis—provided that we heed the call for action which, if ignored, can set off a crisis distinctly our own.

► Midlife Crisis or Call for Change?

For many marrieds this is the decade of destruction. The structures of married life are stressed to the breaking point as rigid roles crack, children become teens, and family finances peter out or stretch too thin. As its members struggle to define their individuality within their restrictive family roles, the pressure-cooker family—and a lot else—often blows up in the process. Children bolt from the nest. Divorce settlements may wreak havoc just as college bills are being received.

The single-minded focus of straight men as competitive, breadwinning loners may leave them unprepared when there's nothing more to father. Shorn of their role, one day they wake to less noble realities of midriff bulge and hair loss. Some seek to recapture lost glories with a younger woman.

For many married women, the reduced role of motherhood is just as disorienting. Many refuse to face reality and fall back onto prescription drugs. Others no longer have a lid on their anger at having been stuffed into a stereotype for half their lives. Whatever solution is sought, it's often not a pretty sight. It's no small wonder that the midlife looms large and awful in the minds and lives of marrieds with children.

Just because we're different doesn't mean we're safe. Our forties present different challenges than are faced by the 90%—and the clients I've helped achieve their dream of gay financial freedom most definitely do not live them as a continuation of their 30s. The simplest reason is that we can't; as we hit our forties, our worlds call on us to face some new realities.

▶ 40s Reality #1: *Economic Equality at Last*

Up to now we've had the chance to have a comparatively easy time of it economically—starting with our surplus spendable income. We've also had more mobility, creative circumstances, and an outsider role to help us. For the last two decades the 90% has been strongly distracted, siphoning off their incomes into family. Now, as they disband those families, they too can have these advantages.

The 40s demolition derby of the marrieds can mask the fact that this is the last time they'll be playing life's game with a handicap. The days of our extra discretionary dollars are running out. Our days of wine and roses are over—a change that must be provided for as we view our financial future.

▶ 40s Reality #2: *The Lavender Ceiling*

If that weren't enough, any cover we may have carefully knit together at work is now worthless; it should be clear by now that we won't be marrying. From here on out neither camouflage nor the closet will do the trick—we're out whether we like it or not. As a result, many find that they must spend increasing amounts of time fending off economic exclusion due to stereotyping. Homophobes may now have us in their sights.

If we've been successful as employees we are probably also expensive—so the 40s can be particularly perilous. This is often the decade for employers to clear out expensive employees, before age discrimination protections make the process more difficult. The higher we go up the salary ladder, the more subjective becomes the basis of our evaluations. Antigay discrimination can now be found in many guises; whether we're harassed, passed over, sidelined, or downsized, the net effect, day in and day out, is the same: we are economically penalized for being gay.

▼ ▼ ▼

Janet is proud of her progress at XYZ Corp. She's had diversified assignments, added skills, acquired mentors, and produced well. At about thirty-five she started to notice a slowdown in assignments. She was no longer included in some regular staff meetings. Finally one of her mentors asked some oblique questions as to whether she intended to have children. At about forty, her division was dissolved—and she was among the few who never seemed to find a new berth.

▲ ▲ ▲

This happens just as the organizational pyramid narrows the more we advance. Marrieds may now pull privilege as card-carrying heterosexuals. At some point we'll bump right up against the lavender ceiling. The murder of our careers will be bloodless—as invisible as we ourselves may have been on our way up.

Work itself becomes tougher, more risky, and less rewarding. If our strategy up to now was to be the best, hardest working, or most loyal, this is a tough act to follow. Even baseball players miss most of the time—and our strikes now may bounce us right out.

▼ ▼ ▼

Alice has been a lighting designer for two major network shows now for ten years. She is also at age forty, two years back from having had breast cancer. One of the shows now has a new producer who never seems pleased with her work. She's tired of waking at 3:00 A.M. to be ready for setup and taping at 4:30 A.M. Yet she is worried about her lack of private disability insurance—and losing her group benefits. She decides to go freelance after getting the one show to continue with her on that basis. She converts her life insurance, which has an accelerated benefit feature. Within three months she's working as many hours but is being paid far more, and—in what she considers her finest moment—signs with a rival show to her old nemesis. She's taking a risk against her financial advisor's advice, but figures it's her life. What tipped the decision in favor of independence, she realized, was the desire to regain the power to pace her own work— and the chance to make a splash in her own field as an independent.

▲ ▲ ▲

If we haven't worked out our psychological kinks by now, we may stay in increasingly untenable situations simply out of loyalty. We may continue to pretend that being gay isn't a factor at work. We may simply try to be better, and work harder. If we do succeed in coming up with a unique skill, unbroken track record, or irreplaceable contribution we may forget to ask why we're still working for someone else.

► 40s Reality #3: *Midlife as Last Call*

Just as in the 20s we didn't have marriage as a wake-up call, now in the 40s we don't have divorce and the disbanding of families as a last call. The straights are again the ones who are clear that change is the order of the day. Again, we may have no sign that reality has changed and that we need to switch gears.

In fact, much of gay culture strives to pretend that we don't get older—that we simply become more of a Man or more of a Woman. Our gay media propagandizes that the party never ends, that we'll always have all that extra money to spend. Even our gay leaders appear at times to fantasize that gay life always slopes up, reaching ever higher heights.

We've climbed those heights, all right. But suddenly we reach a vantage point from which we see both the beginning and the end of our lives. We may have been able to push aside evidence of the evaporation of our advantages, but in the end sheer age makes us open our eyes. If this doesn't wake us up and get us out of that great gay bar in the sky, nothing will. We're going to need every asset we can muster to navigate the rest of the decades before us, especially if we didn't put those advantages to work in financial investments, relationships, and career.

► The Fabulous 40s

Without traditional families gays don't have many automatic moments when we're prompted to take stock and consider where we stand. Our moment of truth comes when we can see what we've done and what we face ahead. The 40s are definitely audit time— a truth-telling about finance.

While the 20s were all about visions and exploring, our dreams then didn't have much financial reality to them. This is our time to revise those visions into rigorous financial plans. Whereas the 20s were years of potentiality, the theme of this round of planning is limits; we're limited by what we've done, and now we see our limits ahead.

This is a good time to seek professional, financial, and legal advice, in part because we're more motivated to take it than ever before. The quality of our planning here is crucial: the better our plans from here on out, the more likely it is we'll achieve them. As they engage in this vital stock-taking, many of my clients have found some happy surprises awaiting them in their 40s. In comparison with the 90%, our journey to the 40s is likely to have included advance work on several principal tasks that come into play as we consider the lasting contribution we are to make with the rest of our lives: crafting a unique identity; forging durable relationships; and developing the entrepreneurial tools that can lead to true financial freedom.

► Gay Plus #1: *Identity*

We've been working our identity issues since our first sexual awakening as gays. With so many "Just say no!" messages our identity has to be pretty strong for us to dare to express it. Tempered by the teen gauntlet, it may be refined in the ghetto cauldron. Each act of discrimination, large and small, tests it.

How different it can be to be swept ahead by the majority's expectations, to lose ourselves in family, and to follow all the signs and signals straight society provides. No wonder the midlife is an identity crisis for the 90%!

Left to our own devices we have all the necessity and opportunity to invent ourselves, to develop our own styles—to individuate. This is part of the reason we're trend makers: our circumstances encourage us to create unique solutions to life's old problems.

With our higher risk of AIDS and breast cancer we have become much too familiar all too soon with the mortality issues that confront everyone—gay or straight—at midlife. For many of us in urban areas, our 30s become a training ground for dealing with these concerns. This priming the pump can make us think that we've been there, done that, and got the T-shirt with the midlife. We may in fact have been distracted and delayed in our 30s by all the death and disease around us. Many have found themselves very much off track by the time they hit midlife. Our challenge is made both easy by its familiarity and difficult by its premature disclosure.

▼ ▼ ▼

Tom is a star salesman. His lover of 18 years, Hal, has AIDS. Both have nurtured plans to retire to Florida. They decide to have Hal apply for his long-term disability benefits and check out what medical insurance options are available when Hal becomes

*Medicare eligible. They put the Provincetown house on the mar-
ket, knowing full well it may be two years before it sells. Tom
resigns, but only after he finds a similar but commission-only sales
job based in Miami. The deciding factor was less travel. "Trust
the Force" has paid off—his sales skills have produced a 40%
jump in income the first year. And he's been able to be there for
Hal during three medical flare-ups.*

▲ ▲ ▲

The central task of the 40s is not to dwell on our death, but
to use the prospect of it to motivate us to probe deeper truths
about ourselves. This is where a good deal of our money and time
get spent in the 40s: on recreating ourselves, on carving an identity out of the material we've collected so far, and on spinning all
that out into a new lifestyle uniquely tailored to our needs and
wants.

The great danger we run is losing ourselves in the wealth of
distractions manufactured by society and by our own gay subcul-
tures. With the midlife it should be clear that in matters of true
importance—starting with the matter of our death—we are alone.
Recognizing this can result in a great economy of effort and
means. No longer do we need to buy our identity at society's
malls, through the company store—or even in gay boutiques.
True identity, we learn, is homemade.

As in most homemade efforts our true cost is time—time by
ourselves. Beware of resisting this solitude and attempting to get
others to do this work. Society's abundant self-help books, seminars, and gurus are of little help, and can divert our efforts from
the necessarily personal nature of this work—the silence, solitude,
persistence, and patience that are called for.

In many ways this is our advanced financial education, where
we personally define and test the attitudes we need for the decisions before us. However you choose to do it, now is the time to
clarify your perspective on the economic fundamentals that come
into play. Ask yourself the hard questions:

• Are you willing to climb the unsure, rocky slopes of risk to
  pursue your dreams of return?

- Can you distinguish between your fundamental needs and the wants you have only tasted?

- Are you prepared to trade in the hard demands of ambition for what truly satisfies your soul?

Economically, this is a crucial decade. After years of exploring the possibilities of *being*, we now define what we want to *do;* where we once struggled to minimize spending and maximize income, we now focus on building assets and minimizing liabilities. The decisions we make during the midlife determine our success or failure in the decades that follow. In short, we take charge of our own lives. We remake our assumptions. We decide whether to work for others or for ourselves. We recognize what work we truly want to do. We set our requirements for relationships, refine our expectations for friendship, and review how extended a family we can support. We strike a balance between work and play, solitude and society, simplicity and complexity.

▼ ▼ ▼

Eli has been a therapist in group practice for ten years now. She reached her maximum salary about five years ago. Lately work has looked more like routine than anything else. One other therapist in the group gets her goat because of what Eli feels certain are her antilesbian feelings. She lays out a battle plan to create her own practice focused on eating disorders, scouts space, begins an intensive effort at getting acquainted with physicians known for their referrals in this area, and settles down to write three articles about the subject. After the first article is published she starts a workshop once a quarter at an adult education group. After the second article is published, she gives notice at the practice. She has also taken the time to note all the journalists covering this field, and has sent them copies of her articles and invited them to use her as a source in future reporting. She's looking forward to her new practice with an excitement she's never felt before—and as a safeguard has cut her nut of basic expenses down to 25% of her net income. She's got about six months of expenses covered, after paying the costs of start-up. It's now or never.

▲ ▲ ▲

With our identities at stake, we must resist the temptation to leave our midlife retreat too soon. One doesn't reject the packaged solutions of straight society without putting in a lot of work. This is our once-in-a-lifetime chance to forge the understanding that makes that possible. The longer we dwell here, the more likely it is we'll end up owning our own lives. The decisions reached here must last decades. Ponder them well.

We'll know we've completed our work when we can see our life easily in our mind's eye. Our descent can be as thrilling as our ascent was terrifying. Soon we find streams—our life themes— which we can ride into the great lakes of our 50s.

Looking back, we now understand why we had to abandon that which seemed to define our life before. In many ways that life has ended, and we have made the transition from a period where we had little control to the age when we have the most control, decisiveness, and direction we'll ever have in our lives. In our 40s we have truly entered our prime—an age of mastery. We are at our mental heights—and as we see the rest of our years unroll before us, it's obvious this is a period of new beginnings.

▶ Gay Plus #2: *Relationships*

The second potential area where we've done valuable advance work on our midlife tasks is in our relationships. Because we don't have the license for an all-consuming pressure-cooker marriage, we frequently develop far more flexible and diverse networks of relationships. We can have an uncompromised, completely personal period of midlife stock-taking without having to destroy our connectedness—and can pursue the midlife's singular path of solitude while still being supported by our relationships.

The diversity and flexibility of our relationships serve us well here. With our ability to yoke independence and interdependence in our relationships, our unions can adapt not only to strong personal needs and styles but to the changes that midlife decisions can engender. Our penchant for age differences can result in less risk that both members of a relationship are going through the midlife at the same time. And our lack of standardized financial arrangements creates necessary room for growth.

It's almost a given that a couple's overall finances will undergo major change after midlife—often in the form of graduation from roommate finance to coupled finance.

▼ ▼ ▼

Pete has just amicably dissolved a twenty-year relationship. Suddenly Thor is in his life—a man with AIDS whose finances are equally complex. Thor, luckily, has high corporate benefits when he leaves on disability, but has real estate with his ex-lover that is worth well below its outstanding mortgage. After being together several years, the two strike agreements that minimize the potential liability of the real estate on Thor—and keep it rented to barely cover payments. They also create agreements that permit them to move in together and assure Thor the security he needs in fighting his illness.

▲ ▲ ▲

Without traditions, rituals, and laws to provide structure for couples in their 20s and 30s, no amount of financial planning, legal agreements, or couple counseling ever seems to make a couple's finances truly joint. After the midlife we're more willing to commit—or more motivated to loosen the ties that bind.

▼ ▼ ▼

Tonya and Anna work in the same field: film production. Tonya's always wanted a country house, and got help from her ex-lover in buying it. Anna's city oriented and is interested in more commercial applications of her trade. These present her with a nine-month assignment a thousand miles away. After discussing its implications they decide to separate financially but stay to-

gether as a couple. The change helps them allow each other to invest in interests that are purely personal—although it takes a few honest fights to get their household-expense sharing on an even keel when Anna returns from assignment. In the process Tonya feels she has become financially codependent with Anna; she seeks therapy to reinforce her newfound independence and insistence that Tonya contribute where they truly have mutual interests.

▲ ▲ ▲

While each relationship is obviously different—and the patterns of change vary—one thing is certain: relationships that survive midlife changes are more likely to have a financial backbone than those of the financially much looser ones of earlier years. After the midlife we've got identity—something real, concrete, and definite to weld together. The particulars of that welding are another crucial variable to be considered in any midlife plans.

► Gay Plus #3: Entrepreneurship

The third possible area where we've done advance work on our midlife is in developing the qualities often associated with the entrepreneurial spirit. This doesn't mean we all have to become entrepreneurs. It does mean that we acquire entrepreneurial characteristics, skills, and experience that can further our career mobility in later life and bring us closer to the level of financial independence that can make our later years a time of true freedom.

Once again, the contrast between the straight and gay midlife challenges is striking. While the family and career structures that earlier served straights so well are under pressure to be dissolved, we are in a position to fashion the flexibility that has served us so well into forms of our own design. We've already seen this at work in our investment strategies, which are built to be continually revised, and our relationships, which we tailor to our own circumstances. In terms of our income, now is the time to establish and activate a money machine that not only can roll for the next two decades but also provide a safety net—or exit options—along the way. When we do that within the context of a career, our entrepreneurial spirit can be of enormous help.

This period is often a moment of truth between us and work—period. Many of our ranks are turned off by work because it seems to be all tied up with heterosexuality, raising a family, and conservatism. Work may not be a very gay place, especially for those of us who have bumped up against the lavender ceiling. No wonder we respond to the entrepreneurial spirit's call to shift gears from being an employee slave to being a master. We may achieve our independence as a master craftsman, a specialized trader, a small employer, or a product director. We may do it on our own, or within a larger company—as an "intrapreneur." All of these options require a 100%, fundamental commitment to financial success. Virtually all the entrepreneurs whom I've helped make the transition report long hours, hard work, and high risk. It's pure work; the investment is total.

Entrepreneurship and intrapreneurship—the birthing, acquiring, and mastery of new domains—can suit our backgrounds to a T. We're already experienced at doing our own thing, following our bliss, finding the grain of our wood. An entrepreneurial bent emerges naturally from our ability to see life truly at an angle, forging handicaps into strengths, finding ways to make gold out of straw. It's all about assertiveness and power, and the boost that comes from exchanging dependency on a few bosses for the diversified strength of many clients. It means forsaking invisibility for total visibility, where our gayness is only part of the picture. If coming out is a bridge to the promised land, being entrepreneurial is the building we do once we get there. It engages us to change ourselves as we go forward. It makes work meaningful and makes meanings, values, and goals work.

If you truly want business success, you should consider putting entrepreneurial assets on your gay balance sheet in some manner, shape, or form. These assets can be intangible—a style, a mind-set, a readiness, a perspective. They can be tangible—a product, a market, a method of distribution, selling, or production. They can be activated both independently and within organizations. They embody a can-do attitude about life, including about being gay.

And the rewards are more than financial. Being entrepreneurial is all about economic power—grassroots, everyday power of our own making, not of some politician's giving. It's the power of financial freedom, the ability to act on the fantasies and frustrations uncovered in our midlife work. By now we've had ample chance to amass a considerable pile of assets—in discretionary dollars, real estate, investments, personal development, networked relationships, and hard-won experience. Now is the time to put those assets to work for us with entrepreneurial vigor.

▼ ▼ ▼

George wonders what it's all about. This year a half dozen of his friends have died. He's forty, HIV negative—and feeling a mixture of guilt and fear. He decides to close down his consulting practice and frankly retreat to the country house. He starts major therapy, sobers up, and after one year starts to write a book about his area of specialization. After four years he comes up with a new direction for his work. He feels up to it but decides to cut out the travel part, and expand his practice to include consulting with individuals as well as organizations. Sometimes he wonders about all the lost income—about $400,000. But he feels he's good for another twenty years of work at a much higher level, and knows he would never have even made it to sixty on his previous path.

▲ ▲ ▲

Life's transitions harness with minimal effort the very forces of what it is to be alive and catapult us onto a new level of living. Successfully making these transitions in a way that corresponds completely to our needs and wants makes us more effective as people, and multiplies our ability to amass resources, apply them, and safeguard them.

Transitions are costly—and they don't always work. But the midlife can be our most successful rite of passage, one we shouldn't miss for the world. We're spared the meltdown and destruction of straight divorce and family dissolutions. Potentially we can approach the midlife with our tanks full, our training done, our networks formed—we're ready. The only question we face is, are we willing?

What if we hold back? Unfortunately the 40s is a do-or-die decade. We can make this transition later, but the financial and personal rewards for doing so will be fewer. The 40s are most productive when we spend them gearing up for harvesting the fruits of our labors in the 50s. It's more than a matter of finance; experts on personal development tend to agree that expressing fully who we are is the best contribution we can make to society, the best gift we can make to ourselves. This is why it's worthwhile to fight any temptation to retreat from the midlife—and why it's worth it to develop our potential to its fullest.

Entrepreneurship and You

We may not think we're entrepreneurial, yet after the 40s our lives have many of those characteristics. And we may have a limited, outdated notion of what being entrepreneurial means today. The growth of the very concept of entrepreneurship has paralleled the growth of gay freedoms. Most of the new jobs in America are now created through small businesses—and small businesses are getting proportionally more support. Big business is also getting into the act, as new product pressures foster intrapreneurship within giant corporate groups—such as the 3M intrapreneurs who were responsible for bringing out Post-Its.

These trends play to our strengths. Immigration and integration have created a steady movement toward diversity, fueling companies' needs for diverse employees to respond to these new markets. As selling and producing go ever more global, straight white married males are about to become a minority among producers and consumers—creating opportunities for the rest of us.

▼ ▼ ▼

Gail's been in the travel business for fifteen years now. Commissions are progressively getting smaller. Anyone can enter the business and undercut. The perks aren't what they used to be,

especially since they're all "family" vacations. Gail gets the idea to
design lesbian-only tours for a major tour wholesaler. They go for
the idea. She lines up and starts checking out local resources,
writes lesbian-friendly copy, and starts launching the packages.
After a back-and-forth first year it looks like she's got a winner—
and this time she even enjoys going on the trips.

▲ ▲ ▲

Meanwhile, the current downsizing of employees and out-sourcing of entire departments can create opportunities for those same employees and departments to sell their services entrepreneurially—using their originating corporation as their first big client. And computer developments now make it possible for those downsized workers not only to use the same technology as the giants, but to look like giants themselves. Finally, computer networks enable even the smallest ventures to access expensive resources formerly out of reach.

All of these developments make it worth our while to determine whether we have what it takes to flex our entrepreneurial muscle as more and more of us do every day. We'll see that many factors in common gay experiences encourage the growth of entrepreneurial traits and that common employment lemons in the gay experience can be turned into salable entrepreneurial lemonade.

An Entrepreneurship Inventory

Entrepreneurship may be suitable for more gays than may realize it, but it isn't for everybody. We can start with an inventory of favorable factors for entrepreneurship:

- Do you have a stash of cash equal to three to six months of your basic needs "nut"?

- Is your nut below 30 to 40% of your income after taxes?

- Are you saving between 15 to 30% of your income after taxes?

- Has your income advanced by at least 5 to 10% per year?

- Are you earning half again as much more as five years ago? Twice as much as ten years ago?

- Do you pay off your credit card bills monthly?

- Have you applied your savings with an overall investment strategy?

- Do you own real estate where you would realize a profit if it sold tomorrow?

- Do you have openness and clarity about your relationship with your family?

- Would you say you have a wide circle of both personal and professional friends?

- Do you and your partner live together? Do you have some shared expenses?

- Do you have a partner who would support career change?

- Is your alcohol and drug use clearly occasional, costing under 1 to 2% of net income?

- Have you used job or career moves to advance your skills? Experience? Income?

- Did you earn money to pay your own expenses growing up? To pay your college education?

- Do you watch fewer than five to ten hours of television a week?

- When you travel, do you plan your own vacation instead of buying a package plan?

- Have you been an officer in a nonprofit or community organization?

- If asked what you had to shelve to earn money at the outset, would you know?

- Do you have a written plan for at least five to ten years out?

- Have you taken any adult or continuing education?

- Have you traveled to more than ten American cities or spent more than three weeks abroad?

- Have you taken more than six months off to go back to school?

- How long have you talked about starting up a small business?

- Do you plan on working part-time well after age sixty-five?

Total your yes answers. There are twenty-five possible. Make your own scale to rate your answers. (You might as well start setting the rules now.)

▶ Our Gay Entrepreneurial Assets ◀

Those gay differences that help us in the corporate world can be just as valuable in an entrepreneurial setting:

No or Few Children

Without the distraction of child rearing we can amass the skills and experience entrepreneurship requires; we can work our buns off while straights are preoccupied with raising families. In these times where technology makes entrepreneurship possible much earlier, our creative enterprises can be our children—and also legacies that will live beyond us.

Greater Discretionary Dollars

Our higher discretionary incomes permit much greater savings early in the business game. If we invest these aggressively we are already venture capitalists, investing in other companies. From here it is but a few steps to investing in our own entrepreneurial efforts.

Relationships

With our partners we can pool discretionary dollars, multiply our networks, and profit from combining flexibility with commitment. Then we can move from Me, Inc., to We, Inc., with significant tax advantages because our relationships are regarded as "arm's length" by the IRS. We can employ each other, sell things to each other, and in other ways take advantage of the fact that we are in reality together but legally apart. The crumbs of domestic-partnership benefits now being offered from straight benefit packages pale beside the creative coupleships we can forge as dual entrepreneurs.

► Turning Handicaps into Entrepreneurial Strengths ◄

Finally, even the handicaps we've faced can in fact equip us for success in entrepreneurial roles. Here are nine negative factors that can become advantages in business when turned to entrepreneurial use:

Discrimination

Society's hatred can result quickly in total inhibition. But watching our *p*'s and *q*'s may result in becoming the "Good Little Gay" and the good little employee: skilled, loyal, hardworking. If we become a corporate star, it may soon be clear that adulation is not the same as the financial incentives that only entrepreneurial or intrapreneurial roles can provide. Our choice is then between being used or being a "Me, Inc."—whether we like it or not. As we practice independence we may unleash our self-expression, and realize that our own business is the best corporate shield.

Isolation

Many of us grew up isolated, surviving in the closet because it very well might have been dangerous to come out. But such restrictions may have led us to network in gay life as if there were no tomorrow. If we become rich in contacts and sources, we may also develop political astuteness. Then we may find that we can operate better outside the organizational caste system as Merlins and Richelieus, prophets and seers, experts and designers. As we acquire a domain of power, influence, or expertise we may come out as well—and know now that when people trust, care, and support us, it is for whom we really are.

Hiding

The magic shield of childhood—imagined acceptance—can betray us in adulthood, leading us to seek illusory allegiances and live in false security that can be brought crashing down with a single (true or false) accusation. But hiding may bring us to operate on the fringe of the organization, permitting us to safely multiply our organizational value and exposure by taking on risky assignments, pioneering new areas, and responding to any opportunity to acquire skills and education. As our mobility and experience base increase, we may see more options, both in the organization and in our careers. Eventually we may come to see that having our own organization affords us the best privacy, and that talent is the best shield for remaining in the organization.

Rejection

When prejudice reveals its ugly face, we may react in a knee-jerk way, playing the outcast who rejects society and its worship of success. But we may instead find ways in which we can channel our anger into action and see that success is the best vengeance. If we set a short-term goal to be the one who rejects, instead of the one who's rejected, we may come to refine this into discriminating choice. We may become quite skilled in selecting those whom we can thoroughly trust, and thereby solve the entrepreneurial challenge of successful staffing. We can further pour our anger into business assertiveness with single-minded focus.

Shellshock

Prejudice can feel like bombardment, resulting in a bunker mentality that has no room for future vision. But it can also result in one's always having backup plans, in guerrilla-warrior-type skills, and in a wariness appropriate in a time when business is conducted more and more as war. This mind-set may then easily embrace such radical modern business techniques as zero-based budgeting (where every item must prove every time period its right to exist), management by wandering about (knowing what's going on behind the scenes as well as down on the sales floor), and take-no-prisoner ways to stay lean-and-mean to match downsizing, outsourcing, and divesting actions by larger organizations.

Aloneness

No matter how big our families and peer groups, many of us have simply grown up alone and lonely, feeling that we don't fit in, or that we have few models to turn to. But this emptiness may result in a freedom to develop sophisticated individual style and values—and possibly a unique vision. If we come out in the process, we may quickly attract not only other gays but society's "fringe" people: its poets, artists, writers, rebels, and thinkers. That in turn may enable us to tap new ideas and products. It may also enable us to invent organizations that even we would feel comfortable in—groups that may possibly knit together individual actualization, organizational effectiveness, and innovative social agendas.

Invisibility

Many of us grew up grateful we could act straight; often we used this invisibility to buy us time to spot safe havens where we can come out. This extensive experience as actors can help us again—to understand what our staffs need, what our customers want, and what our competition might do.

Illegality

Our illegal status and its resulting fear can shut down our assertiveness, dampen our drive, or simply turn us off to business and money matters. But it can also prevent us from getting fat, dumb, and content—and can spur us to figure out ways we can work within, without, and around all kinds of systems where we just don't fit in. As a result, many of us come to see that only by running our own show can we both protect and express ourselves. If they say we're illegal, it's in our interest to stake out domains where we set the rules.

Homophobia

Homophobia is easily internalized as shame, especially if we don't come out. But participating in pride events and the acting-up of AIDS activists may show that banding together cannot only protect but advance our issues. We may discover economic ways to band together and find entrepreneurial ways to work the gay agenda. We might end up launching products and services unimagined and unprovided by straight society. These services may then not only serve our own community through organizations of our own making but lead and fashion markets in ways that are equally disproportionate to our numbers.

As we've seen, the entrepreneurial spirit can grow naturally out of the gay experience, but it doesn't suit everyone, and should not be pursued without serious thought—just the sort of stock taking that the midlife transition asks us to do. Enough of my clients have become successful entrepreneurs at this stage of their lives that it merits the investigation I've offered here. There may be no fuller expression of gay financial freedom than the self-sufficiency that entrepreneurial self-employment can bring. I confess that I'm biased—I've been self-employed for half my working life. But given the advantages it can offer, any midlife transition is not complete without a consideration of the role that the entrepreneurial spirit can play in our creating and safeguarding the legacy that each of us wants to leave.

▼▼▼▼▼▼▼

The Fifties—
Harvest Time

▲▲▲▲▲▲▲

▼ ▼ ▼

Elaine's worked with handicapped kids nearly all her life, but in her 40s she decided to go freelance and specialize in bilingual education. After a slow start her practice has been going full steam ahead. As an independent she earns far more for her time and has become expert at managing her finances. She's got her life on a personal finance program and has her later decades pretty much mapped out income- and expensewise. She's been with Pat for over five years now. They moved in together last year. Gradually they've become the center of their community's lesbian social swirl, staging several parties during the year and enjoying some friendships that are now over twenty-five years old.

Pat's playing catch-up with her 50s. She had been married, divorced, and only just got her kids on their feet. She's got a steady job in insurance but sometimes it seems like she lost twenty years in the process. Elaine's been urging Pat to move into sales, but Pat's more than a little burned out. She worries about depending on Elaine's assets and is thinking about taking the sales training program the company offers. It would mean a steady haul of heavy selling right up to retirement. She's got the contacts to probably make it work, but does she have the energy and drive to do it?

▲ ▲ ▲

With the midlife work of the 40s behind us—and incorporated into the way we see the world and our own road ahead—we're prepared for the final years of commercial productivity. We may now move on what the 50s are best for—plunge ahead and get done this last great work of our lives. This is production time, and any time off for reflection, second guessing, or remaking our plans is productive time we will never recoup.

▼ ▼ ▼

Jackie started out in word processing but stayed on top of every technical change as she became first an in-house consultant and then manager of support for the city's largest legal firm. Along the way she's founded an informal working group of managers with similar professional responsibilities and came out one by one to key partners till being lesbian was a nonissue. She's now phasing in computer networks and is working on a firmwide plan to make partners computer literate. Her battle plan is to retire with extremely rich benefits at fifty-seven—and use these years to build a base for a consulting firm specialized in this area upon leaving.

▲ ▲ ▲

With our newly won vision we can now see that proverbial fork in the road of our 60s ahead. But we can't get ahead of ourselves; this is a very be-here-now decade for working and *doing,* where efficiency counts. This is clearly a time for those inspirational *little* books urging us to action—one saying or one page per day. We face a workathon straightaway with little to impede us from raking in the results of our lifelong labors and materializing our dreams.

In some ways career life cycles parallel product life cycles:

- There's an initial investment stage that sucks up cash, hones a competitive edge, and identifies a market niche—like our 20s.

- There's a rapid rise in income accompanied by dramatic changes in productive capacity—similar to our 30s.

- There's a faltering, shifting gears, and redirection of operations—akin to our 40s.
- And now there's a high-volume, little-change, high-efficiency cash-cow time.
- Next: Either replacement by more shiny products or "classic" status—esteemed and valued.

As a result, the impediments we do face are potentially more damaging than ever. We must pay special attention to managing our liabilities, which should be well known to us by now. This is our last chance to put into place insurance and other preventive arrangements. Risk management and asset protection must go hand in hand with our peak productivity. Like so many other financial moves, many of these actions should have been done much earlier. But we're human, and late is, in this case, far better than never.

▼ ▼ ▼

Robin was downsized as controller of the chemical industry's largest firm at forty-four. He used his considerable savings and investments to try to build a private tax practice helping people with AIDS with taxes. Although it proved enormously challenging and satisfying, it cannot support his lifestyle and has begun to eat into his nest egg. His hypertension remains high, and maintaining private benefits is proving to be a burden. He decides to ride out the 50s as an in-house consultant with an investment firm, milking his expertise on the tax consequences of investment and insurance plans—a lucrative specialty, which will in turn enable him to maintain his individual practice on a low-key basis.

▲ ▲ ▲

We need to keep the 50s a level playing field, and can do so by making this a period of acceptance, adaptation, and accommodation. This is not a good time to remake ourselves, or the world. Our goal is to keep our momentum. Yet forces are at play that will tip the balance dramatically in favor of the 90% at the workplace unless we take action. It's time again to monitor our environment carefully.

► 50s Liability #1: *Lost Economic Advantage*

After years of having surplus discretionary income, we must now recognize that straights are no longer pouring their income into family making. That's a red flag, because that surplus was our major offset to their economic advantage as the 90%.

They not only pull even, they pull ahead, especially in the area of spending. Due to their insatiable needs for cash over the past decades, their spending is by now very efficient. We, on the other hand, may have become used to extra spendable income, growing diffuse in our focus, or expecting more of the same. We are in for a rude surprise. Our incomes may slow, stagnate, drop, or stop. The time to be tight is now, and we may not be used to it.

We must also remember that they are very much the majority. In business relationships it's their world, and their councils are largely closed to us. After all the money they've spent on family, they may be hell bent to squeeze every bit out of their 50s—even if that means pushing us aside, tossing us out, or running us over if we get in their way.

► 50s Liability #2: *Full-Throttle Discrimination*

If we have not secured a market niche, organizational lock, or entrepreneurial haven, the 50s can be open season on gays. It's downsizing time in America, and we are often the first to walk the plank. At this point we are definitely out in fact if not in name. As we rise in income and responsibility, two dangers emerge: We become more visible targets, and our reliance on increasingly subjective performance appraisals makes us more vulnerable to the homophobia that can be cloaked in job evaluations. Guess who stays—and who often gets bounced.

Most of us are not supermen or wonder women; we're human beings. Superperformance isn't an option anymore. We've become expensive. The organizational pyramid gets narrower with each year toward retirement. It's either up or out.

What to do?

▶ 50s Defense #1: *Career Insurance*

If our track record is superb and our employers deem our skills, knowledge, or contacts are essential, we may survive the pressures of this period. Welcome to shark-infested waters; get ready for golden parachutes, insurance lifeboats, and entrepreneurial life-jackets. Careerwise the stereotypes of age are already against us: that we're rigid, tired, out of touch, and expensive. Add homophobia and we're first out the door.

In this kind of situation rules don't help as much as individual career attention and aid from a trustworthy source. If we needed therapists in our 20s, brokers in our 30s, planners in our 40s, we especially need career coaches in our 50s. Among the suggestions I've seen work, where we're flexible enough to adopt them:

- Reinvent ourselves intrapreneurially by seeking special assignments.

- Seek training and mentoring opportunities.

- Adopt foretelling and catalyzing roles—the old Merlin/ Richelieu power-behind-the-throne routine.

- Retread the gay stereotype of being the bellwether or the creative type.

- Start a sideline to fall back on or expand in later years.

- Hire a computer coach and flaunt newfound computer skills.

- Seek project responsibilities outside the hierarchy, stressing your treasure trove of experience.

▼ ▼ ▼

Mike had reached the top banquet job at the top club in town. But he knew management would never grant him further responsibility as a gay man, and he wanted wider opportunities for practicing his art. He contacted a contract management firm that managed several major museums, proposing that his experience with special events be added to their in-house restaurant operations. As a consultant to the museums, his homosexuality became either irrelevant or even an addition to his cachet as he created this new market and specialty.

▲ ▲ ▲

A smart tactic would be to mimic the moves of feminists at the workplace, for whom the 50s are a golden opportunity. This is the time for assertiveness, for multiple career paths, for riding market trend waves, and for finding new ways to add value.

▼ ▼ ▼

Teri saw her home sales stalling at Avon. She decided to aggressively sell in offices—recruiting reps at the workplace, sponsoring career-oriented dress-for-success seminars. Whereas her lesbianism had always been a question in the home market, at the office it became seen as adding to her assertive image. Her sales took off, and she was tapped to export this experiment into other regions. She stayed with Avon because she saw it was one of the only Fortune 500 companies with a majority of women in senior executive positions.

▲ ▲ ▲

This is the time when we come up against the very real lavender ceiling. If we're hit by discrimination, fighting it can be costly, the rewards minimal, juries antagonistic—and our time is already running out. On the other hand, in those cases when manage-

ment realizes the potential impact of discrimination charges, negotiation has produced more than a few sizable settlements.

If a buyout is in the air, it may be a good move to take it—
and rev up those entrepreneurial alternatives. Downsizing can
sometimes be a blessing in disguise if we use that parting package
to fund an entrepreneurial opportunity. Have one ready in the
wings. One increasingly viable solution is to outsource ourselves,
or our entire department, into a stand-alone enterprise whose first
and prime client is the ex-employer. None of this can be done
without negotiation—or the cooperative atmosphere that makes it
possible.

▼ ▼ ▼

*Al handled the human resources for a staid insurance firm.
Year after year budgets and ideas got cut. Yet the firm allowed Al
to assemble a first-rate team. Finally Al proposed that his department be launched as an independent provider of human resources
services to the firm, and be free to market their services to other
firms. He negotiated advantageous use of corporate resources, got
equipment either free or at greatly reduced cost, got free space for
nearly one year—and had a guaranteed client for three years.
After a year's shakeout it looks like it's going to work. One of Al's
first moves was to install partnership benefits and the equality
principles in the new firm's policies.*

▲ ▲ ▲

▶ 50s Defense #2: *Asset Allocation*

Whatever our investment strategy is, it should be in place by now,
busily multiplying our assets at high rates of return. We can now
see approaching the once distant days when this hitherto second
job will become our primary occupation. If we're short on assets,
this is our last chance to play catch-up—to cut again our basic-
needs nut and search out overlooked opportunities for putting
away money and optimizing returns. Frankness and honesty are

vital in any effort to assess what we have and what we need. After this great accounting we may not be able to correct imbalances again.

Like the 30s this is a decade of putting away and putting off. We'll be in better shape if for now we shelve distracting desires such as travel. This is our glorious fall, with richness, abundance, and great wealth—and it is best hustled away into our barns. We're wise to tend our fields carefully. Any holdover behaviors from our spending decades must be held at bay.

► 50s Defense #3: *Income Maximization*

This is harvest time in our lives. If we've survived downsizing and discrimination, we should have found our vein of gold by now—so the only option is to work it for all it's worth. The hours are long, the work is hard, but the conditions are hopefully ideal. We have now taken our place at the table. The cards have been dealt. This is the performance decade, where all that we have learned and all that we have accumulated come into play.

We do well to recognize this as our last great income push. It's not time to slow down yet; the 50s can be a period of volume and great intensity in our careers—a decade when great works get accomplished, and we experience competency to our greatest extent. Many clients have described these as the years when they're totally into what they're doing, losing themselves in work for hours. In terms of maximizing their income, this level of involvement could not come at a better time, for this is often the final decade of our being able to work 110%, our last extended intimate connection with the world of commerce, of work for pay. Make the most of it.

► 50s Defense #4: *Self-Expression*

Fortunately, our dedication to our work is often motivated by more than money. We've been at this long enough that our work should by now be an expression of our selves. Our most profound application of our assets takes place when we make this the decade of our most profound self-expression. If the 20s and 30s are popular decades for creating families, the 40s and 50s are prime time for creating art, organizations, products, services, methods, and ideas. This is the pinnacle of the psychologist Maslow's pyramid, where after security and social relations are in place we are well positioned for self-actualization.

The greatest bonus of all occurs when we begin to experience what the psychologist Mihaly Csikszentmihalyi calls *flow*—the time in life when we feel in the groove, when we are so expert, we can get lost for hours at a time practicing our skill, when we look up surprised at the end of a day that the hours have flown so swiftly by. This hard-won synchronicity with life itself can be one of our greatest achievements—and a powerful motivation when we need it most.

Insurance—The Ultimate Defense

As appealing, or exhausting, as that all may sound, we cannot afford to forget that our being gay means that our well-being is always at risk—medically, socially, and legally. One way to assure that our lives do not come crashing down around us is to insure against those risks. But first we must acknowledge them.

Gay Attitudes about Risk

We can develop very peculiar attitudes about risk, perhaps because the extent of the risk we face can often seem overwhelming. It helps to keep track of the risks we know about: violence, discrimination, and the myriad possibilities that result from having no legal protections. Even then, we do well to expect the unexpected.

- We suffer insidiously invisible damaging discriminatory action at work, in lodging, when traveling—in public, period. We can lose our jobs.

- We have no legal safeguards in our relationships unless we fabricate an expensive, sophisticated legal safety net (see the chapter on the 60s). We can lose our loved ones.

- As illegals we may have to defend ourselves from legal harassment.

▼ ▼ ▼

Bruce took in his sister's son, Tim, while she spent time in a mental hospital. The son made great strides until she came out and reclaimed him. Instigated by her jealousy of Bruce's wealth, Tim, now seventeen, threatened to make accusations that Bruce had molested him, unless a six-figure payment was made. In shock Bruce had to seek costly psychiatric and legal support and ended up making the payment in return for signed releases. He was so shaken, he felt he had to move from their community, sold his house at the bottom of the market for a third of its value— and took two years to recover emotionally.

▲ ▲ ▲

Small wonder that we often split into two groups: the highly risk-averse, who pay dearly to avoid it through lost opportunities and fortress living; and the risk addicted, who tempt fate, getting excitement out of running risks, and even eroticizing risk.

These peculiar attitudes about risk can lead us into particularly dangerous risk-taking and risk-avoidance actions. We may avoid risk through corporate conformity, seduced by the promise of continuity and paying for our overinsurance with lost opportunity. Or we may continue adolescent illusions of immortality, confusing body culture with health, discounting the possibility of disability, and entering our 50s dangerously underinsured.

What's significant is that neither group—those overwhelmed by risk, those embracing risk—sees risk as manageable. Neither thinks of risk as simply something to prevent, manage, or insure against so that we can get on with our lives. Either mind-set can lead to needless financial disaster.

Realities about Medical Risk

As a community we owe it to those with AIDS to heed the lessons they've learned about insurance. They've discovered that disabling illness can strike at *any* age. Breast cancer teaches that we can be struck without any warning. Both teach us that battling disease has become incredibly costly, sometimes equal to more than we would earn in our lifetime. And we need to remember that all of us will have a catastrophic, fatal illness someday: it's as certain as death itself.

Being smart about insurance pays because our friends have found out the hard way that insurers are cutting back wherever they can. They've discovered that most coverage is written for old, established disease—and that when new illnesses strike, treatments are automatically labeled "experimental," i.e., unpaid for, running up out-of-pocket expenses that may be greater than any amount we would ever get from Social Security.

The rest of this chapter will focus on risks specific to us that insurance will cover. Let's face it:

• In many ways our risks of falling ill, not working, and dying are higher. (See the chapter on health.)

• We have far fewer social resources to fall back on. AIDS has also taught us that as gays we're not only outside the fabric of society, but we're also discriminated against in prevention, detection, and treatment. With AIDS we've had to take care of our own; not only are there holes in society's safety nets but our nest eggs often make us ineligible for public benefits. AIDS has demonstrated too often that family support is unpredictable at best.

• We prize our independence, and paying our own way is the only way we're going to keep it. We may not want family care if it means giving up our independence. Our partnerships are geared toward independence and interdependence, and may not include promises of bedside care. Our rich extended families may not have the geographic closeness or financial commitment to be of much help. And many of us wisely don't want dependence on unpaid care, period.

We've fought hard for our independence. We have the ability to salt away considerable savings; but in the face of these costs, they can disappear fast. The financial insult on top of our injuries comes when the hospital social worker talks to us about spending down those assets at thousands of dollars a clip so we can get society's booby prize: Medicaid and increasingly poor welfare.

Risk Insurance

When risk is too expensive, not predictable, or easily detectable, it's better to pay someone else to insure it. We simply cannot achieve these levels of protection on our own.

We're used to having to pay for the quality we want. Why should that stop with the incredibly intimate needs of illness? Only hard insurance contracts can give us the assurance we require.

Any gay who's not insured should be; we run higher risks. Any gay who's underinsured should start here in his or her financial planning. If the cost of insurance is the issue, then forego freelancing and get the free insurance that many paid jobs provide. If those jobs aren't available, then get the skills or go to where they are. Insurance is basic. Good finances start here.

► Gay Insurance Action #1: *Get Medical Insurance—and Get It First*

The simple fact is that gays have higher risks. Our men have a higher risk of AIDS, our lesbians have a higher risk of breast cancer—and all of us have a higher risk of addiction and mental illness. We cannot afford to skip medical insurance. If you don't have it, get it.

A recent GMHC study shows that most of their long-term AIDS survivors had private insurance—not Medicaid. Medicaid is no safety net; it's bad for our health. Do you think you'd get great care from a doctor who's getting $12 from Medicaid when she could get $84 from private insurance? If you presented yourself at a hospital with pneumonia-type complaints, with Medicaid paying $64 or an insurer paying $640, under which coverage do you think you would get a few pills for pneumonia as opposed to a more expensive—and more accurate—bronchoscopy procedure?

If not for yourself, think of medical insurance as spouse/friend/family insurance—to make it easier for them.

▶ Gay Insurance Action #2:
Imagine What Could Happen

You know a lot more about your health than you'd like to admit. To plan for the worst in financial and medical realities requires a useful kind of schizophrenia. Just do it—a little at a time.

Start with patterns of past illnesses; the best indicator of the future remains the past. Don't overlook family history, a big indicator with such risks as allergies and cancer. Note preventive actions taken—and not taken—whether it be exercise, rest, nutrition, or diagnostic tests. Inventory alcohol and drug use, and instances of abuse. One key: this is a time not for moral vows but for accurate assessment.

Take any test that will tell you your real risks. But do *not* test through your doctor or under your own name. Just as it's too late to get fire insurance when the barn is burning, it's often too late to get medical, disability, or life insurance when risks are documented.

▼ ▼ ▼

Horst just tested positively—anonymously—but is asymptomatic. He has just taken the CKR5 protein gene test—again anonymously—to determine whether he's in the 18% group of people with HIV who are long-term survivors. This test will not tell him whether he'll live or die with AIDS, but it will help him see whether he has to prepare financially for the long haul.

▲ ▲ ▲

Think through what care options might exist *when* calamity strikes; yes, the question is *when,* not if. How many months of basic needs could be met? Is money available from a partner's income or assets? An extended family's? Is the family of origin close—geographically, personally? What level of immediacy, care, pampering, do you require? Are you the kind who really wants to work till you drop? Would work support you or spit you out? Would your profession leave you behind? What kinds of career fallback do you have?

The motto here is: Hope for the best, prevent the possible, and insure for the worst. Why assess, prevent, and insure? To keep our options alive. Options is the name of the risk-management game. The more you have, the better hand you have to play.

▶ Gay Insurance Action #3: *Check and Question Your Coverage*

Simply finding benefit booklets and insurance policies that are up to date is half the battle; banish the administrative stuff to a separate folder. Once you've found them, run a likely scenario to see what might be covered, and what you'd have to pay. This might suggest specific key topics to probe such as Incontestability, Preexisting Conditions, Authorizations, and Deductibles/Copayments.

When your eyes glaze over, ask questions of your agents until you can say what you need to know in your own words. You've certainly paid them enough—let them do some of this work. Pick up a good overall money book, but read only the slim section on insurance.

Don't stop here. Consider the options you don't have. Don't drop them until you can write out a short statement as to why you don't need them. This, by the way, is what they call planning.

▶ Gay Insurance Action #4:
Seek Group Insurance

If you are at risk for serious illness and don't have insurance, put benefits before salary at your next job move. Why? There are usually no medical questions on insurance gained through employment. Group premiums are often paid by the employer or are much lower due to your being part of a healthy group of working people.

In 1996 substantial protections were legislated to ensure that medical coverage is immediate, guaranteeing that you can go from job to job and take it with you. These legislative changes were enacted none too soon, since most HMOs, or managed care plans, are specific to only limited geographic regions. Still, there are exceptions; find out if those protections apply to *you*.

Be wary of launching an entrepreneurial venture without top-flight—and expensive—medical, disability, and life insurance. If your venture has three or more people, it may be possible to get all the insurance benefits you need without medical screening. All that may be necessary is to wait a year for coverage to include any preexisting conditions.

▶ Gay Insurance Action #5:
Get Private Insurance

Many gays are in freelance jobs that don't include group medical benefits. Private coverage is also totally portable. It works whether we work or not. This, plus our higher risks, are reasons alone to get private medical coverage if no other insurance is available to you.

Even for those with group medical benefits, private disability coverage is usually worth its high cost, since it's paid *in addition to* what group plans or Social Security would pay. Given the higher costs generated by today's diseases, this is a necessity, not a luxury.

What's most important to us in the end may be independence. That's the ultimate argument why gays should load up heavily on private medical, disability, and life insurance.

▶ Gay Insurance Action #6: *Get Extra Insurance*

We need more insurance, not less, and extra, private insurance should be considered as early as possible.

Even though straights can get by without catastrophic medical policies, we should strongly consider them. They're cheap and, as we've learned with AIDS, can be vital supplements to existing policies. And with the new ability of life insurance to provide cash if life-threatening illness strikes, it's easy to think of this expense as the investment in our futures it can be.

We've got the extra discretionary dollars exactly at the times when insurance is the cheapest. Move it in the spending plan from being a discretionary item to a necessity.

▶ Gay Insurance Action #7: *Seek or Request Domestic Partnership Benefits*

One of the most blatant insurance problems for gays is benefit discrimination against gay couples. Domestic partnership benefits, apart from the awkward name, are a genuine concrete benefit of gay activism. Their spread indicates that discrimination may be more readily ended in the boardroom than in the courtroom or the voting booth.

Few realize, however, that these benefits are listed on the employed partner's W-2 reports as extra taxable income. That can negate the value of the benefit. Yet if the receiving partner is self-employed, he or she can pay for the benefits received—and get a deduction. This is a good example of how tax code considerations also need to be equally taken into account when deciding insurance issues.

► Gay Insurance Action #8:
Get Disability Insurance

The worst shock for gays is the fact that disability causes a drop in discretionary income—usually from lots to little. Yes, we may be able to get by on the average Social Security payment of $875 a month. But after all those discretionary dollars, would we want to? Do you want to spend illness time fighting paper battles, standing in line for public entitlements, and subject to the jealousy of underpaid clerks who listen to religious radio's accounts of how rich we are?

The second shock is that *nonreimbursed* medical expenses alone can easily total over $10,000 a year. This includes insurance premiums, alternative treatment, medical travel, healthier food, moving, home modifications, home help, and professional fees of all types. Add to this the increased cost shifting through higher deductibles and copayments from insurer cutbacks. Three major expenses are reimbursed partially and poorly: psychotherapy, home care, and prescriptions. Yet these are major strategies for dealing with many complicated illnesses.

Over half of all of us are disabled over three months at some point in our lifetimes. And gays may have much higher risks. Our decisions here are simpler than sizing up the risk in sex: all it takes is some stupid action on the part of a stranger wielding two tons of Japanese metal—and we know how stupid Others are. Would our families take us in, and would we want them to? Do we take vows that include stuff about sickness and health? So add disability insurance to the armamentarium—as an income condom.

Our incomes are the bulwarks of our independence. Protect them with disability insurance. Not all group plans are alike; watch out for maximums like $2,000 a month—not much more than what Social Security pays. And keep in mind that group benefits are usually taxable.

If there's a choice, choose employment that offers long-term disability where you pay the premium, making the payments tax free and perhaps equal to your previous take-home pay.

Get private coverage first; that allows you to get maximum

coverage. But beware of agents who don't take application questions seriously. Some companies screen people when they file a *claim,* not when they file an *application.*

▼ ▼ ▼

Jill's agent encourages her to lie about her income to get the most coverage. Now, seven years later, she needs to make a claim. To her horror the company requested her tax return from the time of application and reduced the amount of coverage to what was appropriate to her real income at the time. Her income is now much higher—but instead of raising her coverage as her income rose, she relied on false security.

▲ ▲ ▲

▶ Gay Insurance Action #9: *Get Life Insurance*

For years gays were told not to stock up on life insurance. Now it's an asset that can be cashed in if life-threatening illness strikes. With that catastrophic possibility covered we can truly plan financially for life, knowing we're covered for illness. See the chapter on health for how these brand-new benefits work.

Gays may be easy prey to agents who play the gay card. Remember: their loyalty is to the company paying their high commissions. Our loyalty is to ourselves—so shop insurance aggressively through competitive bidding.

▶ Gay Insurance Action #10: *Check Spousal Coverage on Homeowner, Car, and Liability Insurance*

Joint ownership is rarely wise protection for gays, but joint insurance coverage is. There are three areas where we have liability:

• If you own a home singly, you may need an extra endorsement or renter's insurance for a partner. What if your partner has friends over who fall—and sue? In the world of insurance, the point is to cover any kind of weird exception that can occur; for if you don't, it will.

• Beware of joint ownership of a car; that gives one additional person for an opposing party to sue. True, partners should be listed as additional drivers, but jointness stops there. If the owner is the one having the accident, the liability stops there too.

• What gay couples should get is joint umbrella liability coverage. But beware of agents who point out that umbrella liability coverage simply extends the coverage on car and homeowner insurance—because if those coverages are in one name only, the other partner is uncovered.

► Gay Insurance Action #11:
Get Long-Term Care Insurance

Given our high risks and all the reasons why we might not get or want family-of-origin care, we should get long-term-care insurance much earlier in life than straights, for whom it's normally not economically justifiable before the 60s.

We do have one advantage: our partners are strangers in the eyes of the law. While this means we must have health proxies, powers of attorney, and living wills in place, it also means we can transfer the ownership of our assets to our partners if we feel our high risks may result in our needing public care. Many a couple with AIDS was able to keep home and wealth intact when private insurance wasn't in place and the sick partner had to depend on public benefits. Our ultimate fallback is that we can impoverish ourselves to qualify for community Medicaid with no spend-down period—but this is truly a last recourse, since it puts us at the mercy of potential homophobes.

When nursing homes are in the picture, we need, like all Americans, to have Medicaid Qualifying Trusts in place. Even there we may have considerable advantages, since our relationships are unrecognized by the government; our spouses may have considerably more leeway in the eyes of the law than marrieds.

We want to avoid nursing home care in any case. Too often a nursing home is run by lowest-common-denominator conservatives now with *in loco parentis* power. Nursing homes already act as if older people don't have sex lives—do you want to spend your last years neutered? This can add insult to illness and end a gay's life with the same degree of dependence, secrecy, powerlessness, prejudice, and harassment as we faced in our teens. We can insure against this; being a private payer may be our last defense.

Our best strategy in this area is to become highly expert on home care to avoid nursing home care. With long-term-care insurance, and knowledge about how to make the medical system work at home, we can ensure our independence as well as insure our care.

▼ ▼ ▼ ▼ ▼ ▼ ▼

The Sixties—
Generate or Stagnate?

▲ ▲ ▲ ▲ ▲ ▲ ▲

▼ ▼ ▼

Bob was one of the first to innovate in catering—and expanded that idea into a steady corporate party-planning firm for the last twenty years. He's had a tough time throughout getting staff, especially someone to handle the kind of marketing he does. He's just bought a house with his ex, Jeff, in Vermont, and nothing would please him more than to make the transition from Manhattan to New England life. But the business is even more the monster that must be fed to be kept alive—and it represents a solid source of income, a possible chunk of equity if sold, and a constant worry. Bob tried to get his employees to take the firm over in his 50s but that failed miserably, setting the business back about three years. He wonders now if he should have pursued that convention planner, Alice—to bring her in as a partner and successor. Now the people he talks to always question first whether he's going to stick around to make sure the business survives the transition—a question he's not even sure he can answer yes to.

Jeff has clearly had it with hair—and hair has been his life for the last twenty-five years. He kept on top to the bitter end—about ten years longer than he'd planned—but chose to pile away another $250,000 in investments. He's glad now he did it, for Vermont certainly has changed from the inexpensive retreat he found in his 40s. He's even decided to be a stylist emeritus at one of the few good salons up there—training, promoting, and servicing its prestige clients. He wonders when Bob can, or will, let go *of the business. But in the meantime he's been spending quite a bit of time with Jack, a teacher who's nearing retirement and who has a tourist hiking and biking business in the summer he wants to expand.*

▲ ▲ ▲

Welcome to another great fork in the road of gay life. Like the other even-numbered decades our sixties are a decade of change. We get used to building our castles in our 30s or plowing our fields in our 50s—and then come the demanding midlife 40s and now the fearsome 60s. Like it or not, the harvest is over and the cash cow runs dry.

The 60s are another even-numbered dividing-line/bottom-line decade. It's time to tote up what our 20s–30s young adult and our 40s–50s midlife adult have produced, to see whether our nose is still above water and whether we can relaunch ourselves in the twenty years ahead.

The 60s introduce the idea that our very lives are our chef d'oeuvre, our masterpiece, our contribution to society. It's time to ask ourselves what we have to show for our lives. If we're uncomfortable with the answer to that question, the 60s and 70s are probably the last decades we have to change that answer, and to probe that question and the answers our lives offer up more deeply.

► Freedom from Earning an Income

The golden ring of the 60s is financial freedom. By unlinking income from work we can express ourselves in both work and play as we wish, free from the tyranny of having to earn money. Its indirect offspring, our investments, are now more important. Entitlement income from pensions and Social Security should enable the earning of money to now take a backseat. Even if alternative sources of income are small, these are years when our core and discretionary spending can be greatly diminished.

Since our teens most of our lives have hung by a single financial thread, whether that be an allowance or a monthly income. And that thread could easily be snapped if the person spinning it didn't like our being gay. Gradually we created stronger financial independence by knitting safety nets out of our various threads of income: real estate, our own businesses, employing each other, partnership benefits, insurance, corporate consulting, financial investments, tax-deferred compensation, pensions, collectibles, teaching, individual counseling, writing, and speaking.

▼ ▼ ▼

By the time Ken reached sixty he had one apartment building, a small summer rental agency, and a pension from his teaching. He also has begun quarterly workshops at an adult-education center, has written several paid articles, and is planning a book. Each activity feeds him income, expands his interests, and introduces him to new people. He plans on selling the apartment building in five years to finance a move to the Southwest.

▲ ▲ ▲

At this point we became financial alchemists, pursuing the alchemists' dream of transforming basic elements into something priceless. Therein lies our secret of wealth: transforming income so many times in so many ways that not only does our money multiply but our security, potential, and comfort grow.

Now our very age itself entitles us to wealth through Social Security, Medicare, and a multitude of privileges, perks, and priorities granted simply because we've succeeded in getting this far. Even if retirement funds are thin, entitlements help us snip that last connection between income and work, preparing us for the time when who we are and what qualities we have count as real, hard assets on our balance sheets.

▼ ▼ ▼

Ellen was a tenured professor for nearly thirty years. In her 50s she pioneered research on real incomes of gays and lesbians as a counter to growing hype about our wealth and power. Systematically she also built links to other gay researchers, started writing

*up her results, and began appearing on panels. Upon retirement
she continued her work through an institute of her making and
for the great satisfaction it gave her, as well as the paid opportunities to travel, speak, and meet new people.*

▲ ▲ ▲

Importantly, we are no longer defined by our jobs. And if
many of us were excluded from positions of power by discrimination, being esteemed for who we are rather than what we do can
be a welcome change—as long as we don't make the mistake of
linking esteem to wealth.

Another Change Decade

The real question of the 60s is not the 20s and 30s question
of "Who do we want to be?" nor the 40s and 50s question of
"What do we want to do?" but simply "How do we want to hold
what we *have*?" Unlike the other two questions this third challenge is not expensive to examine or solve; it's largely a matter of
decision, perspective, and interpretation.

This is the decade where we shift our base of power from the
physical preoccupations of the 20s and 30s and the mind matters
of the 40s and 50s to the realm of the spirit.

Unlike the employeeship of the young adult and the entrepreneurship of the middle adult, in maturity it's as if we'd just acquired a company—and our job now is to figure out what to do
with it. This is where we get that elusive feeling that we really own
our own lives.

Our Gay Advantage

It's time to treasure one last legacy from those of us with
AIDS, who have boldly reinvented old notions of retirement.
Some of them have shown how wise it is to withdraw voluntarily
with enough time to allow ourselves to regroup, how rich a variety
of experience is open to us once we unlink income and work, and
how we can move on to new levels of activity and involvement.

We can achieve all of that in our 60s, if we generate a rich enough vision to sustain our later years. That vision probably has a lot to do with independence, since that is the financial baseline of gay life. One extension of that independence is a focus on what we can do for our community and extended family—not expectations as to what family and progeny should do for us.

If we have embraced change, this is our chance to rewrite our scripts, and to think about endings and completions of our own making. Even with most of our lives written, the successful strategy that remains is empowerment. That may take some effort, as it flies in the face of the stereotypes we inherit.

In youth-crazy gay culture the sixties suck; in straight culture the sixties are seen as the end of work, which is how many Americans define themselves. In popular and gay parlance the 60s look like a wasteland where no one wants to be, where no one wants to go, defined in terms of what we *don't* have: looks, money, friends, health, work, fun, support. Is this true?

Our own youth culture notwithstanding, the bad rap for the 60s may be primarily due to the fact that straight men have dominated the debate for decades. The 60s are a disaster for straight males. They leave work—the primary basis of their identity for years—just as their testosterone declines and their impotence rises. Heterosexual women, on the other hand, are on the ascendancy. Many of them are finally equalizing their status with men, exercising both male and female traits as needed, taking advantage of the early separation for retirement that can come from previous periods of time away from paid work.

We don't have to fit any preconceived notions of dealing with the changes age brings, in part because our gay generation has been experiencing and managing dramatic change since the 1960s—change that continues to this day.

We've embraced change now for over a quarter of a century, and nothing since has ever been the same. This augurs well for our future—for our capacity to manage our later years and for our further growth. While straight society continues to be standardized by government and business, we have exhibited a distinct taste for change. This fits well our part in the play as the spice in society's stew.

▼ ▼ ▼

Helen saw in her 40s that she'd never be properly rewarded in a corporate environment. Nor did she want to make those kinds of sacrifices. She saved for and bought a franchise instead. In ten years she'd bought three of them. Subsequently, when the franchisor ran into trouble, she lined up funds to buy them out and has since improved their training and marketing programs. She's expanded the number of franchisees, including among them several lesbians and gay men. Now she's considering either doing a public offering or simply selling out her interests.

▲ ▲ ▲

Change is also what the 60s are all about—a last great redirection and rethinking. If we can continue to embrace change as our liberating angel, we will not be subject to the living death of the heterosexual male or utterly heterosexual retirement communities. Our financial future is based on our continuing to be agents of change—*lovers* of change. Just as our love life is sparked, peppered, and fueled by differences, our economic life is jumped, accelerated, and evolved by our ability to change.

The 60s are not a time for gays to lie down but a time for us to get up, and make one more run for the gold. It's time to develop our own models and draw our own guidelines from our own experience. We can do it. We've reinvented the other decades. We've even come up with rites of passage they don't even have. It's time to do that vision thing, and celebrate our passage into a strange new land called maturity.

► The 60s as Gay Adventureland

The key to making the most of our 60s is the financial freedom that comes with our unlinking of work from income, whether that's by saving and investing our surplus discretionary dollars, or by cutting our needs and wants down to a manageable core. Just as the 50s were oriented toward managing our liabilities, the 60s are oriented toward managing our assets—allocating our resources and applying our funds. Our first asset is that we're alive—that we made it. Just to enjoy this priceless perspective, given all our risks and assaults, is itself an achievement. But survival alone isn't enough when there's so much more to look forward to. Let's see how we're doing.

A 60s Transition Inventory

- Are there satisfying opportunities for part-time employment, consulting, or freelancing?
- Could most income now be unrelated to specific work done?
- Is significant income flowing from simply holding positions (as trustee, director, retainer, pensioner)?
- Would income from Social Security cover basic needs at this point?
- Are housing costs stabilized at a manageable level?
- Are any gaps in medical coverage covered to prevent a drain on assets?
- Are investments sufficient to supplement income needs for likely years to come?
- Is it possible to end savings, maintain investments level with inflation, and begin a small payout from investment?
- Could a financial crisis be met from investment without forcing moving or the sale of a home?
- Are there enough funds to pay for wanted change and redirection?

Waking Up to Wealth

Once we've tallied what we have to work with, we may realize that the time has come to put that wealth to work. Many of us labor under the impression that wealth is about having money; with our lifetime financial position tallied, it's time to graduate to the realization that wealth is now about what we *do* with money.

I've noticed that my clients who feel wealthy are those who believe they have enough in life. Turning it around, one could say it's truly a self-fulfilling prophecy: those who feel they have enough tend to save their surplus, ensuring they'll likely have more than enough tomorrow; those who never feel they have enough tend to spend their surplus, virtually ensuring they'll never have enough.

Ask yourself where you are—and have been—on this scale. Although the past is the best predictor we have, you may still be able to adjust your fundamental notions about wealth in time to enjoy what you have.

Unlinking Income and Work

When we're able to remove income as a requirement for work, this simple change can open us up to many thousands of callings in life. With one paradigm shift we move from a singular vocation to multiple avocations. Those of us who have seen that happen with people with AIDS on disability retirements have some models to follow on this. One lesson they've shown us: Even when people receive windfall sums they often continue to work, finding valuable self-expression in work they enjoy.

No matter what our income level has been in the past, this is a time of life when we have the chance to work simply because we want to get something accomplished, because we have a particular talent, or because we like something. Those of us who have done just that in our careers—either because we had the discretionary dollars to do it or because of our felt freedom as outsiders—already know how satisfying this can be.

What do the rest of us have to learn from them? That we don't have to repeat what we do over and over and over again, as we probably did at work before. That we can work where we like—at home, in a public space, at a nonprofit, at someone else's home—wearing what we please, and working the way we want. In short, we can become our own bosses. Time and again, among those who've lived long in the shadow of someone else's personal power, I've seen this change herald the unleashing of the gay spirit. As long as our money was coming from someone else's hand, on some occasion we've always had to trim our sails, tuck our caps, lower our heads, turn our cheeks, and look the other way. No matter how out we are, not one of us can escape the realities of hatred and violence that some people somewhere may always hold for us.

▼ ▼ ▼

Louis has been a legal secretary for over twenty years. He's also a good storyteller. He sharpens his writing skills in his last ten years of work and collects material that could possibly be of use in his newfound passion of writing legal thrillers. His first stories sell all right, building his experience. When he retires with his firm's rich benefits, he goes full steam ahead with his first book, playing on the image of inside information. Luckily his writing hits big just when Hollywood is impressed by the box-office returns of John Grisham and similar writers. In addition to working when, where, and how he wants, he's decided to start teaching a course in writing at a local university as a way to connect with the younger generation. He's also become a writing tutor to several lawyers in town who've been thinking along the same lines.

▲ ▲ ▲

If we are indeed able to unlink work and income, we finally have the chance to have work our own way, custom designed to our specific wants and needs. Our financial freedom can be as stunning as any liberation we've felt before. Except now we are smarter, richer, skilled, connected, and infinitely more mature. This is a dream worth working for, saving for and investing for.

▼ ▼ ▼

Tim honed his skills in administration in his 20s in a foreign country, returned for a graduate degree, became a hotshot consultant in his 30s, founded a company in his 40s, and consulted with individuals in his 50s. He identified a small consulting specialty in his 60s that paid his travel around the country, a small series of workshops that kept him intellectually on his toes,

*kept a small part of his practice going helping those who could
really use his help, and began writing articles and a book. He saw
that as he moved into the seventies he'd probably drop the corporate work, cut down the workshops, keep the individual work,
and increase his writing.*

▲ ▲ ▲

The 60s may mean retirement from paid work so that we may
have creative work. Work shifts from earning income to generating satisfaction. We've learned by now that the security of safety
nets is a direct function of the number of threads in them; having
many threads of interests is the key to satisfaction in the 60s.

Wealth as Time

One of the best things we can buy with our discretionary
dollars is time—the ultimate luxury.

The discretionary time saved from child rearing and pressure-
cooker marriages has been as important an advantage to us as our
discretionary dollars. Starved for time during the family years, the
90% often appears not to know what to do with themselves when
they hit the 60s.

By now we've learned that investing time pays high dividends.
Taking time to recycle and retrain ourselves is solid protection
against discriminatory surprises while we're working—and it's a
lifetime habit that pays off in the 60s. Why should we stop now?
We made sure we were never boxed in in our careers by networking, by multiplying our skills, and by outsourcing ourselves early
in our careers. We learn how to make a business out of a skill, a
niche, an advantage—or a dream. We use our private practices to
increase who we know, and what we know. We mix teaching and
consulting, inventing and selling. We come to realize that all businesses are really experiments, and that the best investment may be
in ourselves.

If this has become a lifelong habit, when the 90% finally have
discretionary time away from their families and lockstep careers
we can simply shift into high gear. Now we can write articles,

conduct original research, test ideas, reach out, travel, and vary our experience even more. We never had fixed, traditional obligations to follow any one track or to make conventional sense of our lives. In the 60s this freedom needs continued exercise—just like our physical lives. It's a case of use it or lose it.

Reinventing Notions of the Extended Family and Gay Tribes

The straight stereotype, born of finite biological families, is that we lose people as we become older. AIDS certainly taught us that we have to continually create a family of choice, an extended family of friends, and membership in numerous gay tribes all through our lives. These social networks are another gay safety net that took plenty of time and money to construct. Now those networks, too, pay their dividends.

The 60s are a good decade to invest even more in close relationships. Change is in the air, we've discretionary time—and we're prime catches. What is true wealth to us but our relationships?

We'll need these relationships, families of choice, extended families, and tribes, as we grow older. When we do exit our lives, we will require every bit as much care and support as we did when we entered them. In this decade we get to choose who will give us that care and support, and to invest our time and attention in them now.

The old Me, Inc., that got expanded to a We, Inc., now expands even more to an Us, Inc. We invest in people, starting with ourselves. The 60s are all about community.

The 60s Reward: Gay Liberation

Given all this preparation, what can happen when a person thus primed hits the chronological trigger represented by the number sixty? Takeoff! If financial independence from earning has been achieved, what further freedom for expression is to be had!

Part of the 60s stereotype is that we're written off. Good! Let them think that. Being written off can give the opportunity to do exactly what we want, without much interference of social pressure. It can also be an invitation to enter unexplored areas—with less competition.

In this period of life we become inventors in all kinds of domains. This decade is a good time to read up on the literature on inventors or entrepreneurs. New ventures succeed more when the financial requirements laid on them are as loose as can be. This means we can make our 60s into enterprise incubators. Since many formal incubators of this type are attached to universities, it may be a good idea simply to take a course, and thereby get all the privileges and resources of an entire university to power and test our ideas.

The 60s are a time for gays to run amok in the lifework arena. With our financial security we can readily explore society's fruitful fringe areas. Our nonmainstream status also enables us to explore nonmonetized modes of economic exchange. Since we're probably highly networked, we might start with barter exchanges, where we can trade what we know and do best for what others know and do best. We can also trade resort condo time-shares to explore cheaply, and in depth, different areas of the world.

Likewise we now can price our creations high simply because we value them greatly or to get people to take us seriously. This is not a period for giving away our time or our stuff. Philanthropy is at least a decade away. The 60s are a time to reinvest our time, money, and resources, not deplete them.

Beware the nonprofits who equate 60s with cheap labor or think of us as easy marks. Dump their solicitations into a folder marked "Philanthropy"—to be reflected on carefully later and not just reacted to now. A lifetime giving program is what generates the most satisfaction and gives the best results. Those flyers may have some data of interest, but planned giving usually requires much better information than that. It's time to start thinking of your estate as your final statement to the world—your *estatement*. We need a much grander vision for our estatements than can be had from clever slogans designed merely to get us to open the envelope. We're by no means dead meat yet—so scare off the vultures.

In fact, this may be the time to create our own nonprofit

organization. We're free to band together with others simply to get a job done. And we might even cover expenses along the way, and give birth to a new enterprise in the process.

▼ ▼ ▼

Marie is a long-term survivor of cancer and addicted to exercise. She takes long-term disability early so that she can pull together resources for a nonprofit focused on exercise and cancer. After ten years she enters retirement and expands the organization to focus on the special needs of children with cancer. The organization pays many of her expenses and allows her to do what she loves most: exercise with others. Because she is the founder and not the executive, she's escaped the pitfall of becoming a captive of her own organization. She maintains her control through her effectiveness in fund-raising. And she has a growing sense of a legacy.

▲ ▲ ▲

In the Alice-in-Wonderland 60s, play and work intermix. Play is very important at this time. We should use this freedom and time to re-create ourselves; we've had enough serious decades.

The 60s benefit from being viewed as a career change, a transition to joyous lifework opportunities. If we worked ourselves into ruts in the 50s and have difficulties following the Eleventh Commandment—Imagine!—we may benefit from job-changing tools such as computerized inventories of interests, skills, style, and experience to rediscover who we truly are. It's time to reflect and to take down off the shelf old dreams, passions, and ambitions—and to invent new ones.

A frequently productive step is to seek the support of a career counselor. But first make sure that you're in agreement on three vital points: that the 60s can be a new career phase; that there are distinct and wonderful implications to work no longer fettered by income; and that our lifework is no longer based on the physical or the mental, but on the soul.

Lifework: Our Key

Work can be to gays what families are to straights—something in life into which we pour our time, money, passion, and energy. When we unlink work from income, we must replace the key functions that work provided. It's important to create new rhythms and regularities, to provide new opportunities for regular social contact and support, and to find new outlets for self-expression.

Where paid work is often neutral, corporate, and profit-driven—dictated by needs more than wants—any lifework refined, created, or discovered in the 60s should be intimate, personal, and meaningful. The line we cross in our 60s—between a life driven by needs and a life inspired by wants—is as momentous as the peaks we faced in our 40s. Financially, the 60s should see a whittling down of basic needs and a high refinement of wants into passions. If the focus is on needs, something is awry.

To reconnect with our dreams we can turn to career planning tools such as interest, skill, and style assessment. A better approach may lie in a field called "values clarification." Books in this area are full of forced-choice and structured-comparison exercises that show where our values lie.

Another approach that can be more fun is by storytelling: telling stories from our lives, or even making up stories about our fantasies. The focus should be on those incidents where we were engaged, where we experienced life flowing through us, where we had fun. If our listeners note down on small standard-sized cards the strengths, themes, qualities, and characteristics common to these tales, we've created a set of clue cards to where our focus should be. We can then spread out those cards, and with meditative focus begin to group them. Names for the groups will emerge—perhaps whimsical, surely concrete—along with a picture of our competencies, interests, and values.

These seemingly touchy-feely exercises are crucial if they result in our financial redirection. Later years are all about the application and allocation of what resources we have. Focus, goals, and values are our tools for doing this.

▶ Retirement Funding: Pulling It All Together versus Watching It Unravel

The 60s are when the results of all financial action, and inaction, come home to roost:

> savings started—or spent—in the 20s,
>
> investments built—or blown—in the 30s,
>
> money managed—or stagnant—in the 40s, and
>
> surpluses harvested—or missed—in the 50s.

If we work through these four challenges, we should be well along in funding our later years. Let one example indicate the overall challenge in retirement funding in our 60s: to make whatever we have amassed stretch over thirty years, we should not withdraw more than 4 to 5–6% in any one year. This figure is very tight. In fact as you near 6% there's a 60% chance you run out of funds.

If this universal constraint weren't enough, we have some gay-specific hurdles to overcome before we can pull our retirement funding together.

▶ Gay Hurdle #1: *A Tidal Shift in Disposable Income*

What unique financial reality faces the gay who's gray? No matter how pulled together, any gray gay has seen the evaporation of the one financial advantage over straights, our extra disposable income. As our spendable income gradually aligns with theirs, we may have the same worries about Social Security and the same concerns about retirement income. Age appears to be, in the end, the great equalizer.

For those of us for whom gay meant being special—that is, especially flush—and for those of us who derived satisfaction from keeping up with the Joneses, this may be a great comedown after years of extra discretionary income. For those of us who tried not to live life as a function of how the 90% lived theirs, this change is hardly noticed. Once again, we come back to the importance of the spending strategy developed and practiced over the years. The bottom line? If a financially secure life isn't already in place, gray gays need financial surgery—and not just a financial face-lift.

The 90% may in fact be at an advantage. They're now on a par with us as far as disposable income is concerned. Many are facing life for the first time without children or divorce settlements—a first breath of financially fresh air. Accustomed to being financially strapped all their lives, they may have the frugality that seems to work best in later years. Their children can make them feel more secure. They're more likely to have stayed with companies that offered generous pension plans and retiree health benefits. They probably have large homes that are paid off. They may have been frantically pouring excess income into investments since their late 40s or early 50s. This greater overall financial momentum can clearly put the 90% at an advantage compared to the average gray gay.

► Gay Hurdle #2: *Forever Single—Our Lack of Spousal Rights in Pensions*

Gays should have a peculiar rule underlined in their pension-plan booklets: Don't die before retirement. Why? Unlike marrieds, the law gives no rights for our partners to our employer-paid noncontributory pensions—*if* we die before we start to receive them. Once we start receiving pensions we can usually structure some way to ensure our spouses are protected, but not before.

The problem is worse with Social Security, which impacts more of us. Whereas private pension payouts can be rearranged to provide a survivorship benefit for the nonparticipant partner, it's simply not possible to do this with Social Security. Once we die, the benefits stop.

► Gay Hurdle #3: *Risk Aversion and Underallocation*

Many of us are our own worst enemies when it comes to risk. We need education that gets us more comfortable with investment overall and with risk taking in particular. There is a remarkable literature on the subject of life's risks, and for many gays it's required reading.

Investment is a two-step dance: savings and allocation. The irony is that the supersavers sometimes never quite see the importance of the second step. Retirement funds in particular get their maximum power when allocated to investment vehicles that provide greater stability and higher returns over the long run.

► Gay Hurdle #4: *Survivor Guilt*

To survive to one's sixties has always been an accomplishment for gays. Gay seniors have truly run a long gauntlet. But HIV can make it seem almost selfish to survive, much less thrive.

▼ ▼ ▼

Tim's lover has left him with an estate worth over $250,000, but Tim worries about the lover's children even though they've been left $250,000 each as well. The son in particular dissipates his share quickly, yet Tim gives him more money. Tim leaves the apartment unsold for nearly a year and doesn't aggressively invest the money he's received.

▲ ▲ ▲

A greater problem may occur when AIDS has distracted us from proper preparation for retirement. Some have given all they had and are irretrievably behind in their financial preparations for their own lives. Perhaps we simply didn't think we'd make it.

► Gay Hurdle #5: *Surviving AIDS and Cancer*

With increasingly effective treatments PWAs face the ironic problem of outliving themselves. For nearly a generation well-meaning social workers told them to spend down or give away their assets to qualify for public benefits.

Likewise survivors of cancer spend years in a financial never-never land surrounded by financial chaos, where even if investment was possible uncertainty kept funds liquid and poorly producing. Now, as survival and remission seem increasingly likely, survivors find their skills are out of date, they've lost the routines of work, and the labor market has tightened up.

As in a war dramatic financial redistributions have taken place. Some of us have inherited from lovers while many of us are impoverished. Debts that might have been forgiven in disability loom large and may require the harsher solution of bankruptcy. The longer-term danger in these financial dislocations is that we may easily forget the basic path to financial security: Save and invest.

► Gay Hurdle #6: *From the Ghetto to the Tribal Community*

Before AIDS our community seemed poised to take care of its own, to redress the discrimination previously shown gray gays by their juniors. Now several generations of urban gay men are decimated, and many lesbians have silently died of cancer. Retirement concerns no longer seem to figure much on the gay agenda. But the central question of the 60s remains: Where do we want to live?

We have many choices: urban ghettos, traditional gay resorts, and now AIDS disability retirement magnets like South Beach, Tampa, and Key West. The latter are especially attractive, since they gather together all age groups, are low cost, and have excellent medical care.

It is no accident these Florida communities, the Southwest,

and the Pacific Northwest are experiencing an overall surge in population. Many gay men with AIDS pioneered relocating in these areas to opt out of urban violence, expensive living, and bad weather.

It is entirely possible that a by-product of AIDS may be the adoption by gray gays of the developing infrastructure of widespread care, inexpensive housing, and new community organizations in these new locales. The influx is drawing in medical resources, renovating housing, building community, and changing the cultural climate of these areas. It makes every bit of financial sense to follow the tide.

▼ ▼ ▼

Heloise shared a country house in Connecticut with Bart and Tom for over ten years. When Tom developed AIDS, he and Bart decided to move to Fort Lauderdale, selling the house all three owned. With new drugs Tom's doing much better; he and Bart have invited Heloise to move to Florida in anticipation of her retirement as a legal secretary. Through the gay grapevine they find a good job for her, house her while she finds a new place to stay, and get her introduced to the local lesbian community.

▲ ▲ ▲

Financially this shift is extremely beneficial to gays in their 60s. Instead of facing retirement in urban ghettos geared toward the needs and wants of gays starting their careers, they can gravitate to newly developing communities with lower living costs, greater security, better medical resources, a wide span of generations, and better weather. These may in fact be the new geographic focus for gay community in the next millennium.

▸ Gay Hurdle #7: *Structures versus Systems?*

When the time comes that we're asked to invest in residential gay retirement communities, we'll do well to ask ourselves if we need to invest in this heterosexual-style solution. Considering that our community cores just need systems—not structures—adapted to the needs of gray gays, we may find we simply need gay-friendly services, not gay-friendly facilities.

To invest in a gay retirement community, particularly one marketed as symbols of wealth, would be just another exploitation of gay money. Our purpose ought to be to integrate, not segregate, our gray gays.

The wealthy need services, support, and flexibility. Buying into a gated community, especially one that does not offer an integrated program of medical care, simply multiplies the number of moves we must make as we grow older.

More likely than not, our first needs are for services, not facilities—for portable systems that promote and guarantee our independence, not communities that will kick us out when we're sick. We should pay attention to the scandals breaking about the lack of independence in retirement communities, assisted living residences, and even nursing homes. Such communities are usually run by rules upon rules—yet the 60s are all about freedom.

Heterosexual retirees seem to like homogenized gated communities. Would we, in all our diversity? Our aging gay population offers us the opportunity to create senior systems that are the backbone of true communities—not enclaves where we get stacked away simply because of our age.

► **Gay Hurdle #8:** *Remedial Actions*

Plainly speaking, retirement funding is either there or it isn't. The 60s are the proverbial bottom line. There may be gold watches, but there are no rabbits to be pulled out of retirement hats.

What actions are open to us? Those we should have taken years ago.

Save early and save more. Plan as if we're single. Aggressively allocate those savings to maximize long-term returns.

Or retool our careers to continue working into our 60s and 70s. Take time off to retrain, recycle, and rest. If we have already done this, then we've successfully integrated retirement planning into our lives, fulfilling a basic requirement of having a good life. To do this now may make us perfectly paced for our later decades.

▼ ▼ ▼ ▼ ▼ ▼ ▼

The Seventies— On Making an Estatement and Leaving a Legacy

▲ ▲ ▲ ▲ ▲ ▲ ▲

▼ ▼ ▼

Irene is amazed she's alive after her earlier respiratory problems—but in a way they were a blessing, for they prompted her in the 50s to use her disability income and settlement from her ex-husband, Jack, to launch Silicon Valley's first gay paper. It was tough, but as long as she had enough advertising to get an issue out she was happy—and now the paper's big enough to give her writers a chance to do award-winning features such as the latest two-part series on breast cancer. The paper ties her into the valley's life, and thanks to electronic mail she's over that hair-raising first period of physical strain, the oxygen tank, and occasional visits to the hospital. She works her staff hard, and they love it. Keeping it a kitchen-table operation, she makes sure it stays focused on the issues—trusting that toward the end of her 70s she'll be able to pass it on to someone who will manage its transition to something that can stand on its own feet economically.

Irene's ex, Allyson, completed her lifelong stint teaching art and is comfortably fixed. She doesn't really enjoy teacher travel anymore and is irritated that she hasn't made good on her promise to herself to paint now that she doesn't have to teach. She's been teaching some adult ed evening courses in the local two-year college, but it's more about her past than about her future. Sometimes students come back, usually hanging out at Irene's, who puts them to work on the paper. Irene's been asking Allyson to illustrate the paper and do an overhaul of its graphic look. Maybe she should accept that offer of an advertiser for free use of their computer graphics facilities and, with the help of a course, see where that takes her. This knocking around smacks just a little too much of the end of life, and she's obviously got some decades to go—but where?

▲ ▲ ▲

With the 70s we enter virtually unmapped territory. In the past, few people even made it to this age. Notions of the 70s have largely been based on old realities and outdated concepts of age. Until very recently old age itself was popularly regarded as a disease and many of its ailments "incurable."

People now in their 70s are increasing in number, health, and prosperity. However, we're probably seeing the last hurrah of the 70s financially based on increasingly generous Social Security allotments, company pensions, and the postwar generation's unique prosperity.

Though they may have had drastically different life experiences from younger generations, our seniors have much to share with the rest of us. Gays with HIV or cancer are suddenly faced with 70s-type issues—no matter what their age. Simply put, the question is: What legacies do we leave if we've no children? What kind of impact do we have on the wider web of life? Yes, any actions are ripples whose effect seems never to end in the pond of life—but if we want to make waves we need gay money.

After all the change of the 60s the 70s can appear like a calm sea. If we used our 60s freedom to reassess and reinvent our choices, those explorations have probably resulted in a "legacy agenda," and not merely a list of senior-sized complaints. It's sunset time with enough light for one last decade of life's work. It's time either for boredom or for culminating achievement.

This is another production decade. Gays still hung up on youth-culture values may have a lot of trouble with the work of this particular decade, since it's all about completion.

And what is the product? Soul work. In our 30s we worked

for others, in our 50s we worked for ourselves—and this is where we work on ourselves. We may try to escape this through distraction, but in many ways we're forced by our growing limitations to this focus.

We mine the soul and process our life's experience to find what we have to give back to life. This inner work may become as all consuming as any of our jobs were in early life. The true irony is that we gain as much pleasure in giving now as we got in getting then; the more we have to give, the more value we have and the greater our life's satisfaction. We often achieve this by deepening our networks, extended families, and friendships. The flow that we experienced in the 50s and the simultaneity we discovered in the 60s both benefit from the meditative focus we can bring to them now.

The most popular professions of the 70s are those of teacher, mentor, storyteller, and writer—spirit-to-spirit communications. This is the crying market and spiritual need of the gay community—to understand the diversity and uniqueness of our experience. These are the ones who can help. May we have a golden time when we value and reward our elders in these occupations!

▼ ▼ ▼

Lenita's greatest commitment has come to be her local Quaker meeting. Over the years, she's initiated the meeting's adoption of a minute endorsing gay marriage, prompted the meeting to add gay antiviolence to its annual donations, and has encouraged the meeting to reach out to potential gay members. At her own expense she's compiling a collection of taped stories of other Quaker elders in the meeting and is writing up profiles of them in the quarterly newsletter. She's been named to the Annual Meeting and proposes to gather stories of gay Quaker elders across the state in a specialized collection. She plans to then take these stories out to gay community organizations again at her own expense to raise consciousness, not only about profoundly religious gays, but also about the role religion can play in the lives of gay seniors.

▲ ▲ ▲

With decades of knowledge, skills, and contacts to pass on, we are in a position to give our time, our resources, and our selves to others. We often assume the role of the spiritual trainer—often one on one—who knows the ways to get things done through others, the leverage of knowledge, conservation of energy, the reframing of insight, and efficiency of action. This is our time for philanthropy—to endow the offspring of our soul work with resources that they may have a life of their own. Even though we may well see our uninhibited 80s and noble 90s, the time to ensure our work is either completed or continued now.

If we still control organizations, the time has come for succession planning, and the hard work of teaching and passing on that entails; if our achievement is enduring enough, we may want to view the 70s as the time for nonprofits with a purpose.

Still, it's time for ourselves as well. While it was wise, and of little loss, to cut comfort in our 20s and 30s in order to save and invest, the 70s are the time we were saving for—the time when we can appreciate those efforts. It is a time to pamper ourselves. In fact, as our needs continue to dwindle with time, this may be the best time to truly enjoy spending.

As this is often a decade of profound understanding, spending in the pursuit of this is also a major item. Books, experts, and the Internet may become our work companions. We may return to school. Whereas it may have taken great effort to meditate in our midlife, we can gaze into a candle or mirror now and use these and other ways to see deeply into the meaning of our lives.

▼ ▼ ▼

Mark and John have now been together twenty-three years. First John retired, then Mark cut back his legal practice and has taken up an old love—architecture. He's bought professional-level software and is thinking of professional training as an architect. They now spend much of their time in the country, where rather than travel they've made their current project a spa/gym equipped with swimming pool, whirlpool, and sauna. They've rented the city apartment but have an arrangement by which they come in for theater nights and use the guest room. Since he's become so involved in house projects, John's decided to enroll in a local university for interior design. He plans to spend an unpaid internship in a local gay interior-design practice. Together they enjoy the idea of becoming a free-wheeling macro/micro-design team unhampered by fee considerations—following their bliss.

▲ ▲ ▲

► Asset Protection: Continuity, Control, Choice, Conveyance, and Contribution

We started out life dependent on others. As gays we learned quickly how important independence is when the world around us hates who they think we are. In later years we again become dependent on others. A gay priority is to keep the independence we worked so hard to win.

Defensive measures are in order. One of the first questions I ask of clients is "Who is your attorney?" Nine times out of ten they respond that there is no one—to which I respond that they should hire one, immediately. Attorneys are so much more effective when used in a preventive role. Yet legal training—and rewards—often emphasize litigation instead, as do clients' tacit expectations. All of us—our attorneys included—need to understand that gays need good legal management of our concerns before and during a crisis more than legal disposition of our stuff after we're gone.

Without tailored legal protections the most effective financial preparation in the world can go down the tubes in minutes. The most solid legal protections after death are meaningless if our affairs go unmanaged while we're alive. The unique requirements of our situations and our relationships demand a team approach.

Only financial prevention and legal protection will ensure that our increasing physical dependencies do not compromise our independence. Gays especially may suffer assaults on hard-won independence from family and other forms of would-be authority. This danger is especially grave as our technocracy increasingly hides its authority behind symbols of supposedly higher competency. Beware of the nurse, social worker, insurance reviewer, or managed care provider with an ax to grind.

Without children in the picture, it makes sense for gays to focus on asset protection while we're alive rather than on traditional estate planning for distribution of our assets after we're dead. Asset protection for gays should include these goals:

assuring **continuity** in our relationships through explicit *agreements,*

enabling **coordination** of our affairs through *training* of our power holders,

providing **control** when we can't act on our own behalf through *powers of attorney,*

seeking alternative forms of **conveyance** other than weak *wills,*

ensuring **choice** by protecting assets through *trusts,*

creating a **contribution** to our community of choice through an *estatement* that makes sure that what we value lives on in some form after us.

In general it is wiser for us to create tools specific to our needs rather than borrow techniques based on blood relationships that assume the applicability of centuries of family law. This is why we rely on contracts and specific instruments of control rather than on such tools as wills. And as AIDS has taught us, it's never too early to address these concerns.

Are you protected enough? Keep these questions in mind as you read on.

If you have joint financial dealings with anyone, are they documented with an explicit financial agreement?

Do you have an attorney? a financial advisor?

What kind of crisis might hit that could result in your not being able to handle your financial and legal affairs for at least several weeks?

Have you thought through what kinds of practical problems might be caused by a crisis?

Do you have a durable or springing power of attorney? a health proxy? a living will? a guardianship directive?

Do you have a will, a living trust, or some other form of asset management trust?

If your accounts permit it, have you labeled your accounts in trust for someone, to pass funds outside of probate?

Have you discussed and determined what probate fees would be on your estate?

Do you have someone you trust enough to manage your affairs should a crisis hit?

Have you discussed crisis management with those who hold your powers, trust management with your successor trustee, or probate administration with your executor?

If your estate is subject to state or federal estate tax, have you examined how to reduce those taxes with an estate-planning professional?

Do you have a sense of legacy, of mission, of purpose—and have you taken steps to endow some expression of that with your estate?

Continuity: Agreements

The true advantage of agreements becomes clear when we realize that we gays, gay brothers, often have many relationships—with past lovers, close friends, lesbian sisters, and business colleagues. Whatever the relationships that we have, we need agreements to prevent and manage the crises that happen in life.

We build the structure point by point, document by document. This can be a gay financial advantage because legal marriage is a one-size-fits-all artifact of heterosexual history. Without its oppressive uniformity we get to choose by the nature of the relationship we have created what arrangements are appropriate, under what circumstances, for how long—and which are not.

These agreements serve as a good vehicle for protecting our partners, friends, chosen family, colleagues, and kin and for providing a structure for sanity in case of an emergency. They're a financial necessity in the case of death, disease, or temporary incapacity, to facilitate and keep our joint financial affairs orderly. As society becomes more bureaucratized, this kind of foundation for continuity is essential.

When do we create such agreements? Without the trigger event of marriage it's largely up to us. Often the best time for such contracts is when commitment reaches a point where we want to celebrate and reinforce it. Another trigger can be a life-threatening illness or a peace-threatening family of origin. Another trigger is age itself. Specific details on these contractual agreements are given in detail in the couples chapter.

Not having the grab bag of marriage permits us to tailor our partnership agreements to the unique kind of relationship we have grown. Straight prenup agreements and marriage law, for example, adhere to a focus on breakups and divorce that don't suit our needs. If our agreements focus on breakups, we're using the wrong model. We need this kind of structure for keeping our relationship alive—creating backbone for our crisis periods, and spelling out practical and financial arrangements. More money has been wasted in breakups, incapacities, and deaths because of fights over small but personally important details. Only you know what they are—so prevent a brawl by making such things clear now.

▼ ▼ ▼

Leticia has a house that she bought with Lee some years back. She's been living with Alice now for four years, and they have a partnership agreement governing use of Alice's apartment and the country house. Leticia has given a general power of attorney over her financial affairs to Jim, whom she's worked with for years. She has provided that her lifelong friend, Tammy, would be her guardian in case she were incapacitated.

▲ ▲ ▲

Regardless of our current romantic relationship status, we always have, to varying degrees, circles of friendship, chosen family, and kinship. We need to give backbone to these living spheres of relationship or these living creations can collapse without us. There is no reason why we should not be excruciatingly clear as to our needs and wants in these instruments. And, as with retirement planning, we have to plan as if we were legally single.

Coordination: Training

Since good agreements are likely to be nonstandard, our partners and power holders need instruction in what our wishes are and how to carry them out. Since we love the people to whom we give such power, and since they must love us a great deal if they accept it, it is only considerate to make their job as easy as possible. We may wish to use nonbinding letters of instruction to inform our powers where things are, what has been changed, and what specific small wishes we may have. Getting into a habit of writing these wishes down is extremely useful and appreciated later. It is extremely important to let powers know where all documents are, to give them copies, and to let them know who else has copies.

Good self-help and power-training material is available through NOLO Press (1-800-992-NOLO). It is especially important to acquire readable references as to how to best use the powers and agreements we forge, and to make these resources available to those we appoint. Annotating these references may not be legally binding, but many a power holder is grateful for having guidance of any kind. The process may reveal many simple actions that can be identified and carried out now, which might be impossible or extremely difficult later.

A good use of our attorney's time is to put her to work training our power holders *before* a crisis comes. We should include those we appoint in sessions with our attorneys so as to educate them as to how these instruments work—how to use them in confronting stubborn bureaucracies. A good working relationship with our attorney beforehand will pay off handsomely later.

If there are multiple agreements, it's a good idea to coordinate them through one person or the attorney, to inform the parties as to who has what job, and to do some training in how it all might work smoothly. Letters of explanation can do wonders when we're not there to speak for ourselves. However, we need to make clear what's simply explanation versus what's a legally binding document. Likewise, keep a crib sheet of key account, contact, and phone numbers to help those who would help you.

▼ ▼ ▼

Jon knows he's going to beat both his diabetes and AIDS— and he also knows he may be in for some rough times ahead when premiums or key bills may not get paid. He's prepared a master list of policies, utilities, rents, and his mortgage-payment dates, addresses, accounts. He's noted where things are kept, his usual way of doing things, and who has keys. Also included is a master list of agreements he's forged with different people, as well as dates those agreements were revised. He sees as safeguards for living— not preparations for dying—a reassurance that the quality of the life he's so carefully crafted won't unravel simply because of a serious illness episode.

▲ ▲ ▲

Homoignorance I

Making sure our powers are recognized by strangers requires that we take steps to ensure that these people aren't strangers to the documents. Powers should be forwarded to any person who may have to recognize the wishes they articulate. Lists of these people should be maintained in a formal manner. Doctors, therapists, lawyers, brokers, agents, and bankers should be sent the document and asked to keep it on hand; they should be asked to acknowledge receipt of the document and that they have instructed their clerks and marked their files accordingly.

Since third parties are likely to be concerned about being sued, it's vital to include language that holds them harmless if they act on the basis of the powers we've given. We should include a copy of our power's signature (called an "exemplar") with our notification so they can recognize the authority of those we appoint. We need to periodically renew our powers, since dated documents may make third parties anxious.

Lastly, if we change powers we absolutely must make this known; if not, the entire edifice of credibility we have built may be weakened by the resulting confusion—and inaction may result. Care must be taken in canceling powers; often specific legal procedure must be followed.

It is all too easy in a crisis for our dear ones, uneducated in the ways of this part of the law, to assume that glitches are due to homophobia and not just homoignorance. Train them to understand that it's possible that simple inexperience in dealing with our documents and situations may result in foul-ups.

It should be clear by now that the choice of our power has to be very careful. Some of us may have no one we would trust in this capacity. In this case we should review our long-term goals regarding friendship and extended family and, in the short term, choose an attorney as our "professional power."

Control: Powers of Attorney

It is especially important that we establish *durable* powers—meaning powers that explicitly continue their authorization during periods of incapacity or incompetence. That kind of situation is what these measures are all about.

Many gays, betrayed in the past by bad reactions when they came out, are hesitant to entrust general powers in someone. Remember that most states have a great deal of legislation and case-law experience governing power holders, especially in the case where a short form of a durable power of attorney exists. The short form, often available in stationery stores, taps into all that precedent and expects power holders to be acting only in your interest—and would judge them severely from that perspective if they didn't. Beware of attorney attempts to customize where a short form exists; customizing can result in your no longer being able to tap into the legislation and case law that are tied to the short form alone.

We may need not only a general power of attorney but specialized types of powers of attorney, including springing powers of attorney, guardianship directives, burial and body disposition directives, health proxies, and living wills.

Powers that spring into action if something happens are useful and protect the holder of the power more. They're like apartment keys kept in a sealed envelope, so the holder can't be recklessly accused of theft. However, the trigger event needs to be carefully defined and discussed; power holders are more likely to hesitate, inadvertently causing a loss.

▼ ▼ ▼

Tess is an exercise fanatic who, one day while jogging, is side-swiped by a car and knocked unconscious. She's been in a coma now for weeks. Her ex, Linda, has a general power of attorney and has been paying Tess's bills and holding her financial life together. Tess's childhood sweetheart and best friend, Martha, has Tess's health power and is fending off that part of Tess's family that wants to "take her back into the fold." Luckily Tess had signed a guardianship directive after reading about a scary case of family abuse—and she'll be safe from similar problems no matter what the physical outcome.

▲ ▲ ▲

A common bottom-line problem is that even after we have painstakingly built a family of choice there remains the danger that our biological family may attempt to take over our lives if we're incapacitated or if we die. AIDS has taught us that relatives are unpredictable with death and disease.

Gays are often unprotected legally as to hospital visits, lose survivorship rights in apartments, are denied access to safe deposit boxes, are excluded in the disposition of personal property, and are discriminated against in insurance matters. Examples abound where we suffer for a lack of delegated powers.

Standard, inexpensive forms can be used for many of these situations. In fact sometimes the very form of health proxies and living wills is state mandated and therefore readily accepted—and nothing else is required.

Homoignorance II

Even when we create powers, we must pay attention to whether or not they will work in practice. In many cases invisible bureaucratic conservatism, bungling, and homophobia can wreck much of our planning.

• Most banks will not recognize a general power of attorney, but instead require that their own form be used with regard to banking transactions.

• Many clerks refuse powers almost as a matter of course; few holders of powers realize this and may not push their rights, unaware that they should always appeal any refusals.

• Our health powers must specifically state who gets to see us first and who has the right to screen and keep out anyone from our presence.

• If we have any feelings about how our body is disposed of—plain or fancy—we need to write it out and inform our families of origin in writing. If there is any chance they may wish to impose their own values, we must take multiple measures to ensure that our wishes, not theirs, are respected.

Conveyance: Wills

No matter how carefully we construct our powers, they all cease upon death. And remember: no power of attorney can write a will or create an estate plan.

The will is the most common estate planning technique. That

alone should make us cautious from the outset. The case law backing up the interpretation of wills assumes heterosexuality.

Most gays are unaware that even without having written one, we already have a will: one written for straight people by the state. This will gives all to our family of origin—not to our family of choice. It's ironic that we have this incredible ability to make virtue out of necessity and choose our own families—yet many of us allow the state to put the counters all back to zero and give all our wealth back to our families of origin.

Sometimes wills seem to function like lightning rods, drawing out homophobia that wasn't expressed during the person's lifetime. A family that seems unconcerned about our gayness or shunts aside mention of it may hide major homophobia or, just as dangerous, homoignorance. When death strikes, behavior is unpredictable, and past behavior is of little value as a guide. Assume the worst—and take legal steps.

▼ ▼ ▼

Enrique and Hans knew that Enrique's family were uncomfortable with his being gay. When he died, however, Hans was unprepared for the vengeance with which they attempted to eradicate the gayness from Enrique's life. Hans couldn't immediately find the will—which named him executor. While he was away the family got the doorman to let them in as family, and they made off not only with almost all of Enrique's things but their joint and even Hans's things. They not only refused to return these things but destroyed Enrique's personal phone book—so Hans couldn't reach many friends with news about the memorial service. Hans has spent over $60,000 in the will contest, which now includes the family's claim that Enrique was not in his right mind when he changed the beneficiary on his $250,000 insurance policy at work to Hans. Hans is in therapy, on antidepressants, and now his work performance is failing because of interference from his new full-time job: defending the wishes of his lover from attacks by the family.

▲ ▲ ▲

While wills may give legal rights, they may also offer little practical protection to gays if a family of origin wishes to contest them. Contesting a will costs the family relatively little, but it can cost a great deal to defend. Rarely does a surviving partner or executor have the stamina to fend off family. Either the lawyers get most of the assets and the contest drags on for years, or the family wears your protectors down and wins by default.

There are ways of making wills hard to contest. Multiple wills may deter mischief; each of them has to be fought individually. Videotaping can help, if it confirms the impression of competency. Confirmations of competency by therapists and physicians taken at the time can be used to make such wishes stick. Clauses can be put into the will that automatically reduce legacies to token amounts if a will contest is raised.

The pitfalls can be numerous. Caution needs to be exercised in passing on such items as a co-op apartment that have restrictions; if the inheriting partner is not listed as an owner, he or she may not be able to inherit the apartment without going through the same review given a stranger. Even innocent loving, parting statements of the dying partner in the will have been used against us by antagonistic blood-relatives of the deceased, attempting to show incompetence, or to demonstrate undue influence, by asserting that a bequest was in consideration for sexual favors. Other pitfalls to look out for include:

▶ Will Pitfall #1: *Will-Writing Software Package Traps*

Some gays may think it is gay neutral to use software to make last wishes clear. As with financial software, this is not true—most software is written for the 90%, not us. Formula advice is treacherous for gays, no matter what its source. If it comes in a book, at least it's visible; if it comes in a software package, its inapplicability will not be obvious. The consequences with wills can be final indeed.

Will-writing software kits focus on the typical household,

with legal spouse and children. For example, kits fail to advise on whether to make bequests to a partner outright or via a trust to keep assets out of the hands of a partner's family or a partner's creditors. Kits wouldn't catch the co-op example above. In a situation where beneficiaries are from a family of choice, not a family of origin, we need carefully crafted language and sophisticated procedures not provided for in software packages.

Studies show that wills-by-kits are more likely to be contested, thrown out of court, or inadequately executed—no matter what our orientation. Moreover, software tends to focus on the document, not on the overall will-creation process. For example, it often doesn't advise on the will-signing ritual. This ritual—specified by state law—usually provides many subtle bits of legal evidence that the will signer was competent and that the will was totally legal. For example, an attorney would usually require affidavits of witnesses, whereas the program may be mute on this point; this avoids his having to track witnesses years later to confirm they indeed witnessed the will.

Anticipating such circumstances, interrelationships, and interpretations is what professionals are for—not programs. Gay financial relationships are full of such twists and turns that can add up to potential legal trouble with major financial consequences.

▶ Will Pitfall #2: *All-Purpose Wills*

Wills are but the iceberg's tip of an entire body of law evolved over decades and based fundamentally on families of origin. Wills are all about property conveyance—and the continuity of families—stemming from times when families were society's fundamental economic unit. This is one reason why probate is so much quicker, easier, and cheaper if property is *not* included.

A common error is to make wills do everything when it comes to wishes. In fact, separate agreements and targeted powers may be better for gays. Wills are only about final wishes; we need protections while we're alive.

Given these limitations, gays need to realize that wills are often "loss leader" products for attorneys. Attorneys may write the will for cheap in order to bring in highly profitable probate business. This motivation, plus the fact that 90% of the time wills work okay as all-purpose documents, means that gays should resist being steered toward simply doing wills.

Estate planning for gays is usually much more than writing a will. For gays a will is often simply a backup document for a trust—to be used as a catchall document in case some asset is not put in the trust. Estate planning is all about protecting our overall finances while we're alive; a straight attorney may be oriented toward what happens after we've died. An attorney may have a bias toward the tools of his trade—legal documents—not toward preserving our financial health.

▶ Will Pitfall #3: *Overdetail*

Wills are megawishes—big, final decisions. If our interests are more in the present and not so much in the hereafter, we may tend to load wills down with too much detail. That creates many more ways a will can quickly become out of date. Then the temptation is to fix that with what's called a "codicil"—a bad idea, because in probate lawyers have to sort out whether the codicils conflict with anything in the will or with each other, causing legal bills and delays to mount. However, the better alternative—rewriting the will—also multiplies legal bills and therefore prompts people to delay the rewrite.

The way out of this is to trust—and train—our executors. Executors should be part and parcel of the will-thinking-out and will-writing process. We should then not hesitate to pour all those specific wishes ("That hearth rug goes to Harry and the tea set goes to Leslie") into numbered letters to our estate administrators. The will gives them discretion to ignore these detailed wishes, but more often than not will managers appreciate some guidance from the departed when it comes to divvying up the loot. Without these detailed letters from the grave, if conflict emerges—and it always does—the common escape route for administrators is to give it all to charity. And *that* will probably get you all riled up on your little pink cloud.

▶ Will Pitfall #4: *Probate*

Homophobia and homoignorance are hard to deal with, but for the most part they're out in the open. An archenemy that largely lies invisible is probate.

For years probate courts have been antigay. Often they've used the sexual nature of our relationships as a basis on which to reject our final wishes, as subject to "undue influence." Probate courts can be loaded with personnel and judges who are not only political appointees but self-appointed enforcers of conservatism. Beware.

Probate can be hell under any circumstances. For example, even without prejudice the probate of simple wills can average eighteen months in some states. Probate state law may encourage or even specify that probate attorneys receive a percentage of the estate—up to 4–8%—and under some circumstances may give attorneys multiple fees. We have many reasons to not route our assets to our loved ones through probate. Probate attorneys do valuable work—so pay them by the hour and negotiate the rate (or the percentage) while you're living as a favor to your will executor.

Choice: Trusts

One way to avoid probate is to use an alternative to wills—a trust. This, too, is part of the legacy of AIDS. For gays this is a legal tool that suits many of our special needs *during* life, not just after death.

Many trusts exist, each tailored to the problem to be solved or the purpose to be achieved. Trusts may not only replace wills but function as umbrella documents to replace powers of attorney as well. In some states trusts can be implemented as easily as labeling financial accounts "in trust for. . . ." If this is permitted, the money in that account upon death passes directly to the person named.

For gays, trusts are better than isolated powers of attorney, because total control of all assets is under the trustee and because only one document is used. For continuity in financial management, trusts offer many other advantages; they are truly flexible crisis-management tools. Trusts can avoid attempts by blood relatives or outsiders to impose guardianship. The creator of the trust is the first trustee, and a succession of authority is provided for. The trust already owns everything while you're alive, so there's nothing to contest; this is why the main weakness of a trust is when some assets are inadvertently left out of it. Trusts offer much greater discretion and are less subject to court supervision than wills. Trusts are especially reliable and flexible in making final arrangements for our remains. Trusts assure confidentiality and keep transfers out of the public record. They are the only way to carry one's financial secrets to the grave.

By centralizing authority, trusts can prevent the neglect of investments or nonpayment of important bills (such as insurance premiums) during a crisis. Trusts can define what the grantor considers to be a crisis and can outline procedures for determining it swiftly if there is any doubt.

Trusts may cost much less to create than what attorneys ultimately charge for probate. Trusts can prevent the costs and delays of a will contest because the trust continues to own its assets despite disability or death. The trust doesn't die except by agreement.

A trustee is likely to accumulate experience in administering the grantor's affairs before death, can discuss decisions with the grantor, and has the written instruction of the trust document as guidance. Trusts are clearly a case where prevention pays.

Trusts tailor language to reflect the subtleties of gay relationships. They can mobilize tax laws where our differences can be made to work to our advantage—as with charitable lead trusts (discussed under taxes). Wills are not designed to offer such specialized and sophisticated capabilities.

A popular trust is called the "living trust," because it's used to protect assets while we're alive. Beware of the overselling of living trusts, especially through packaged approaches. Because there are so many trusts, and because the best trusts are tailored, a trust specialist experienced in our specific needs and wants should handle this task.

Conservation: Estate-Tax Planning

The central problem for gays with assets worth as little as five figures is how to deal with heterofriendly estate taxes. It must be remembered that the estate-tax code was rewritten by the Reagan Republicans in 1982 to suit their own type of heterosexual retirement plan—not that of gays.

Some state estate taxes penalize us even further. A state may tax an inheritance from a parent or grandparent at 3% but up the tax to 10% on our partners.

A complication may arise if we have property in different states—which may be much more common with gays. If estate tax is charged in those states, our estate-tax situation becomes very complicated. This is especially true if the states start trying to prove that they are our true home state, so they can collect the most tax.

This is one area where gays do get hurt—by the lack of a marital exclusion. Someone dying can pass on any amount of goods to a surviving legal spouse; we can't. Extra estate-planning work has to be done by gays to work around or compensate for this missing right. As with income tax, one way to do this is to take advantage of areas where our relationships are *not* recognized by the IRS. And again we need professionals experienced in our special tax situations—not just gay friendliness or general competence.

Remember: professional counsel in these areas is required. The artificial regulations that drive them are often counterintuitive, and they shift with every small state and federal change. It's enough here to identify our needs and wants—not also to solve these highly technical problems. The information given here is purely from a financial perspective and requires review by an attorney to give you its essential legal perspective.

Contribution: Estatements

Where is all this largesse going? It makes sense to value what we've achieved by putting in place instruments of control and conveyance such as those described thus far. But why not go that extra 10% and translate this meaning into an estatement about our life—one that continues to nurture what we've come to value well after our death?

In a well-prepared financial life there comes a time to commemorate and endow those things we have come to value in our lives. Most of us have no desire just to make someone else rich by our efforts—certainly not our Uncle Sam. There is an alternative: establishing a true legacy rather than simply passing on stuff or giving it away.

If we have no children, we can continue to make a difference even after death. This is a time to respect what we've created in the laboratory called our life and to distill some part that may live on, that may continue to contribute, that may continue to build. This is the ultimate in self-respect, in taking ourselves seriously.

Not to take this last simple step is to climb the mountain without enjoying the view—and not know why the climb was worthwhile. Without this capstone our financial lives are reduced to mere money, just as we are reducible to earth's basic elements. In endowing the people, organizations, or values we've come to cherish, we have an ultimate reassurance that our lives indeed had a point to them.

► Refinement #1: *Values Clarification*

How do we take this out of philosophy and make it practical? The following exercise can help you start identifying and ranking the values that will shape your legacy decisions.

Draw up a list of what you have come to cherish, what has contributed to your own life. This list might consist of names, locales, things, achievements, values, characteristics—whatever comes to mind. (This exercise is similar to the one used to focus our careers.)

Identify natural categories to group together these items, just as we gave concrete group names to items in our spending plan.

Rank these categories in order of importance.

Give each category a percentage such that all of them add up to 100%.

Within each category identify specific people or organizations that manifest, carry out, exemplify, nurture, or promote the values of that category.

▼ ▼ ▼

Thad was a teacher who couldn't leave his building alone. He renovated, gradually buying building after building on his beautiful street, on his teacher's salary—and with all that teacher time. By age sixty he had not only become a real estate maven but had succeeded in having his street declared a historic district. With AIDS he felt a need to complete this work and somehow recognize his achievement.

He created a trust agreement by which the properties would be held by the foundation in a trust for the benefit of the district. The trust would dedicate a certain number of apartments to gay seniors or gays with disabling illness, keep rents stable, and use its excess income to continue to preserve the district.

▲ ▲ ▲

These people or organizations can be your ultimate beneficiaries—in a will, in life insurance, or in a trust. Alternatively, these categories and percentages can be specified to your executor, since specific individuals and organizations may change over time.

If you wish to repeat, deepen, or expand this exercise, look for books or workshops in the field of values clarification to help you identify and use values to direct other areas of your life.

► Refinement #2: *Community Trusts*

Just as we may not think we have enough assets to be hit by estate taxes, we might not think we have enough value to practice philanthropy.

Here, too, AIDS has much to teach us. Part of the AIDS legacy has been the prodigious growth of gay community foundations in over ten cities in the U.S. A community foundation is a nonprofit that consolidates philanthropic funds of virtually any amount designated for a purpose. Because funds are pooled, the cost of managing them is kept down, financial return is maximized, and protections are more extensive—just as in a private foundation.

As with any nonprofit these groups need to be monitored and screened carefully. After all, you'd be relying on them to carry out your wishes after you're gone.

These groups are the gift that keeps on giving. They ensure that your giving stays targeted to your purposes even when people and organizations change. The donor can usually name people to be involved in the continuing giving process.

▼ ▼ ▼

Sally had amassed a cash cushion of about $150,000, but it was a cold comfort. She started thinking about her life and remembered with delight her awkward but intense first years in dance, abandoned now for decades. She realized that modern dance was her favorite, and identified a particular dance company that she both enjoyed and respected for consistent dedication to schooling young dancers. Sally wondered, though, whether the school would be able to survive in the harsh world of dance. She decided to create a trust under the Stonewall Fund dedicated toward modern dance in general and the training of young dancers in particular. The trust was charged to give an annual grant

*to a dance company, a smaller grant toward her beloved dance
school, and two scholarships for promising young Asian dancers,
in honor of her Asian lover.*

▲ ▲ ▲

Wealth: Empowering Our Values

What is wealth? There are so many answers—health, friends,
time, possessions, money. What is usually meant by wealth in
each is abundance, increased capacity, and potential.

What does our life amount to? Professionally, our achievements may add to life's abundance. Physically, our bodies break
down into their chemical components and become part of the
earth again—or we may donate our organs to give others new
capabilities. Psychologically, our impact on the lives of others is
like ripples in a pond.

But as most emperors have found, none of this has lasting
value.

Perhaps this is why heterosexuals love children, nurture them,
and endow them. And many of those children do the same—and
so forth. That's wealth expanding.

What can we create that may have a life of its own? When
should we start the process of advancing the purposes and values
we've come to love? If giving is the purpose of life—and this
becomes intensely felt in our 70s—philanthropy on any scale is
indeed the gift that keeps giving—as it endows others with a
further ability to give in return.

If the point of our lives is to create this kind of wealth, this
kind of legacy that parents the organizations and people which
embody what we've come to truly treasure, then our gay money
may be our most lasting gift to the world.

PART II

Gay
Issues

▼ ▼ ▼ ▼ ▼ ▼ ▼

Double Differences:
A Note to Gay Women

▲ ▲ ▲ ▲ ▲ ▲ ▲

Before we go any further, let's address a question that may already have occurred to you. Can I, coming from the gay tribe but belonging to the gay male clan, advise lesbians on personal finance? The compromise I have struck is to focus *Gay Money* on gays in general, noting differences between gay men and lesbians as they occur.

I've learned enough in my practice about our respective perspectives to know that we're each trying to describe different parts of the elephant—even though sometimes we're not sure it's the same elephant. I am a man and the majority of those I help are gay men, so any bias I would have is obviously toward the gay male experience. To offset this, let's focus here on issues I've seen in my practice that crop up in particular for lesbians.

The greatest help I can give both clans of our tribe here is simply to encourage and structure our dialogue. Then we need to shift our focus from philosophy to practicalities so we can refine our planning tools in this additional important dimension of the gay financial experience.

▶ Sitting Targets

Lesbians face double discrimination—as women and as lesbians. What seems to count most, economically, is what the outside world discriminates against first: being a woman. For this reason I have strongly urged lesbians I help to avail themselves of the well-developed armamentarium of the feminist movement. It's much more prudent to master feminist finance 101 before taking off the veil and attempting to process lesbian economic issues.

Both gay men and lesbians are tempted to remain invisible, and that kind of invisibility is a silent economic killer eventually for both. But lesbians don't have the option of keeping their gender invisible. They must fight two battles: one as women, one as lesbians.

▶ Double Discrimination

Feminist finance comes first—and starts with the financial hurdles placed before women. Lower salaries, exclusion from male networking, and job stereotyping are just a few of the economic handicaps set into the very grain of society.

Lesbians face discriminatory money issues as women. Although gay men may earn slightly less than straight men, it's still more than lesbians, who in turn may earn slightly more than other women. Overcoming this income handicap is any lesbian's top economic challenge. The answer usually lies in two areas: cutting expenses more to create a greater discretionary income, or escaping employee discrimination by pursuing entrepreneurship.

Under fire as women, lesbians often get street smart earlier in a man's world; they know who the enemy is and, unlike gay men, don't have to deal with the contradiction of loving their economic rivals.

Gay men are more likely to sail along under their gender's flag, not realizing they may be thrown off the ship when they're older and their homosexuality has become increasingly visible. It's easier for gay men to pretend that being gay doesn't matter economically, losing many years of countermeasures in the process.

Many lesbians may gain a financial leg up over straight women by having no children, or by having them later in life. But lesbians have far more children than gay men, further increasing their economic disadvantage. Child rearing is an extremely expensive investment, and an economic decision of incomparable magnitude.

▶ Double Discrimination: Careers

Coming out at the workplace is very different financially for lesbians, and tends to be far more carefully managed by lesbians than by gay men. Career is the economic pivot point for lesbians. Society's messages still position careers for women as secondary to being a wife and mother. Lesbians generally cocoon more in their relationships and report conflicts between relationship and career.

Yet for lesbians career is the primary way to get out of de facto second-class citizenship. Many lesbians choose high-tech paths that are more protected from income discrimination and male stereotyping. Many wisely choose to keep gearing up with skills and credentials to gain authority in a world dominated by men. And lesbians strike out in private practice and entrepreneurial ventures far earlier than gay men, seeing the writing on the double-paned glass ceiling. The double discrimination that lesbians face extends to the workplace, and the less dependent they are on male-dominated organizations the better off economically they will become.

Gay men face a radically different challenge. Lulled into complacency by the expectations and priorities society places on men, with few outward signs of discrimination, gay men may be more likely than lesbians to use their 20s to catch up on adolescence. While their straight counterparts are acting out society's scripts about male breadwinners, gay men can easily be tempted to sacrifice career to ghetto life.

The problem gay men may face is lack of evidence that the glass ceiling exists, or of its effects. Gay men may be much more tempted to stick around the organization—motivated by the superficial perks of their male membership card—suffering far greater loss when they hit the gay glass ceiling.

Most lesbians I've helped have ultimately chosen the entrepreneur's route. In the end it's just too uncertain to pin one's economic future on an employer's attitudes at the top. For starters the high-level sponsors and mentors we cultivate can all too easily disappear, leaving us in their wake as just so much flotsam and jetsam.

▸ Doubling Our Differences

As couples, same sex can mean doubling the differences between male and female. While gay male couples merge two incomes that may on average be higher than their female counterparts, lesbian couples must cope with the double discrimination of often equally low salaries.

Perhaps that's why lesbians seem more willing to help each other careerwise by pooling their resources to finance additional training or education for first one member of the couple and then the other. It's extremely important to put into place safeguards and provisions for the payback on such investments if the couple breaks up.

Gay men tend to practice a peculiar version of the Golden Rule whereby he who has the gold makes most of the rules as to how it's spent. Studies show that lesbians, on the other hand, are more likely to strive to equalize financial decision-making, especially if incomes differ.

While gay male couples tend to do too little to take advantage of their double discretionary dollar advantage, I've seen lesbian couples get too diffuse in their financial decision-making by bending over backward to practice equality. Lesbians may need the strength that comes if we act interdependently when this is an advantage, and independently when that's an advantage.

▸ Different Dollars

Gay men and lesbians exhibit differences not only in making money but in spending it. With higher incomes and temporary (if illusory) membership in straight-male-dominated society, gay men are strongly tempted to be spenders. Like many minorities, gay males may act out fantasies about power with what they have at hand—their discretionary dollars. Gay men often take their careers too casually, save less, and invest less. I've seen many simply get lost in present pleasures. When their discretionary incomes equalize with straights' and their jobs disappear out from under them, many don't have the skills, savings, and investment experience to shift easily to entrepreneurial careers.

With lower incomes and an immediate experience of discrimination, lesbians have strong reasons to save. If lesbians can channel their drive and energies into career building, saving, and investing, they have a winning formula for economic power.

I've seen lesbians get financially sidetracked by security concerns: putting too many resources into illiquid and poorly-performing real estate and too few resources into financial investments with higher performance potential. While the gay men I help sometimes seem to have a cavalier attitude about risk, lesbians appear to be more prudent but less risk tolerant.

While lesbians benefit from feminist experience in remaking the role of women in a man's world, it's clear that the economic status of lesbians and married women is not entirely the same. Married women have two assets in particular that many lesbians do not: alimony and inheritance from married men. It is not an accident that *Lear's* magazine was started with funds from a divorce settlement. Lesbians need to be wary of adopting the assumptions and expectations of married women if they don't have their kind of assets. Especially complicated financial disparities exist between lifelong lesbians and the increasing number of women becoming lesbians after marriage, children, and divorce in later years.

► Different Diseases, Similar Strategies

Many health differences exist between gay men and lesbians, although the health chapter outlines some powerful strategies that apply to both. We share one major risk equally—our 30% addiction rates. (In contrast, straight men are five times more addicted than straight women.) On the basis of sheer cost our prevention and recovery from this costly epidemic should top any of our financial agendas. We need to root out and revise the many roles it has played in our culture.

The real shocker is how few lesbians are aware of their increased threat from breast cancer, and how little focus the gay and the lesbian communities have put on this key health problem. As much of the wisdom of succeeding in the straight world offered in this book owes a debt to the lessons learned from AIDS, we can hope that these lessons will now be applied to cancer—especially now that new treatments are making AIDS much more similar to cancer financially.

▼ ▼ ▼ ▼ ▼ ▼ ▼

Financial Health
and Illness

▲ ▲ ▲ ▲ ▲ ▲ ▲

Health care issues have a bottom-line brutality to them. Poor health can destroy wealth quickly. Illness can drain resources, disrupt income, and imperil control. Health hits are far worse than other financial losses because they often dry up our income-making capability, drain what assets we have, and destroy our ability to rebound. What's more, the rising expense of ever more sophisticated treatments means that having a health crisis now equates to having a financial crisis. Money has become as potent a treatment tool as technology.

With so much riding on our health, we can ill afford to make a financial plan without taking into account gay health assets and liabilities. On the plus side we have the opportunity to earn the discretionary dollars it takes to keep us in the middle class despite a health crisis. But as the recent past has taught us, our liabilities are considerable, beginning with our being significantly more at risk for AIDS and breast cancer, but also encompassing our much higher rate of mental illness and addiction, and the painful reality that we receive widely varying treatment because we're gay.

Our liabilities compel us to employ two principles immediately or watch illness erode our wealth: we must plan for the worst and hope for the best, planning for the day when illness happens, not if it happens; and we must act before the barn starts burning, putting our defenses in place *before* disaster strikes with major financial losses.

Let's cut to the quick: what do we need when illness strikes?

- Medical insurance without limits
- Disability insurance that continues our incomes
- Life insurance that can be turned into cash if things turn terminal
- The maximum credit available, insured for disability and death
- Total legal protection through powers, wills, directives, proxies, or trusts

We have one ace up our sleeve. If we're missing any one of our crucial insurances, even when illness is apparent we can usually get them by finding a job that offers them in its benefits package.

We have one megadecision: private care or public care. Do we wish to protect our lives as we know them, or merely survive? This has been called the thruway/truck-route decision—our great fork in the road. Both ways will get us through life. The public-welfare truck-route exacts payment in kind—in discomfort, disrespect, and delays. The private insurance thruway demands constant feeding of premiums and rejects those with less than perfect health.

Illness Planning = Transition Planning

The key to managing illness financially is to recognize it must have a beginning and an end. Illness is a transition. Its essence is unpredictability and uncertainty. Just as the goal of medicine is to stabilize our condition, our financial goal is to limit the highs and lows of economic uncertainty and to make this transition as financially smooth as possible. The purpose of insurance, credit, and reserves is to ride out the storm without having the structure of our financial lives torn apart.

When illness strikes we need radically different financial tools from those that traditional financial planning offers. That's why I cofounded a nonprofit called Affording Care—to create the crisis-management tools we need to weather serious illness financially. Without these tools a sudden hospitalization can often result in

AIDS and cancer patients being naively told to strip themselves financially to qualify for Medicaid—adding financial insult to medical injury.

In the chapter on our 50s we highlight what preventive measures are needed—before the barn is burning. These are mostly focused around insurance. In our chapter on the 70s we define what protective legal measures are necessary before we lose our ability to manage on our own. Here we'll identify the extraordinary health assets we might have, and then see how we can manage our risks financially if they flare up as a gay health crisis.

► Illness and Cost Prevention

Let's first speak to the importance of minimizing the health risks faced by all of us in general but especially by a particularly vulnerable portion of the readers of this book: sexually active, HIV-negative gay men. Though you face many risks, you must remember that it is not inevitable that you will be cut down before your time. Regardless of the optimism now emerging from the AIDS treatment front, it is crucial that you remember that you can remain HIV-negative—and that your financial future may depend on it. Now some may survive HIV. But few with HIV will escape its financial devastation.

In fact, some of the skills developed in thinking about our financial futures can help us envision and pursue our future health too. As we've seen, from our position on the outskirts of society, with homophobes taking random shots at us, and with many of us dying before our very eyes, it's easy to fall into all-or-nothing thinking. In personal finance that leads to focusing on the present instead of the future. In money matters, short-changing the future for present pleasures or because of present pain can be costly; in sex it can be deadly.

We've talked a lot about risk management in personal finance, learning how to trade off costs for returns. We've seen that our decisions on how we handle risk in our lives are informed by our changing, moment-by-moment assessments and guesses about potential pleasure and pain, costs and returns.

Why should our handling of sex be different? It certainly doesn't have to be. Beware of shifting our focus from what we're doing to who we are. And once how we have sex becomes our identity, and stops being simply yet another activity we do, we're in trouble both medically and financially.

We've seen that our gay money gains power when we set aside inherited notions of what society says we are—outcasts—and focus on what we and our gay money can *do*. Similarly, risk management in sex is all about what we do, not who we are.

Size up situations on the fly, just like all the other things we do—with the simple question, is it worth it? At several points in earlier chapters, we've explained methods of growing more familiar with how we assign worth in our lives. This is how we make our financial decisions, and our sexual decisions too. If we're bombed or drugged out at the time, it's a fair guess we're fair game for someone else to make the decision for us—and we may want to consider trading off drink and drugs for self-directed sex.

The rest of the time we observe, deduce, intuit, reflect, wonder, guess, conclude—just as we do in the supermarket or the stock market—and decide what's appropriate right then and there. We trust our judgment because we exercise our judgment, as we do in most everything.

The point is that we make hundreds of decisions about risk daily in this way, grappling realistically with ever-changing, complicated realities. We do a good job. We learn from our mistakes. You've gotten this far in one piece, so there's no reason you need to falter now.

Sex as a Financial Proposition

Just as risk management is a financial skill, sex is now a financial proposition. The financial consequences of unmanaged risk can be more frightening than the medical consequences. And where it may be hard to imagine ill health, it's often easier to understand impoverishment—a distinction that can help us here.

If you find poverty is more vivid than illness you may consider the following financial argument for managing sexual risk.

In our lovemaking ahead, given what I know about you and me, is the penetration part of our having sex—let's say about fifteen to thirty minutes of intense pleasure—worth these following possible costs?

> *The extra ten to fifteen to two hundred medical visits per year to a primary-care physician, neurologist, dermatologist, oncologist, internist, nutritionist, psychotherapist, psychiatrist, pain specialist—for the next five to fifteen years.*

> *The $2,000 to $3,000 per year in out-of-pocket copayments and deductibles plus the $5,000 to $10,000 per year for nonreimbursed costs for alternative treatment, nutrition supplements, pain management, taxis, chiropractor, acupuncturist, legal, accounting, financial, and other professional fees.*

> *Career impacts in the form of cutting back hours, holding off promotions or transfers, maybe getting rated poorly because of absence or fluctuations in performance, not being able to switch companies because of insurance, getting laid off or fired, or never being able to work again.*

> *The uncertainty of not knowing whether disability benefits would be granted or when.*

> *Limitations on investing for fear that some episode might require liquidation of stocks, bonds, real estate, or collectibles.*

> *The inadvisability of buying real estate in general because of its up-front costs, illiquidity, and the costs of getting out of it too soon thereafter.*

> *Strains on existing and new relationships with a likely curtailing of sex.*

> *Side effects from ten to twenty medications at any one time plus the rigid requirements of taking medications exactly as required or suffer the development of mutant virus.*

> *Missing out on the harvest of life, losing years of happy life, never*

being able to make it financially, always having to live on public benefits.

This is what's now at stake with gay male sex. This is why sex has become a high-priced proposition. Making estimates as to how much is at stake is what financial life is all about.

► Our Health Assets: Fitness, Street Smarts, and Individualism

We're into our bodies; we've survived the streets; and we pursue individuality with a vengeance. These gay twists on health should be assets, but they can end up as liabilities.

Body Beautiful—for Show or Go?

We could not have run the gauntlets of growing up gay without coming out of it with special skills, and special scars, in special places. For decades the only way we could survive was for our men to be feminine and our women to be men. Stonewall's double dividend was for us to reinvent our masculinity and femininity, and to rediscover our bodies beautiful.

Our common bond is sexual attraction, in which the physical plays no small part. Our delayed adolescences add to this an overall emphasis on youth.

We're also scared to death to watch our men age with AIDS and our women lose their breasts. It's no wonder that all this has moved us out of the baths into the gyms and out of the bars into the coffeehouses.

Does our trimming and toning make us any healthier? Does it add to our health bottom line or is it just another expense item on our income statements?

If our gyms lead only to bubble butts and ornamental muscle instead of cardiovascular fitness, little has been gained financially. If it leads to an illusion of health and reinforces an adolescent attitude that we're immortal, we're in for deep financial trouble.

Fitness has to go more than skin deep to prevent the risks and costs of future illness. Otherwise we've just invented another spending category and left our health flank wide open.

Exercise can pay through increased energy, endurance, life expectancy, and resistance to illness and stress. We need that solid contribution—not just steroid strength.

Lesbians banded together on women's health issues long ago. Gay men relied on a seemingly endless supply of medications to fight off the infectious by-products of sexually transmitted illness.

The bottom line remains: Is it for go or is it for show? The first is an asset; the second, a liability.

There's a lot we can do here to buttress the health sector of our balance sheets. We can use the fact that the gay community embraces the body beautiful to overcome that common barrier to exercise: motivation. But we need to go well beyond bulking up to cardiovascular fitness and flexibility. If we do that and can remember that muscle isn't shielding against risk, we'll be well ahead.

Street Smarts

Gay life often starts in the school of hard knocks—literally. The teen gauntlet can teach self-reliance and skepticism real fast. In today's soft society that's often a blessing in disguise. In a homogenized society stripped of its rituals we also have a unique rite of passage: coming out. In mythological terms it's a kind of hero's journey in a society that doesn't have many heroes. We dwell in the wilderness with little but our wits to guide us, and most of us survive. With this rite of passage we are giving our men and women survival skills society can't match.

Many, of course, don't make it out of the closet. Many of us are hardened, twisted, and beaten down by our treatment. And a startling percentage of our teens never make it.

It wouldn't hurt to reinforce our entrepreneurial bent by exploring what myth has to say about the gay experience—for example in the writings of Joseph Campbell. And let's remember: the closet is no place for a hero.

Individualism

Excluded from the mesmerizing mainstream, we may stand a better chance of individuating, of finding our own bliss, of owning our own lives. Our early isolation can lead to self-reliance, questioning, and independence—coming to our own conclusions, making our own decisions, and choosing our own options.

These results can in turn foster clear vision, and powerful drive. It can lead us into more self-directed, enterprising, self-defined ventures that support the emotional good health that fosters good health overall.

Independent thinking is a key financial skill that can be helped by time-honored tools such as individual retreats, meditation, and disconnecting from the mass media. It's a major positive shift when we go from a strategy of lying low to expressing our individual needs, wants, and values.

► Our Higher Risks: Bad Treatment, Mental Health, Breast Cancer, and HIV

The figures describe a brutal health-risk bottom line:

- Two thirds of physicians don't feel comfortable with us.
- One third of our teens commit and attempt suicide.
- We are three times as likely to be addicted.
- One in seven lesbians has breast cancer—a much higher rate than for women in general.
- In major cities between one third and one half of gay men are HIV positive.

► Risk #1: *Poor Care*

Today's illnesses require high levels of complex care. The times when "time, nature, and the body do the healing" are few and far between. Highly qualified care is literally our lifeline.

Yet most of us hold back vital information from our physicians. And when we do reveal ourselves we get short shrift. This is a major threat to our financial health.

Invisibility = Poor Care

In 1990 studies typically three quarters of lesbians and half of gay men admit that they do not identify their sexual orientation to doctors; many report abusive reactions when they do. Nearly all of those who don't tell feel they would get inferior care if they did.

The problem is compounded by the fact that only one tenth to one third of primary-care doctors routinely take a sexual history; fewer than that even think to ask about sexual orientation.

We're not talking about a simple communication problem here. This is our prime asset—our health—that we're playing with. What you don't say can hurt you. Many gynecologists assume that lack of heterosexual intercourse eliminates women's health problems, including breast cancer, when in fact it makes them worse.

This injury is compounded by closeted figures. Up until AIDS, authorities of all types—medical, legislative, administrative—have not seen fit to tabulate our ills or crimes against us. Lesbians by far suffer the most from underreporting; without figures we don't know the extent of the lesbian breast cancer problem, though it's safe to assume that it's worse than the already dire statistics indicate.

Visibility = Poor Care

If we do come out, we risk getting the booby prize: poor care.

In 1990s studies of general practitioners, typically only one third say they feel comfortable with gay men. Doctors are conservative; over a third thought we should not work in schools and that homosexuality is "just plain wrong" while two thirds felt that gays should not be recognized as normal.

Two thirds of Gay and Lesbian Medical Association members believe gays receive substandard care. Over half have seen medical peers reducing care or denying care to patients because they were gay.

No More Gay Docs?

In the 1990s we face a much greater challenge: managed care. In but a few years most of us are being forced into insurance plans to which our gay doctors may not belong. No prepaid health plan recognizes gay health as an area of specialization.

Even with AIDS, a high-profile well-defined area of practice, gays outside a few major metropolitan areas find themselves in the hands of doctors utterly ignorant of AIDS, much less gay-specific health problems and practices. This makes the prognosis for gay health in the 90s very poor indeed.

Gay doctors have been further handicapped by the medical profession's discrimination against its own gay members. The AMA has turned down three times in three years a proposal to add sexual orientation to the nondiscrimination policy in the association's bylaws.

Nearly two thirds of Gay Medical Association members report discrimination, harassment, or ostracism. This isn't paranoia. Half of all orthopedic surgeons feel that a highly qualified gay or lesbian applicant should not be admitted to medical school.

Physician Action

The costs of the present don't-ask/don't-tell situation are untenable. People with AIDS have much to teach here.

We have to take charge, not only of our individual medical care but also of these larger social issues, which set the context of the care we receive. This probably means shopping for our physician—researching, interviewing, and evaluating him or her. Since few physicians can be expected to be expert on sexual-orientation issues and their impact on medicine, we need to become our own experts in this area. We also need to choose physicians who are comfortable in sharing information and mutual decision-making. Lastly, like it or not, this means explaining physically and in detail what we do in sex so they can know what to prevent, what to monitor, and what to diagnose.

▶ Risk #2: Mental Illness—
Suicide, Depression, Addiction

Just because we got the American Psychiatric Association to realize in 1973 that being gay isn't itself a mental illness doesn't mean that we don't face mental problems. Gay doesn't necessarily mean happy.

Suicide: Gay Roots

What happens to teens is a bellwether of gay mental health, and it indicates the psychological context in which we live. Studies report virtually total rejection of gay teens by their parents— by 80% of mothers and 90% of fathers. Reports confirm that self-disclosure still results in loss of a friend over 40% of the time; 80% of gay teens have deteriorating school performance. Often over a quarter of gay teens drop out.

Violence hits our teens first and hardest. Although grossly underreported and concealed by fear, studies have uncovered sexual abuse rates of 35% for gay boys and 21% for lesbian girls. A further 24% of lesbian girls report physical abuse. It doesn't stop with childhood for lesbian adults: 15% report sexual abuse and 16% physical abuse in adulthood.

In Los Angeles 25 to 35% of street youth are estimated to be homosexual; the estimate for Seattle is 40%. Among the estimated 500,000 homeless youth in this country, gays may total one third or nearly 170,000.

In 1986, 5,000 youths and young adults up to age twenty-four committed suicide. A 1989 government report found that gay and lesbian youth are two to three times more likely to attempt suicide than other youth and suggested that they may comprise up to 30% of completed suicides by youth.

One way that adolescent homosexuals cope with their problems is by using alcohol and drugs. In one 1987 survey, 58 percent of gay youth reported substance abuse as a means of coping. Other estimates are in the 30 to 35% range—"normal" for gay adults, but still *three times the average* for society at large.

Compassion aside, why should all this matter to us if we're past our teens? Because it adds risk, costs, and financial handicaps to our lives. The mental health of our neighbors, friends, lovers, playmates, and pals is part of our baggage, like it or not. This is the "goodwill" or "ill will" on our balance sheet. This is our infrastructure; if it's solid, we can prosper, but if it's not, someday the bottom may fall out at a very inopportune moment. We don't need added risk in our lives.

Depression

It's not surprising that therapy can be a major budget item for us. This has great financial impact on those of us who make money mostly with our minds, not our muscle. Our attitudes shape our ability to invest. Our moods impact our spending. Our clarity informs our short- and long-term thinking. It's no wonder that mental health belongs in our financial equations.

Study after study documents our greater incidence of depression. This is especially true in teen years, with gays of color, and with people with HIV.

Yet we face the same problem with therapists as we do with physicians. One study reports that a quarter of the psychiatric faculty of a medical school admitted they were prejudiced against gay men and lesbians. It wasn't until 1986 that the American Psychiatric Association deleted "egodystonic homosexuality" as a diagnosis for gays who are overly concerned about their homosexuality as a result of an unaccepting society. Even without prejudice almost no training in our special therapy issues is given. Even if we go with a gay therapist, we might want to ask ourselves what impact that possible professional ostracism might have on their competency.

This means that in therapy we can play Russian roulette in our choice of practitioner—and then end up with a compromised professional no matter what. Since we're talking about our psyche here, we have to be that much more exacting in researching, interviewing, and evaluating our would-be helpers.

Alcoholism

Alcoholism is the number-one financial gay killer. Why? Because alcohol has been the very fuel of gay life for so long, because our alcoholism rates are three times those of the 90%, and because virtually all experts agree that over 30% of our community is alcohol impaired.

Alcohol is the elephant in the gay living room that nobody talks about. The traditional center of American gay life remains the gay bar/disco, especially when we're just starting out.

Faulty Treatment

As the treatments we need become more specialized, the likelihood that we won't be well served seems to increase.

Studies show that we seek alcoholism treatment four times as much as the 90%. But once we get it, our problems often get compounded by prejudice, ignorance, and mistakes.

To begin with, a survey of gays receiving in-patient treatment for alcoholism and addiction shows that fewer than half reveal their orientation in treatment, even though a majority in treatment see gay life as a causal factor in their substance abuse. Of those who did come out in treatment, fewer than half felt that their sexuality was taken into account at all. Including a spouse is key to many treatment approaches, yet in one study fewer than 8% of lesbians and 4% of gay men were even given this opportunity. It's not surprising that fewer than 15% of gay men were satisfied with their group therapy. It's not surprising either that follow-up on recovery reveals far lower success rates than with the 90%.

The Finances of Addiction

While the medical cost may remain camouflaged for years, the financial tab for alcohol builds inexorably. It's our most quantitative indicator as to whether, overall, pain is outstripping the pleasure we seek.

As with estimating life's other small but repetitive costs, the key is to frame the whole picture, and not simply move from moment to moment. Perhaps we can start with a weekly recollection, and then move on to a month's perspective, a season's overview, a year's tally, or a decade's buildup.

Reframing our time perspective is necessary because of the impact of drugs on our very ability to think clearly, our body's increasing tolerance to them, and their cumulative effect on our will to act. Financially this dictates taking the long view.

Let's check the common costs from alcohol, drugs, and other addictions:

Is cash simply unaccounted for the morning after?

Are health food store costs mounting for home remedies?

What are bar bills running in a month? delivery bills? restaurant bar tabs?

Are there costs from damaged, broken, burned, or lost possessions such as cars, furniture, clothing, and accessories?

Are there financial complications from mishaps, accidents, or snafus where alcohol's played a part?

Are there symptoms of headaches, mental fogginess, disinterest?

Are medical situations developing that might get complicated?

Have there been incidents of unprotected sex with risky partners?

Is there a growing disregard for risk of street violence, of venturing into poor sections of town, or of a temptation to dare risky things?

Is there loss of time from work, especially on Mondays and Fridays?

Have there been mistakes, accidents, indiscretions, or missed deadlines at work?

Have there been any driving violations, mishaps, or alcohol tests?

Have there been any legal costs incurred related to an incident involving alcohol?

Have there been incidents of sudden violence?

Have work colleagues, clients, or suppliers withdrawn or grown distant?

Are performance evaluations or salary increases declining?

Is work becoming less important?

Have there been friends lost, relationships damaged—or growing isolation?

Drugs: Financial Crashing

If 30% alcoholism rates are scary, and the financial erosion of alcohol sobering, drugs are terrifying in their fast financial fallout. Drugs escalate costs not just several steps further but into whole new dimensions of disaster:

It's far easier and quicker to get addicted—and harder to get off them.

They're exponentially more expensive—and wreak financial havoc swiftly.

Their impact on career and job performance—our money machine—is more unpredictable.

They build tolerance more quickly—and make overdoses much more possible.

They act on the brain with more immediately irreversible effects.

Individual Solutions

What are the chances of keeping drugs and alcohol out of our balance sheets? Take a look at the costs tallied on the checklist above. If there are a few primary areas where damage is high—such as Sex While Intoxicated, or SWI—then an alcohol-reduction approach might work. This is a new strategy that works best where alcohol isn't such a central part of the overall culture. The traditional tactic is to try out a twelve-step-based recovery program, most notably, Alcoholics Anonymous. Major urban areas now have full-blown *gay* AA programs that offer gay support in a gay setting. In fact New York's largest contingent in its Gay Pride Parade has often been the sober group. If professionals are engaged to help, the figures above indicate this may be one case where gay professionals have an edge. A person in recovery shouldn't have to educate medical personnel; let's put that item on our social, not our personal, agendas.

► Risk #3: *Breast Cancer*

Experts project that one in seven lesbians gets breast cancer as compared to one in nine women in general. In fact the unpublished National Lesbian Health Care Survey in 1985 indicated that over a quarter of all lesbians have experienced some breast abnormality.

The big problem with cancer for lesbians comes from the delays in detection, for over 75% of women *with late diagnoses* die within four years. And many factors delay detection with lesbians:

- the prejudice of the medical professions

- the extra invisibility of lesbians

- a possible hesitancy of lesbians to discuss sex

- lack of finances

- lack of partner insurance

- an understandable reluctance to seek regular checkups and to come out to physicians

Pap smears and lower pelvic exams are often the only effective ways to be sure there is no cancer. Yet lesbians let three times as much time go by between Pap smears as heterosexual women do. The National Cancer Institute notes that 45% of lesbians don't have regular obstetric-gynecological care and another 25% have only sporadic care. As many as 10% of lesbians either have never had a Pap smear or have had just one in the previous ten years. Many lesbians incorrectly assume that with fewer or no children they do not have to do breast self-exams—when the opposite is true, as it is not having children, along with above-average smoking and alcoholism, that is believed to contribute to the higher incidence of cancer overall.

Lesbians are more invisible than gay men, report worse experiences with physicians, and often won't come out to physicians. This compounds the secrecy already surrounding gynecological health concerns and its automatic focus on childbearing—on top of shame issues around women's body issues. Further problems can occur among lesbians who reject traditional medicine in favor of more personable practitioners of alternative medicine offering unproven remedies.

As we've seen with AIDS, many insurers reject treatment advances as "experimental." Most insurance will not reimburse alternative treatment, or reimburse it for only short periods of time at extremely low levels.

Medical research reflects the high health cost of lesbian invisibility. Only four general studies of lesbian health have been published in peer-reviewed obstetric and gynecological journals since 1966. No health surveys and no tumor registries identify lesbians, making it impossible accurately to identify health risks or events unique to lesbians.

Progress is possible. The American College of Obstetricians and Gynecologists updated its brochures to patients and doctors in 1995 to include information on lesbian health. The Harvard Nurses Study and the Women's Health Initiative of the National Institutes of Health are both large-scale surveys that include data on lesbian participants to document whether lesbians are at high risk and what preventive measures they can take.

Cancer Costs: Immediate, High, Career Fallout

If cancer strikes, financial chaos can follow.

The high risk of cancer impacts lesbians extra hard, since the costs of cancer usually hit immediately upon diagnosis. Patients are often whisked into surgery; if insurance is inadequate, money quickly vanishes simply to get treatment, with little time to recoup.

This is one reason why lesbians should build substantial borrowing power. This may take the form of an equity loan on the home, carefully cultivated personal borrowing facilities with banks, already existing credit arrangements on personally owned businesses, and high personal credit card limits. The key task upon diagnosis is to muster the cash to get treatment as soon as possible. How to pay for it is a problem we'll discuss under credit in the section on life-threatening illness below.

Every illness has its own cost curve. With cancer most costs hit up front, followed by a less costly but protracted and uncertain period of treatment and remission.

Unlike the case of chronic illnesses, there is little chance for financial preparation, planning, or preventive measures. Since the essence of planning is advance time, little preventive action may be possible. This sudden, unanticipated cost can upset financial arrangements and plunge lesbian finances into debt.

If treatment is successful, the long waiting period begins. A cancer diagnosis eliminates most chances of getting insurance after the fact. Without domestic-partnership benefits this can result in many lesbians being without insurance when they need it most. And that can in turn force impoverishment to qualify for Medicaid.

To be eligible for Medicaid an individual usually cannot have more than $5,000 in resources. Transfers between nonmarried people will not impact eligibility for Medicaid home care, but will impact eligibility for nursing-home care. Consult an attorney!

The real fallout can come in careers. One of the few advantages lesbians have over childbearing heterosexual women is the continuity they can bring to their careers. Cancer brings a sudden end to continuity and leads to job loss more often than you might think. Uncertainty about remission can keep people from going back to work and cancel out budding careers. Cancer stories abound where employers fire employees with cancer, refuse to hire them, or will only bring them on in lower-level positions.

There are protections from the Americans with Disabilities Act and under the Family and Medical Leave Act. However, the awards are small, the delays are large, and litigation diverts resources at the exact time when they are needed to offset the financial damage caused by the illness.

After cancer's initial cost onslaught, the pattern of its costs approximates more closely the cost impact of other life-threatening illness such as HIV. Since much more progress has been made in mapping out actions to deal with this financial fallout with HIV, let's move on to that discussion. Most of these follow-up ways of dealing with the costs of cancer are covered there.

By their 30s lesbians simply have to plan finances. Domestic partnership benefits can be a boon to a lesbian couple where one doesn't have conventional employment with benefits. With statistics like these and the swiftness with which cancer strikes, having credit, insurance, and legal protections in place is a basic survival strategy.

► Risk #4: *HIV-Related Disease*

HIV has wrought financial havoc in our community, with no signs of slowing down. In major urban centers one third to one half of all gay men have HIV. In small cities it's one in ten. And there's more to come. Over a third of gay youth and over half of bisexual and multiethnic men have unprotected anal sex.

HIV—or just the possibility of HIV—remains the crucial financial challenge for gay men. HIV has not just revolutionized the way people fight disease; it's spawned new techniques and resources in personal finance as well. Let's look at how we can solve the financial problems presented by HIV—and use this as a lesson in how to fight financially other illnesses as well.

Providing for Catastrophe: Last Things First?

The most fundamental financial change with HIV has been to shift thinking from catastrophe planning to crisis management, from a last-things-first mentality to a first-things-first focus.

What are we providing for, anyway? Up to now the job of financial planning has been seen as providing for our last days. Nursing-home care is the bogeyman that insurance salesmen, investment brokers, and financial planners have used to convince us to save for that last great battle.

On the surface it seems logical. A medical frenzy accompanies life-threatening illness and our days of dying—our last big blowout. About 20 to 30% of all medical costs are expended in those last days before death. For years now this has been the great unspoken purpose of personal finance: to pay for this modern-day parting party, as if going out in glory was worth using up every last cent we have in some great financial funeral pyre.

Yet most of us don't really care about how we spend our dying days. At that point we're simply beyond feeding the medical machine—and even if we don't, the government will.

As people with AIDS have found out, the real financial impact of illness happens during our lives—when disease suddenly stops our money machine, when we care as much about comfort as about care, and when the costs of fighting illness count.

Cash as a Treatment Tool

Treatment for HIV averages well over $100,000 and often runs up to $1,000,000, totals that can easily go beyond health-insurance policy maximums, approaching average lifetime earnings.

Simply put, cash is now a major treatment tool against serious illness. In the olden days when little could be done, cash didn't matter. As our medical arsenal enlarges, each advance costs money. Luckily we have financial resources that can help. Disability is a valid basis for tapping tax-deferred retirement funds, even with the 20% withholding for taxes, although pension benefits are more often locked in place until normal retirement age.

Crisis Management: First Things First

Illness can make finances seem unreal. We become a battle-ground not just for microbes but for medical providers and insurers fighting over large sums.

Our only practical defense is crisis management. Cash and credit become king, and cash flow estimating is key. Preapprovals are crucial. Mistakes in billing and reimbursement are widespread. It may pay to have a technical specialist take over the claims payment and reimbursement process. Some guidelines to keep in mind:

- First determine how much cash will be needed, and on what likely timetable.
- Nail down tax considerations before taking any action.
- Think through the impact on estate planning.
- Keep your options open; the more choices you have, the greater your chances for substantial savings and better care.
- Remember that the sequence of action is as important as the actions themselves.

Truck Route or Expressway?

How do we get that kind of cash when disease hits in midlife? We have two choices: the public welfare truck route or the private insurance expressway.

Welfare just isn't very gay. We not only lose choice, we lose dignity, turning control over both our finances and a wealth of information about every detail of our lives to a potentially uneducated bureaucrat of unknown homophobic tendencies.

Group or individual insurance now becomes an asset greater than any real estate or investment holdings we might own. In fact those traditional focal points of personal finance must take a backseat if illness strikes, since their long time frames are ill suited to the need at hand.

• Employment benefits are now as important as salary or the job itself if we're seriously ill. They're cheap, and they don't require medical screening.

• Medical insurance is priority number one. We need to make sure it won't disappear if we change a job, lose a job, go on disability, or become eligible for Medicare.

• Disability insurance is priority number two. Fighting illness is a full-time job, and we can't do it if our income tank is nearly on empty.

• Life insurance now ranks number three, offering the possibility to get cash out of life insurance if our illness is seen as life threatening.

• It now makes sense to buy what is otherwise needless and expensive insurance: catastrophic medical coverage and old-fashioned hospital indemnity plans that literally pay cash when we're in the hospital.

• Liquidity becomes primary. Credit records must be impeccable, credit limits must be expanded, and otherwise expensive and needless disability and life insurance options on credit balances may now be appropriate.

Jobs: the Back Door to Security

What if key insurances are missing? If we already have a serious illness, our best bet is to search for jobs because of their benefits, not just their salary. Follow the benefits, the money will follow.

Certain industries, such as finance and computers, offer liberal and luxurious benefits that are often effective soon after employment starts. Medical insurance is usually cheap and with few limits. If the employer is large enough, we can take the insurance with us for eighteen months under the COBRA laws—and if we leave on disability, our COBRA coverage will continue right up to the point where Medicare kicks in.

Corporate coverage is not without pitfalls. Beware of maximums on pharmaceuticals and even specific diseases. Look out for poor-quality managed-care offerings, because you usually can't change plans more than once a year. And keep in mind that if the company goes out of business while you're employed or on disability, its group-based medical insurance will also disappear.

Disability benefits are offered by fewer than half of all employers, mostly in prosperous, "benefits-rich" industries. Get to know what those industries are in your locale. Look for plans that pay 60 to 70% of current compensation, including bonuses. The best plans make you pay the low premium, making the benefit tax free and usually near-equal to take-home pay; in portable plans the coverage can be convertible to an individual plan if you leave. Finally, life insurance benefits may include a basic employer-paid plan plus supplemental coverage equal itself to several times salary, increasing the amount of funds available for possible sale.

Those of us who own our own business, even as small as three employees, can find surprisingly low-cost group disability and life coverage with minimal preconditions that usually last only one year.

▼ ▼ ▼

Anne's breast cancer is in remission. She has a catering business that has four employees. She put in a group disability plan that would not pay preexisting conditions during the first year. Because of this coverage the insurer granted the firm's employees guaranteed-issue group life insurance coverage worth $50,000 each.

▲ ▲ ▲

It's time to remember the lessons of Maslow's pyramid: Human motivation is sequential. Security comes first, social support second; *only then* can we focus on self-actualization.

Upside-Down Credit Debt

Illness often prompts worries about debt, leading many people to cut up their credit cards in one last attempt to be good. In fact, this is the opposite of what should be done. What's crucial with illness is liquidity. It's time to buff up that credit record, pay bills promptly—and get *more* credit. Unpredictable expenses, slow reimbursements, and insurer disputes make cash and credit golden.

It is often possible to get disability and life-insurance coverage on card balances with *no* medical screening, although it usually needs to be in place for six months before it's effective. If illness forces expenses onto cards and forces you onto disability, this back-door insurance will pay off the balance. But some coverage stops after one or two years. And you'll need to stay on top of the relentless paperwork parades many policies require—including monthly forms signed by your doctor.

If you insure your cards you can reduce premiums by keeping your card balances low, ideally using them only once a year to keep them current. If you do have outstanding uninsured balances at the time of disability, you can sometimes argue that the sudden shift to disability income is a valid basis to negotiate extremely low repayment plans, to freeze interest, or to forgive accounts—especially if individual card balances are but a few thousand dollars. Sometimes much disability income is exempt from creditors.

Often simply a lawyer's letter results in a debt being canceled and shields us from harassment and stress. In fact, if a creditor ignores an attorney's no-contact request, there may be a basis for a lawsuit with triple damages based on the harassment.

Lastly, federal student loans and many other types of student loans are often forgiven automatically on disability. If this is true, it pays to keep payments minimal until disability starts.

Health Insurance: the Buck Stops Here

We need insurance we can take with us from job to job—insurance that'll stay with us if we leave a job or become ill. Modest health-insurance reform has in fact now made insurance more portable. But in many states restrictions remain. Many gays fighting illness cannot leave their job without the risk of being slapped with a preexisting-condition waiting period, during which time there's no reimbursement for that illness.

Over half of all major employers are self-insured and beyond the reach of state regulation. While most of these want to offer attractive medical benefits, there are few barriers to prevent them from discriminating against us in their coverage.

As someone trained to run HMOs, I recommend managed care only for people who have little need for the medical system. HMOs are taking power away even from physicians, much less consumers. They see sick people as costs—to be eliminated.

We can fight back. Find out if the HMO has an ombudsman—and become a squeaky wheel. We are, after all, ultimately in charge of our own care. One of the great revolutions of HIV needs to be repeated. In New York the major disease groups banded together to change state insurance laws. For the first time in history representatives of people with heart, lung, kidney, blood, HIV, and cancer problems converged on lawmakers. Think about it; this is an incredible lobby—if we will but band together.

Medicaid Hell

What about Medicaid? Only as a last resort. Its low reimbursements are incentives to providers to channel patients into low-cost treatments; its delays can literally mean poor care. It is no accident that three quarters of long-term survivors have *private* insurance.

▼ ▼ ▼

Lyle has symptoms of pneumonia; with Medicaid he's given some pills and told to go home. His friend John has pneumonia, too, but with Blue Cross he's given a $750 bronchoscopy, fully reimbursed, and it's discovered that he has PCP, which requires hospitalization.

▲ ▲ ▲

Well-meant advice to "spend down" (i.e., get rid of assets and income) to get onto Medicaid is a bad bargain financially as well. Poor is not gay. It is far preferable to seek health insurance through work, domestic-partner benefits, or, after legal consideration, a marriage of convenience.

One of the tragedies of life-threatening illness is the revelation of how social workers are trained almost too well to play the public system—because they end up ignoring privately funded benefits that gays should rely on instead to stay free.

Disability Insurance: Funds for Life

HIV teaches that health insurance without disability coverage is simply not enough. Often *more* income is needed than was earned before: many expensive treatments of new diseases are poorly reimbursed, if reimbursed at all.

Disability benefits can also help us build a bridge back to life, to realize the dreams that acquire a new urgency when time becomes precious. Clearly, they are resources worth planning for—but are far more difficult to acquire after the barn is already burning. People whose illness has already progressed to disability levels can still get these benefits through group plan employment benefits packages, and are encouraged to do so if health at all permits.

There are two other methods that people have tried, but both are fraught with risks so high and success rates so low that they cannot be recommended.

• The first is to lie on a private disability policy application form and not make a claim for the two years that the incontestability clause runs. In fact, unscrupulous insurance agents often encourage applicants to skip over questions—i.e., lie—on application forms. The policy writers are a step ahead of such schemes; since 1990, insurers put escape language into incontestability clauses, such as "except in case of fraud," that can render such policies worthless.

• The second approach is to find questions on an application form on which all medical screening questions could *possibly* be answered no. You are urged to do this only if you have a lawyer review the form. Practically speaking, this is a poor course. Some disability policies are easy to get because those insurers screen out people when they make a *claim*—not when they *apply*. Then, of course, it's too late; the applicant could have applied the money to other actions, but relied instead on this illusory protection. It may be possible to get a nuisance settlement, but anyone seriously ill is unlikely to want to spend his time and his health in a lawsuit.

Life Insurance: Catastrophic Funds

The greatest news for people facing life-threatening illness is the invention in the 1990s of two ways to get cash out of life insurance: acceleration and viatication.

• The idea behind acceleration is simple: the insurer pays out some part of the life insurance *before* death.

• The idea behind viatication is even simpler: an insurer's promise to pay upon death can be sold by the insured—just like any other financial promise to pay.

No other change has turned personal finance more on its ear. If viatication or acceleration is possible, the focus of financial planning can shift from catastrophic planning for dying to crisis management for living. Financial planning suddenly becomes more than a question of how we rob the present just to pay for our finale; with more to plan for, there's more incentive to plan.

And planning is certainly called for. These two techniques are new, they're poorly understood, and mistakes here are extremely costly. There's almost no useful written information about them. Let's take extra time here to see how they work—and how to use them effectively.

As with disability insurance, life insurance is best acquired when we're healthy. If our potential risk falls mostly during our working lives, it's best to get our life insurance under cheap term rates. Term insurance stops at retirement age but if our risk is low then, it will have done its job.

If we're facing life-threatening illness, it makes sense to get coverage through employment. In fact, since most workplace life coverage is effective immediately and must by law be convertible to private status if employment ends, each job we get may now pay us a life insurance bonus, although converted life insurance carries very high premiums.

▼ ▼ ▼

George was a wanna-be actor and temp. With HIV and without life insurance he joined one of the firms he'd temped for and immediately was eligible for $185,000 in life coverage—five times his salary. He and his lover decided to move to the country. George converted the coverage into an individual policy, paying term rates the first year. Two years later after the suicide clause expired, his financial advisor found two viatical firms to bid on it; one bid 53%, the other bid 70%. His few months of employment netted him an extra $130,000. The country didn't work out so George returned to work and got another $200,000 in coverage—effective immediately.

▲ ▲ ▲

Acceleration Complications

No one has calculated how many policies offer acceleration clauses these days. We do know that acceleration is rare on group policies, sporadic on individual policies, and virtually nonexistent on policies smaller than $25,000. Only about two hundred of the two thousand insurance companies in the U.S. have added this feature to their new policies as a rider—although this two hundred does include many of the nation's largest companies. Many companies do not apply them to existing policies.

Our first task is to find out if they exist on our coverage. Make many calls, starting with your carrier's claims department. Insurance agents and customer service personnel are likely to be misinformed on such a new kind of benefit. I call the president's office to find out if they're being considered, and the state insurance department to see if they've been applied for.

Many insurers require a physician to attest that the insured's life expectancy is twelve months or less. Keep in mind that life expectancy is a notion subject to fierce debate, and that your physician may have a natural tendency toward optimism. This means you two need to have a chat only about this—and about how much good the funds will do. It won't hurt to remind the physician that this is all about the worst that could happen, and that little if any review is made of his form by the insurance company. (I've had physicians balk at signing because they falsely thought the insurance company could hold them liable—if the patient lived longer than the estimate!)

▼ ▼ ▼

Thorsten hit bottom fast with his HIV. He'd always had a dream of running a gay publication. He accelerated his $500,000 policy—and received $475,000. The money proved to be a restorative; his health improved and he moved ahead with his dream. He's tested now as a long-term survivor, and his publication is in its third year.

▲ ▲ ▲

Insurers determine unilaterally how much of a policy can be accelerated. As with many financial tools, this seems geared to the mythical family with a male breadwinner, nonworking female spouse, and 2.5 children. This hurts gays, since insurers usually restrict acceleration to only a 25–50% portion of the policy. Of the part that can be accelerated, however, the insurer will typically pay more than 90%—charging a small amount for interest and/or an administrative fee; once accepted, the payout is within weeks. One catch: Insurers permit acceleration only once—an inhumane provision, since things change quickly in final days. Unless you have good reasons to the contrary, get as much as you can.

The biggest problem with acceleration is that most of us don't need much cash for personal needs as we near death. We do need it for nonreimbursed medical expenses we can't get except through cash. This means that acceleration is truly a technique best suited for end-stage situations.

Some insurers allow acceleration to be used to pay for long-term or nursing-home care. Beware of nursing-home operators withholding a bed unless you accelerate life insurance. In many states creditors are prohibited from forcing you to accelerate or viaticate. Let Medicaid pay for things instead, since Medicaid will allow you to keep your life insurance under most circumstances.

Viatication: Cash for Life

Any life policy can be sold that permits assignment of rights, including the right to name the beneficiary. Prices paid vary enormously according to the market. The National Association of Insurance Commissioners (NAIC) suggests these purchase rates for these life expectancies: six months, 80% of the policy's face value; twelve months, 70%; and twenty-four months, 60%.

Under the Health Insurance Act of 1996, viatical payments are not subject to federal taxes, provided that a physician signs off on a two-year life expectancy, and the buyer is a licensed company in the buyer's state, or (in unregulated states) abides by NAIC standards for viatical companies. State and local taxes vary with geography, but are often waived in regulated states (such as in California and New York).

Most buyers require that the policy to be viaticated has been held more than two years, beyond typical incontestability and suicide clause periods. Some buyers will buy policies within the contestability period; some will buy individual policies converted from group plans even if they have active suicide clauses. Still, waiting out the two-year period usually results in more bidders and higher settlements.

Viatication can be done on virtually any individual policy, with life expectancies of up to five years. The longer the life expectancy, the more thought required: if life expectancy is greater than two years, all amounts are declared taxable income, and the dollar amounts of settlement fall drastically as uncertainty about life expectancy rises.

Most companies prefer policies above at least $10,000 or usually $25,000, but a few do smaller policies as a community service or to promote themselves. If at all possible tie the sale of such policies to larger policies—or keep asking companies if they know of one that will buy a small policy.

Group Coverage Is the Widest Available and the Trickiest to Sell

Although group policies can be sold, the length and complexity of group master contracts create room for delays and glitches to look out for:

• Some old group policies permit assignment—the mechanism by which ownership rights are transferred—only to blood relatives as a *gift*. This holdover is anti-gay and should be the target of gay activists: gay money is at stake. If "assignment for value" is permitted in the description of the coverage, it can be sold. Only one state, New York, insists that insurers allow viatical assignment if they allow *any* kind of assignment. Even here insurers have objected, saying their group contracts predate the law, a defense that crumbles when they are reminded that each contract renewal effectively creates a new insurance contract.

• Some insurers actively oppose viatical settlements, claiming that their end-stage accelerated benefits alone should be sufficient. Such insurers will take months to fill out insurance coverage viatical questionnaires—and will refuse to process assignments or insist on special requirements. Seek expert legal help if this happens.

• Benefits personnel are already low on the corporate totem poles. They usually do not comprehend what these new benefits imply in terms of coverage or procedure. Get any information from them in writing, and deal with supervisors or heads of departments if at all possible. Beware of inaccurate responses on questionnaires sent by viatical companies. If a suicide clause exists, ask why. That can keep coverage illiquid for two years from the date coverage first became effective.

• When group sponsors change coverage, new coverage is often un-documented for up to one year, and buyers must research whether future changes would make sold coverage worthless.

▼ ▼ ▼

Mort needed funds badly; but with his company's new in-surer he couldn't even find out how much coverage he had, much less whether assignment existed on the contract. Luckily he had been in a seminar with the controller, so he asked him to be his White Knight. The controller found that the insurer had not continued the assignment provisions of the old insurer—and forced them to. He also forced the insurer to remove any suicide clause so the coverage would be immediately salable. He then had to create new procedures in the benefits department that would ensure that the buyer would be notified of any changes in coverage or in the seller's employment status.

▲ ▲ ▲

• When group members go out on disability, they're typically covered by a disability waiver of premium.

If that premium waiver is paid for and held by the insurer, the coverage is likely to be salable, and highly attractive.

If the group member is waiting for the disability waiver to be approved, some companies may not bid.

If the disability waiver is paid by the group sponsor, and the group sponsor changes coverage while the employee is on disability, the old coverage may suddenly reduce to only a few thousand dollars. Result? No sale possible.

This detail is provided to show that viatication is not as easy as the ads would make us believe. This is a new, untried, highly sophisticated technique that can easily go awry—involving large sums of *your* money. Seller beware!

Prices Vary Wildly

Viatical prices are set by a rapidly changing, Wild-West market that generates its profits in part by taking advantage of seller naïveté. It makes sense in such a market to hire help in not only eliminating barriers to a sale, but in negotiating a price.

Viatical prices are market driven. Prices can go up and down subject to rumor, news, conflicting expert opinion, interest rates, funds availability, type of funds—and the judgment of often inexpert entrepreneurs and investors. The market experiences major price shifts several times a year. Like the stock market diseases shift in popularity among buyers.

In the midst of all of this flux, you should know who you're selling to, and who to avoid. *Individual-investor*-funded firms may pay high for middle-term life expectancies, but poorly for short-term life expectancies. Their cost of funds is high, but they don't appear to care what investors get stuck with. Investor-financed firms have been the subject of lawsuits from the SEC, who claim that they are dealing in unlicensed securities—adding to the uncertainty of the market. *Bank- and insurer*-financed firms must rely on conservative funding. When life expectancy is predictable, this financing is abundant, and offers are fair; when breakthroughs occur, these funds flee, and offers are meager.

Licensing Chaos

Because insurance is state run, viatical firms are licensed by state insurance departments. Most states do not yet regulate viatication, yet the states with most people with HIV do. Investor-financed firms often do not apply for licensing in strict-licensing states such as New York and California, where many with HIV live. Yet funding sources must be licensed for funds to be tax free.

Except when it tries to set prices, regulation protects consumers. Regulations usually require that the buyer's money be placed into an independent account held by an escrow agent—usually an attorney—*before* the buyer sends the offer papers to be signed by the seller. They also provide for a period during which the seller may rescind the sale—usually fifteen days after the money has been received.

Some unlicensed firms are spreading doubt about the licensing process. Ads placed by one firm in twenty-one gay publications in spring 1995 claimed that licensed companies had to reveal to state authorities their confidential records. The opposite, in fact, is true. Any claim by an unlicensed firm that regulation hurts consumers should be a red flag to move on to another firm.

Licensing: Key to Tax-Free Status

Viatical income is declared to the IRS as of 1997, so anyone viaticating a policy must deal with the tax issue.

Licensed brokers commonly claim that their license is enough. A broker's license is in fact irrelevant; only the funding company's licensing status counts in the eyes of the IRS. The greatest impact of licensing now is its link to making viatical settlements tax free. Beware of assurances that a simple address change will suffice to sneak by the law. The IRS has strict standards for residency that should be kept in mind when planning any viatication.

Executors for estates where policies have been viaticated should be extremely careful, since they can be personally liable for the tax on undeclared funds. Prior to 1997 many who viaticated did not declare the funds because they were not declared to the IRS—a ruse unlikely to survive an audit. Now viatical proceeds are not only declared but taxable if life expectancy and licensing requirements are not met.

Legal Thickets

Because most states are still unregulated, and state regulation itself varies so much, buyers should definitely seek legal review. However, the attorney should *already* have expertise in viatical regulation and what special protections sellers need. This is no time to yet again educate a naive attorney at our expense.

Most companies are honest, if only to cultivate word-of-mouth advertising. However, we need protection against many hidden glitches. And I have yet to see one viatical settlement go through without a glitch, on the part of the insurance company, a doctor, an employer, a nondisclosure on the part of the buyer or seller, or a simple human mistake.

Are legal costs worth it? Would you sell a house without an attorney? This is on a par with the sale of a house, except the territory is unexplored. These sales are often the biggest financial transaction we've ever done in our lives. Yes, it's worth it.

The Invisible Prices Paid by the Seller in Brokering

The greatest financial pitfall in viatication is to use a broker. Brokers promote the illusion that their services are free, or even that they have their own funds. Yet brokers cost the seller by demanding 5- to 8%-commissions from buyers. This seriously hurts sellers in several key ways:

• Because commissions vary from company to company, brokers have a financial incentive to steer business to the company that pays them the highest commission—*not* to the company that makes the highest offer to the seller.

• Because the commission is paid by the buyer, brokers have an incentive to satisfy the buyer—not the seller—by closing out cases quickly, by discouraging legal review, by claiming the payment is tax free, and by saying an offer is competitively bid when it isn't.

• Because broker fees are calculated on the policy's total face value— *not* the amount received—the broker has no incentive to get more money for the seller and no incentive to competitively bid the policy.

• Because brokers get paid only if a sale occurs, they and the viatical companies have a *dis*incentive to tell sellers about accelerated benefits—which may be a superior alternative.

• Because brokers are paid only commissions, they have a *dis*incentive to encourage other less costly ways of meeting expenses or providing cash.

• Broker fees as a percentage actually cost the seller much more—twice as much in the case of a 50% offer. Here's how: the commission on a $100,000 policy is $6,000. Yet the buyer gets only $50,000, or 50%. The $6,000 commission is actually 12% of the amount received.

• Finally, brokers and purchasing companies frequently fail to inform sellers about their commissions. Only New York requires that they be disclosed—in a tiny paragraph often overlooked in the complex closing package.

In short, sellers are encouraged to avoid brokers, opting instead to deal directly with self-funded or bank-funded companies. If a seller does decide to go through a broker, these precautions are advised:

• The seller should require in writing the company names, phone numbers, and contact names of all companies contacted as well as the opening and final bids of each company.

• The broker should specify for each company the commission promised both as a percentage and as a dollar amount.

• The broker should accept a commission based on the actual amount received—to provide an incentive for higher offers. It is often possible to negotiate commissions down to 1%.

• The broker should agree to true competitive bidding.

• The seller should require that the amount and percentage of the broker commission be stated up front, in writing, and in the purchase agreement—with written assurances by the buyer that there are no side agreements with the broker.

Get Competitive Bids

Why bother to get competitive bids? Bids vary widely. Even with preselected self-funded companies chosen on the basis of extensive past experience, I still receive final bids that are 10 to 15% higher than opening bids—and bids vary 15 to 30% between companies.

Sellers should seek at least four to six true bids from only self-funded firms. To do so requires understanding how the industry is organized—and getting names of firms to work from.

Beware of ads, most of which are placed by brokers who funnel buyers to companies that pay them the highest commissions. Advertisers have been known to deny being a broker even when they are.

The most basic screening a seller can do is to ask if the buyer is licensed, and to check that out with the state insurance department. This is not easy. Even as a national expert I repeatedly have to use the Freedom of Information Act, attorneys, and the press office just to get a copy of the state list of licensed firms in New York and Florida. You may have to as well. Beware: the list is often one year out of date, citing firms that may no longer be in business.

It's probably easier simply to ask the viatical firms themselves for such a list; but be prepared for quite a variety to choose from. There is an association of brokers and buyers called the Viatical Association of America: (800) 842-9811. Their list identifies who is a broker and who is a buyer. The other association is the National Viatical Association: (800) 741-9465. They do not identify brokers and buyers and have many more investor-financed firms.

Sellers should ask AIDS organizations to maintain an up-to-date list of state licensed self-funded firms. An AIDS organizations that recommends a single firm is a red flag, and could signal an arrangement that benefits the organization at the expense of the seller. Some organizations have openly struck agreements with viatical firms to receive a kickback in exchange for publicizing a single firm—and see no conflict of interest in this. Likewise, viatical firms are persuading employers to recommend them as a "preferred provider." Employers have no basis for doing so. Since fair offers only result from competitive bidding, sole-source recommendations are anticompetitive.

Get Expert Help

All these factors teach one lesson: Beware. This is tricky, unknown, shifting territory. Taking the easy path with viatication may turn out to be a very expensive proposition, with tax surprises, high commissions, and poor offers. Seek competitive offers; invest time, money and effort; and consider expert advice.

Your negotiator should be able to:

- Estimate how much the bidding process might cost and how much time it might take
- Estimate your financial needs and define what time frames need to be provided for
- Assess alternative ways to generate cash that are less expensive
- Determine if accelerated benefits are at all possible
- Generate a list of four to six genuine, self-funded bidders
- Develop a bidding package that includes a single simplified application, authorizations, insurance information, and two years' worth of medical records
- Follow up with bidders, coordinate with medical providers, and generate a standardized insurance questionnaire that verifies the coverage
- Get all bids in and inform bidders of the highest bid
- Get second bids in to award the policy to the ultimately highest bidder
- Review contract paperwork and arrange alternatives for legal review
- Follow up paperwork processing, insurer processing, and payment instructions

- Advise on how to hold funds, how to plan spending, and how to handle those who would take advantage
- Do all this for a fee based on the actual time spent and the level of expertness required.

Remember: This may be a final major financial decision of your life, as well as the most complicated. Expert assistance will pay off in more ways than one.

▼ ▼ ▼ ▼ ▼ ▼ ▼

Surprise Survivors: HIV and the Costs of Change

▲ ▲ ▲ ▲ ▲ ▲ ▲

In the summer of '96 good news about new drugs broke at the annual AIDS conference. The remarkable promise of these new drug therapies has deservedly been a cause for celebration throughout our community. However, the financial fallout has been complex and chaotic—and often less than good.

Disability Benefits

Social Security doesn't change their criteria quickly with the advent of the new treatments. Because Social Security's criteria are written, a change is also a political act and may take a long time to take effect.

Few realize those on Social Security already have an elaborate system for returning to work. The trial work-period program allows people to earn virtually anything they can for up to nine months before Social Security undertakes a review—and before benefits might be stopped.

If the income has been less than $500 a month or it's apparent that earnings are not consistent, Social Security may be continued. Even with a return to work, if there is a month in the next 36 months where income falls to less than $500, the Social Security Disability Income benefit may be reinstituted with no waiting period. If Medicare was in place when the return to work happens, Medicare is continued at no charge for the next three years.

In any case, a small income of less than $200 a month is not countable.

There are even programs under Medicaid and Social Security Supplemental Income (SSI) programs that allow disabled gays to stockpile earnings while continuing to collect benefits—if those earnings are for the purpose of going into their own business. There may also be Earned Income Tax Credit benefits available as well—although these are under attack in Congress. These are just examples to show that even with disability and seeming impoverishment, there are ways to redress the balance financially and get back to work with minimum penalty.

There are also government programs that pay the educational fees and retraining expense of people on disability; these are usually run through the states. Other programs exist by which people on welfare can put money aside tax free to start a business, while continuing to receive benefits. Turning to such programs should be a first step when news turns good.

Private disability carriers are neither so structured nor so helpful. Bad insurers suddenly stop benefits whether there's good news or not, effectively shifting the burden of proof to the person on disability. For example, insurers may approve mental health claims—but stop paying soon thereafter. Insurers are very good at putting words in the mouths of physicians and twisting the words on their reports; instruct your physician accordingly. Bad insurers send field hacks around to eyeball people on disability, but rarely go to the expense of hiring detectives. I've had insurers question whether a client's trip to Greece, revealed to the disability insurers, was grounds for returning to work, so it doesn't pay to tell insurers what they don't need to know. We can expect all the worst cost-cutting practices of managed care in the disability field very soon; I've had insurer nurses tell a patient he could return to work without even having consulted his physician.

The real danger is not from insurance detectives, but from panicked physicians and patients. Often both forget that it's their data that determines disability in the end. Physicians have a strong bias toward optimism; that can help in the healing process, unless it results in patients returning to work too soon. Disability-retired patients filled with new hope need to recall the financial planning maxim—Plan for the worst, hope for the best, because giving up hard-won private benefits can be hard to reverse.

The problem to avoid is a premature return to work—and patient panic. Patients read the hype of the drug companies and journalists and feel their benefits are going to be withdrawn as a result. Statistics tell the story: over a hundred people a week called the AIDS Project L.A. about having to go back to work when news of the new treatment broke; yet not a single cancellation of benefits had occurred. Remember that people on disability can volunteer any amount of time they wish, as long as they control all circumstances in doing so and no money changes hands.

▼ ▼ ▼

Joe's employer pleaded for him to return to handle a project on a clearly temporary basis. One week into the project Joe received a letter from his insurer stating that they felt he could return to work and asking pointedly if he had worked in the last year. Joe took pains to remind the employer that his help was purely voluntary—wearing leisure clothes, coming when he wished, and doing things his way.

▲ ▲ ▲

Back to work is often a misnomer, because life moves forward and we rarely return easily to any earlier life stage or job. People on disability aren't put on ice. They grow, they age, they reflect. They often come to appreciate other things of value in life than money making; they come to realize that needs can be very few and wants don't necessarily require money; they move on to new interests. People on disability need new training before working again. The world of work changes in but a few years, especially in high-tech fields. The 1990s have seen organizations downsize and disappear and specialties and skills subside in short periods of time.

Beware of reentering the workforce at a low level; people tend to get pegged where they start. It's far better to learn a new trade, adopt new interests, and take the time necessary to thoroughly plan what role career is going to play in this stage of life.

Medical Insurance

The first dilemma with new treatments for any illness is paying for them. Insurers wait as long as possible before paying for new treatments. I have seen patients wait nine to twelve months before review committees got around to passing judgment on new-medication literature—and they wouldn't have bothered to do that unless forced to. I've seen these committees dissolved when insurers were changed by employers, or when insurers merged. Patients with no money to pay for new treatments literally can't afford such delays.

The new treatments for AIDS have revealed how shredded the public safety net has become. A year after their introduction, fewer than half of the states were paying for the new AIDS drugs for people without medical insurance. Rationing is definitely here to stay—with the last-chance treatments where it hurts most. Now instead of saving up for a last great blast in a nursing home, we may have to save up for a nonreimbursed treatment fund.

People on long-term disability eventually go onto Medicare. Since each state regulates medical insurance, going off Medicare will have widely varying impacts on the ability to get full-scale individual medical coverage again. Only one state—New York— permits people to keep their individual coverage when they go onto Medicare. Most states do not cover pharmaceuticals under Medicare. It is highly likely that people going off Medicare would be hit with a twelve-month preexisting-condition exclusion for drug coverage on their new individual medical insurance—even if the drugs were paid by a state drug program. Study these impacts carefully before making any shift in coverage.

Credit and Debt

When disability seems like it is a one-way street, many people going out on disability either declare bankruptcy or, more likely, write their creditors saying that they cannot pay their bills and that their only income is disability income.

Going off disability means either paying the piper on these bills or—more likely—facing a damaged credit record. Usually old balances have been written off. What many don't realize is that rebuilding credit has become much easier.

Impartial, reliable materials to help do this are available by sending $4 payment to Bankcard Holders of America, Publications (524 Branch Drive, Salem, VA 24153) for their "Building Credit" package. Membership is $24 per year—and worth it if you have credit problems.

Selling Life Insurance

The greatest impact of new treatments is on viatication. As in any financial market, the funding of viatical firms can react to news and hype wildly. Only a few months after the protease-inhibitor news, bank and insurer funding had virtually dried up and private-investor funding had mushroomed with the new AIDS drugs. Sellers overreacted as well, unloading policies without concern for the tax consequences.

The shift in funding has dramatic, unintended tax consequences for sellers, since investor-funded firms often are unlicensed—and licensing is required for settlements to be tax-free in many states where those with HIV live. For example, nine out of the thirteen licensed viatical firms effectively withdrew from the New York market. This meant that sellers could get a tax-free bid from only four firms—two conservatively-financed and two investor-financed.

Elsewhere in but a few weeks the market had reverted back to the Wild West early days of questionable practices of investor-financed firms. Because these firms charge such high middle-man fees and pay much more for funding, their highest offers are often only in the low 70% range—in contrast to 89% and even 90% offers from establishment-financed firms. Conversely, the investor-financed firms can pay much more than establishment-financed firms for policies where life expectancy is mid-range—

twenty-four to thirty-six months. Why? With life expectancy vague they can claim to investors that life expectancy is really much lower—without any easy way for the investors to verify this. Because the investor-financed firms are middlemen, their income derives from making the deal, whatever the price. These dynamics benefit people with mid-range life expectancies and penalizes those who are very ill.

The shift in financing has also increased the role of brokers in the industry—another step backward. Some brokers have claimed that if they are licensed, that's all that's needed for the IRS: wrong. Some funders started quoting fixed prices—and letting brokers get whatever commission they could squeeze out of sellers. Others have increased commissions on non-HIV cases. Since most sellers do not understand how the industry operates, since the industry changes a great deal, and since illness prevents the sellers from fully acting as cautious consumers, much more consumer abuse has resulted.

These events highlight how the sporadic way medical information is released causes artificial overreactions that hurt the seriously ill financially. Medical news is kept under wraps until publication in periodic scientific publications or release at annual medical news events (such as the annual AIDS conferences). This makes progress seem sudden and prompts patients and their financial suppliers to lose perspective. Panicky sellers are a problem in any financial market; in viatication a lot more is at stake than money.

Mixed Pictures

The true situation is not too dissimilar from other serious illnesses. At some point things get better—but not for everyone. New treatments are expensive; not everyone has insurance or funds. They require strict compliance or diet discipline, produce side effects, generate mutant viruses, and may simply run out of steam. Some people can't tolerate them; others are too sick to benefit. In such a situation impulsive financial changes are totally uncalled for, on the part of insurer and patient alike.

• • •

Whether or not an illness is life threatening or chronic has major implications in both medicine and finance. When illness becomes chronic we return to standard operating procedure where planning is possible. As long as illness remains life threatening, crisis management is the order of the day. New treatments can in fact increase uncertainty and shatter time frames, making an illness like AIDS an even greater financial crisis than before.

▼ ▼ ▼ ▼ ▼ ▼ ▼

Gay Coupleship: You and Me—and We, Inc.

▲ ▲ ▲ ▲ ▲ ▲ ▲

Financially, the flexibility of gay coupleships can be an asset in areas where straight marriages can be a liability. Without a cookie-cutter model we're encouraged to grow relationships around our individual differences, to strike our own balance of interdependence and independence, and to change this as we grow over time. The marrieds are locked into centuries of not-so-relevant tradition. They may start their relationships off five figures in debt from a fantasy wedding, pile up six-figure expenses with each child they bear, and then may destroy much of what they've accomplished in an equally costly and time-robbing divorce.

Coupled or not, each one of us is legally single—and because of tax laws we must first plan our finances as singles. This maximizes our flexibility when change occurs, and minimizes the damage when we break up.

We're vividly aware of the preciousness and precariousness of life, of relationships, and of love. This is a lesson perhaps many divorcees wish they'd learned sooner. Think of what it's like to be a divorced man who's neglected male friendships, who poured everything into a pressure-cooker family, who's just been drained financially—and who's now quite alone. Or consider the plight of the divorced woman who has neglected career, poured everything into a family that's now flying apart, amassed almost no assets of her own—and who is now past childbearing age.

By contrast, in gay relationships we tend to keep and develop friendships, make sure each partner has some degree of financial independence, and encourage each partner to pursue his or her own career.

As a result of our fiscally single states, when we do enter into relationships there may be barely a financial ripple. For most of us the state of being single and coupled varies from person to person and from time to time. In one 1970s study of gay white males in California not one of the couples studied were monogamous after five years. Does that make them any less a couple? Not in our world. We may even have stronger financial relationships with our friends—and our lesbian or gay brothers and sisters—than we have with our lovers.

Although we're high on independence, we're weak on structure. We may have an opportunity to custom-design that structure, but we run the risk of never really putting it in place. Lacking financial and legal structures, when the time comes that we are ready to go from Me, Inc., to We, Inc., it's up to us to uncover new ways we can frame our love for each other and commit to each other financially.

Without imposed structures gay relationships are easy to start, modify, change, increase, decrease, separate, or end. Our *flexibility* enables us to transform our relationships as we change. It is this flexibility that allows us to support, nurture, and multiply each other's assets and offset, question, and perhaps change our own liabilities. This is why our coupleships are more like corporate diversifications, instead of straight mergers.

Our coupleships promote a natural diversity and flexibility that can make us balanced economic partners with little financial fallout when the relationship ends.

Gay Socialization

We tend to grow up isolated as compared to our highly socialized straight peers. To escape that many of us gravitate in mind or body to urban centers and the gay zip codes. Beset by high urban prices and low entry salaries, these gay immigrants economically become gay roommates. In rooming with the same sex we may eventually settle down with, we've already begun relationship 101 and have started to experiment with financial sharing arrangements. This is a sharp contrast to the still-prevalent segregation of straights before marriage, and generates two financial advantages:

• We may have already learned quite a lot about same-sex living by the time we settle down in a committed relationship.

• We may have developed a number of financial relationships of varying degrees before we commit. Our partnerships don't have to do it all, and we may have a wider range of potential financial support.

The potential financial advantages of our relationships don't end there. Take a look at the following characterizations of gay couplings to see what hidden benefits may already apply to you:

• More flexible, we may be better at restructuring the relationship around new assignments and promotions. We have to initiate ways in which to keep the relationship alive while apart.

• Without the costs of marriage we can see how our relationships might work before we commit to them financially by moving in together or merging finances. We do need to mark developmental points in our relationships—though copying the heterosexual models of dating, engagements, betrothal, and anniversaries may not be suitable to our needs.

• Our relationships have more freedom to change, making it possible for us to grow into them rather than grow out of them. Financially this means we need to talk about joint responsibilities more explicitly.

• If our relationships run out of steam, we're less financially bound to keep them going. We do need to guard against smoothing over rough periods simply by spending money.

• Without massive financial disruption resulting from a breakup, we eventually are more likely to keep some form of financial relationship with our past lovers.

• We are less likely to have one partner dominate joint finances. We benefit, however, from having one partner take the lead in different areas.

• We're more likely to have separate finances, though the union may grow stronger if we merge finances steadily as the relationship grows.

• By not putting an extraordinary emphasis on family, we have more of a chance to create other emotional and financial ties through friendships and an extended family of choice.

Economic Experimentation

Experimenting with our relationships includes trying out new financial arrangements as well. Copying heterosexual models without reworking them can be as big a mistake as leaving our relationships so loose, they may never get anywhere as financial support. We are free to plan our finances in ways that married couples might never imagine.

▼ ▼ ▼

Joan has known Al and Pete throughout their long up-and-down relationship. All three decide to buy a country house—a dream all wish—reasoning that having Joan as a financial partner will stabilize at least the real estate aspect of Al and Pete's relationship. It does, enabling all three to build longer-term plans with the emotional security and continuity that the house now provides.

▲ ▲ ▲

Gay relationships are prime opportunities for helping each other economically. We bring all kinds of economic facts to our joint table and the more enterprising among us are successfully inventing ways to do more with them.

▼ ▼ ▼

Dan and Dave live separately, but they're lovers. They move in together. They create a joint bank account. Dan starts a consulting practice out of their apartment. They start joint accounting of expenses. Dave makes the down payment on a country house that Dave pays the mortgage on. They start a joint investment plan. When Dave gets downsized, Dan covers half the cost of a two-

year graduate degree program. Upon graduation Dave opens up a public relations practice also out of the apartment. As their practices mature and succeed, both spend increasing amounts of time in the country—and start exploring having a retirement place in Mexico by taking annual trips there.

▲ ▲ ▲

Never have I reviewed the finances of gay relationships where the patterns were the same—if they were liberated from heterosexual copying. The key seems to be spotting areas of mutual advantage to emphasize practicality. Historically this isn't so strange; marriage was an economic alliance long before it became an emotional one.

Although there's no telling which came first, couples I've worked with who achieve a working economic relationship that involves some significant degree of interdependence seem happier. They seem to take joy in creating something that has a life of its own. Diversity and flexibility may also spawn a sturdy adaptability to new circumstances that might otherwise push the relationship to the breaking point.

▼ ▼ ▼

Alice and Libby decided to take an economic break when Libby recovered from breast cancer. Libby went on long-term disability benefits, Alice gave up her massage practice, and they made their summerhouse livable year round. They've developed a new life as temporary retirees where they can enjoy each other's company—and Libby's family, who live in nearby towns. Alice has begun taking on new clients, and Libby's talking about an electronics repair service based in their home. Their level of income is lower by a third, but so are their expenses, and the quality of life they've achieved is incomparable to the rat race they ran in the city before.

▲ ▲ ▲

Many of us have learned to manage both emotional commitment and sexual experimentation. This may introduce change that in a straight marriage would be grounds for divorce but, for us, can point to a new way for the relationship to grow.

▼ ▼ ▼

John's ex-lover Ted has AIDS. Ted's ex-lover George, who came after John, is still living with Ted. John decides to leave his job and care for Ted along with George. He uses the free time as well to launch a new career that enables him to commute and eventually move to the gay resort area where John lives. After doing this John and George decide to buy a multiunit home where Ted can also live to further integrate their larger caring family economically, physically, and emotionally.

▲ ▲ ▲

We should also be ready to let some of our little experiments fail. If our economic arrangements aren't usually identified with the relationship itself, and if their focus is usually fairly narrow, those failures won't have to sink the ship and may even lead to better solutions, or at least deeper understanding.

Our adaptability can lead us to embrace widely differing financial goals, styles, and circumstances in our partners, and to make these work through the principle of complementaries: the wealthy falling in love with the poor, bankers coupled with thespians, accountants with artists, and professors with investment bankers. This diversity promotes growth.

▼ ▼ ▼

When Bruce and Peter met, Bruce wasn't working and Peter's job was in hotelry. Both were new in AA and grew considerably in their first two years. Peter supported Bruce while he was in therapy. In the course of their recovery both eventually undertook serious career testing and participated in career remodeling programs. Bruce started a consulting practice while Peter realized he scored high off the scale in beauty culture. Bruce financed Peter's retraining and first years with low pay in the city. Then both decided to move their practices to the country. Eventually both

decided to return to the city several days a week after getting their
practices under way.

▲ ▲ ▲

Financial Stages

Financial looseness characterizes many gay relationships. Most of my clients discuss as "roommate finance" the idea of maintaining detailed accounting of who pays what to whom, choosing instead to keep a mental calculus of where each stands that leaves room for easy economic separation at any point in their relationship. But relationships do evolve over time, and I've noticed distinct stages along my clients' ways:

Roommate Finance

Basic interaction is usually focused on a joint checkbook and/or credit card that gets supplied regularly by both partners, to pay rent, utilities, cleaning, and basic transportation. In these relationships things, toys, and travel are purchased separately.

Joint Finance

Here the couple moves on to joint economic projects, such as putting a partner through school or buying real estate together. Unless the couple has a written agreement about the specific purchase, they're sowing the seeds of a potential financial crisis.

Merged Finance

Here the couple has their names on everything and has moved on to joint investments, in collectibles, the market, or a business. Such a couple definitely needs a partnership agreement that details their holdings and outlines what would happen to them in case of illness, separation, breakup, or death.

Planned Finance

This is the most overlooked and more productive way a couple can work together financially. They tally their expenses so they know where income is going. They estimate how income will grow. They debate income and spending patterns without regard to whose income or whose spending it is, looking at their union as an economic unit. They project how they'd like to change income and spending over the years ahead, and only then do they look at what individual roles and actions they could take to make that happen. What makes this process superior is that the overall picture is the focus—and a great deal of room is made for individual roles and actions to change as things develop. This is clearly the case where two heads are better than one.

Celebrating Commitment

Gays are reinventing both the purpose and the form of that straight tradition, the wedding.

• Financially our commitment ceremonies make a great deal more sense—they're simple, straightforward affairs, of very little cost.

• Our ceremonies usually commemorate a commitment already achieved, not a contemplated coupling. We celebrate the relationship, not the promise.

The five-figure expense of weddings these days handicaps straight couples right from the start with debt and financial worries—not just their families. It's no surprise that money is often cited as the issue that most of the 90% argue about—yet few of my clients report arguments about money.

Having a commitment ceremony is an excellent trigger for signing a written partnership agreement. This is about the time when such an agreement would be appropriate—and without the ceremony, it often just won't happen for lack of a trigger event.

Should We Marry?

As we'll see in the following chapter, we have few tax reasons why we should marry, and can gain significant tax advantages if we're savvy.

Even the main tax advantage for marrieds—the unlimited marital exclusion—is a mixed bag, as it often promotes sloppy estate planning with expensive tax bills down the line. Financially we can do without the costs of marriage and divorce. Economically our relationships can be highly productive partnerships. Advocates of marriage who look beyond the hype will see: financially, it's the great heterosexual booby prize.

Spouse Protection

If we turn our backs on heterosexual divide-and-destroy divorce, do we have better options to support and protect us if death, disease, or dissolution occur? We do.

Death: Legal Agreements

The chapter on the 60s covers our options here. Suffice it to say that with gays, a will is only a starting point—and often illusory protection. We need much more protection than a will can ever provide.

Disease: Insurance

The chapter on health and the discussion of insurance in the 50s chapter detail what protection we need.

• The most overlooked provision for our spouses is adequate medical insurance. This a major penny-wise, pound-foolish pitfall for gay couples. The worst harm we can do our spouses financially is to short-sheet our medical coverage.

• The second gaping hole in most joint financial fortresses is a lack of income insurance in case of disability—especially for the partner earning the most.

• The third line of defense is life insurance—doubly useful, since it's now a source of cash before as well as after death. Make sure life insurance includes an accelerated benefits clause.

Dissolution: Partnership Agreements

What do we owe our partners financially if we break up? The standard legal solutions that would be provided by divorce would be as financially disastrous for us as they are for the 90%. What we need instead are partnership agreements.

In the beginning stages of a relationship it's true that we don't need ceremonies or contracts. We use those first years to experiment and get to know each other's style with little formality.

As time goes on, it's helpful to protect what we've created from the changes wrought by time, from outside events, from our own emotional bad weather. The financial side of our relationships is contractual whether it's written or not. These contracts should be part of every commitment ceremony.

Happily we have access to good, ready guidance in this area. NOLO Press (see Notes and Resources) has long recognized our need for help. Its guides, *A Legal Guide for Lesbian and Gay Couples* (Hayden Curry et al, eighth edition) and *The Living To-gether Kit* (Toni Ihara and Ralph Warner, seventh edition) have stood the test of time.

Sooner or later we reach the limits of self-help. But guides like these will have prompted us to generate our own ideas of what we want. Because we define our relationships in a very tailored, custom way, forms may not be enough. At that point an attorney experienced in gay legal issues will be needed to make it legal.

What do we write down? A first step is to look where we invest our emotional energy. Ironically, if we have pets, start there. According to gay attorneys this is the one area where tens of thousands of dollars are spent in litigation. Endless anguish can be avoided by an agreement written when both parties were loving, had vision, and were sane.

▼ ▼ ▼

Joe went to his attorney since his lover had cleaned out their apartment and had taken their dog. During the appointment it became clear that Joe was willing to give up the furnishings and electronics. But the attorney had to abruptly terminate the meeting because Joe started sharing his plans for a hit man to ice the lover and recoup the pooch.

▲ ▲ ▲

Take the same precautions for pet objects. Save receipts for jewelry, furnishings, appliances, electronics, and renovations. Agree on a depreciation or appreciation schedule in a buyout agreement. Or adopt a fair-rules auction technique for divvying up the goods.

Keep two copies of everything, but not in the same place, in case of fire—or in case the fire goes out. This is what safety deposit boxes and lawyers are for.

If there are unequal resources or income flows, it might be a good idea to compensate for this with agreements that equalize these disparities gradually over time.

▼ ▼ ▼

Alice has a right to a condo conversion. Her love Deb has excess funds. They struck an agreement whereby Deb made the down payment but Alice was given a percentage of the potential profits that was high in the beginning but through a sliding scale made them both equal after about ten years. This agreement let both acquire something neither could have done alone.

▲ ▲ ▲

With houses and businesses, titling is everything. Yet often it is an afterthought or never updated to reflect changing realities. Consult tax and legal counsel on title transfers to check out the tax implications.

We have a luxury problem with titling. The 90% are subject to common property laws in many states. We're not. We have the opportunity to tailor these important decisions to what we want and not have them made automatically for us by a state statute.

The key is to create partnership agreements that foster partnership. Such agreements are reminders of love when tempests hit. They help us map a joint course with minimum interference from emotional weather. They are concrete measures with which we can literally build a foundation for our relationships. Each provision they enshrine can be a testament to our love.

▼▼▼▼▼▼▼

Gays and Taxes:
Can Gay Advantaged Mean
Tax Advantaged?

▲▲▲▲▲▲▲

Taxes are another area where being gay gives different values to our cards in the personal financial deck. In taxes these cards come into play only if we're two at the table, but since our inventive definitions of what's a couple are limited only by our imaginations, we have more opportunities to play the tax code to our advantage.

Since the IRS recognizes only marrieds as legal couples, the tax system can produce very different results for us. This is true for any unmarried couple; the issues are simply more pronounced with us, and the inequity of our tax penalties is more glaring.

Keep in mind that tax issues have a wealth bias. You have to have surplus income or savings to enjoy any real tax savings. Many of these issues impact only the wealthy. If we've been managing our gay money, we should at least already have enough of a savings surplus for these issues to impact us directly.

Let's look first where we're at a disadvantage and then examine where our differences can be parlayed into tax advantages. Please note that nothing in this book should be considered tax advice, and that specialized tax-counsel is needed when we're trying to use the tax system in ways for which it wasn't designed.

With taxes we're dealing with an artificial world created by legislation and regulation—a world that can change with the stroke of a pen. One of the best tax moves gays can make is to keep abreast of tax policy and practice. You can be sure we're going to figure highly in changes ahead, for better and for worse.

▶ Tax Disadvantages

Their Marriage Bonus

It is true that the traditional single-income marrieds with children are favored by the tax code. But that animal is a dying breed. Most couples now both work, putting straight couples at a disadvantage with the way the current tax code is written.

Congress may also try to confer new tax advantages on couples who pay their children's college bills, which in turn may be taken into account by the colleges and result in greater tuition increases; so it goes in playing the tax game. Legislatures may from time to time propose tax bonuses for having children.

The Shortcomings of Financial Software

The ads look good and the software works, but *family* finance programs may not handle typical situations for gay couples. The programs are based on the IRS's notion of a family—and we are strictly single in the eyes of the IRS. While programs can create separate financial statements, they have no way to portray a consolidated statement for unmarried partners that is not geared to marital tax provisions. Software is currently oriented toward a *legal* joint *tax* unit as the basis for household finances. Neither family financial software, asset management software, nor tax planning software allow two unmarried-yet-joined gays to have separate *and* joint financial records and goals. When queried on correcting this glaring gap, manufacturers have responded thus far that we're too small a group.

While we need software that can deal with our special agreements or arrangements, we can find some value in commercial financial software use. It may not yet address all of the tax ramifications of our relationships, but it can help track our spending and manage our investments nonetheless. Just don't expect to do joint planning with it.

Joint-Ownership Pitfalls

Desperate for some recognition of our jointness, some of us rush into joint ownership as a solution, only to discover serious tax complications later. Home buyer beware.

The most common misunderstanding in joint ownership involves deciding who can take the deduction for the mortgage interest. In many expense-sharing arrangements the live-in spouse pays part of the mortgage, even though only the owner of the property can take the deduction. If the property is jointly held, special declarations are necessary for both to benefit from the mortgage interest deduction.

If a partner dies after a purchase made with unequal contributions that weren't rigorously documented, the IRS will assume all contributions were made by the deceased until proven otherwise. If the deceased was in fact the low-contributing partner, the wealthy partner may end up paying extra estate tax needlessly on his own property.

If one of the partners splits to parts unknown, the surviving partner will have full responsibility for the mortgage—and substantial difficulties in selling the property without the signature of the dearly departed. This could last for years and amount to a substantial financial drain.

The Estate Tax Handicap

The most important disadvantage by far is our inability, unlike marrieds, to pass estates tax free to partners. Keep a watch on Washington on this front, for Republicans continually propose doing away with these estate taxes now paid by the top 4% of the population.

This illustration of how tax rules can dramatically change shows why it's important to include tax-law change in the gay agenda. It also shows why we, as society's small x%, may not necessarily get what we want.

The best we can do is to double up on our planning and counsel. Tax is the hardest area of personal finance. It's a full-time job unto itself. It is so complex and volatile that I choose not to offer tax advice in my practice, instead referring people to specialized counsel. While you can benefit from understanding your tax profile, your best bet is to get advice on how to manage it.

► Tax Advantages

Our Unmarried Bonus

Here's one corner of the tax code that clearly benefits the unmarried—whatever their sexual orientation. A married couple that works and is relatively highly paid suffers a penalty with joint filing that they would avoid by filing separately. If each person in the couple has $7,000 in deductions (other than state and local taxes), for example, the tax for the couple as marrieds is about $1,400 more than for two individuals filing separately. If the couple earns $145,000 each, has two children and about $23,400 in allowable deductions (other than state and local taxes), their tax as a married couple may be $12,000 greater than if both of them filed as head-of-household.

The marriage penalty hits especially hard percentage-wise when children are involved and when incomes are low. Let's assume a partner with two children and a partner with one child, with each partner earning $12,000. Individually, each partner can file singly as a head-of-household and qualify for the earned income credit—and get money back from the government. Married, they both lose the credit *and* pay taxes; and the penalty in a low-income credit state could be $4,300—18% more!

The lesson: Our unmarried status means tax cuts that yield extra discretionary dollars—another source of the gay money we need early in life.

Residence Sales after Age Fifty-five

A much more important advantage awaits gays later in life; if we sell a jointly owned home after age fifty-five, *each* partner can take the $125,000 exclusion on gains—for a total exclusion of $250,000—while a married couple can only take a single $125,000 exclusion. Of course, politicians may eventually eliminate capital gains taxes on all sales of principal residences, spreading this benefit into the straight world.

Domestic Partner Benefits—a Real Benefit?

Another emerging tax issue for us is that of domestic partnership benefits. These look good politically but may not pan out financially. Few of us realize that these benefits are reported on the employed partner's W-2 as extra taxable income, or that the benefits can be loaded with expensive child-rearing features we have to pay for but would never use.

There is one silver lining. If the receiving partner can pay for the coverage and is self-employed, that payment is an allowable tax-deduction in full—as long as this is done in the year the benefits occurred. This is a good example of how the tax code can work both for and against us in ways that are unpredictable at first glance.

Deducting Payments to Each Other as Helpers

Our differences can truly become advantages in the area of entrepreneurship. Transactions that are prohibited or nondeductible for marrieds may be permitted for couples like us, since we're considered to be operating "at arm's length" by the IRS. A helper-partner may help out regularly enough to be paid. These payments are deductions to the business and may transfer money from one highly paid business partner to a partner in a much lower tax bracket.

If the help is enough to be considered the equivalent of full-time help, salaries and benefits for both owner and helper can be very generous. If there are more than three employees, benefits can often include disability and life insurance at very cheap rates.

Just keep in mind that the IRS can scrutinize payments against standards of reasonableness and apply standards of equity as the payroll expands. Expert advice is always recommended. In addition, a good rule for judging the wisdom of our arrangements is never to do things purely for tax reasons, but rather to structure the financial dimension of what we do to maximize tax advantage.

Income, Asset, and Expense Shifting

Because the IRS treats us as singles, we can decide beforehand who in a couple would benefit taxwise the most by paying for deductible expenses (e.g., business travel, books, computers) and who could absorb extra income at a lower effective tax bracket (e.g., rentals, investments).

There are many gray areas where a wealthier partner can redirect income to a partner with lower income but gift taxes must be considered when transferring assets. And remember that since the transfer must be with no strings attached, the level of trust required to do this must be profound.

Technically some say that an unequal sharing of living expenses may constitute a taxable gift, but in practice this is rarely challenged.

Sales between partners of hard-to-value items where there are few market guidelines (such as artwork, rights, and business intangibles) can be a mechanism by which value can be transferred without incurring a gift tax in the long run. A privately held business offers similar opportunities where valuation may be determined to mutual advantage of the buyer and seller.

Gift Tax Considerations

We all have a federal estate exemption that currently amounts to $600,000. When we die, if everything we have adds up to less than this exemption our estate doesn't owe federal tax; if it's more, the federal estate tax rates are mind-bogglingly high.

The most common—and most often forgotten—way to keep our taxable estate down is to gift up to $10,000 per recipient, per year. If we have gifted more, that amount is deducted from our $600,000 exemption. So we need to be careful that we don't inadvertently make gifts over $10,000 to each other—which literally may come back to haunt us if we die.

If we do need to transfer assets over $10,000, we must file a gift tax return, even though no tax is due at the time. When the giver dies, all these amounts given will be deducted from the $600,000 exemption, effectively lowering it *and* increasing estate taxes if the estate is worth more than $600,000.

In any federal or state estate tax considerations of this kind, seek tax counsel. Don't use tax counsel culled from a book.

Interest Deductions on Third and Fourth Homes

A gay couple in love with real estate is wise to have the purchase of a third home be made by the partner who can still deduct the interest on the mortgage from taxes—rather than pile them all up on one wealthy partner for whom the interest on a third mortgage wouldn't be deductible.

Arm's-Length Rentals

Under some special circumstances a same-sex couple wanting country and city homes might buy them separately and rent them to each other instead of owning each property jointly. Assuming this is organized as a bona fide and not a sham rental, the city condo-owning partner would rent from the country house-owning partner—and perhaps, but not necessarily, vice versa.

Each partner now potentially owns a rental property on which can be deducted maintenance, grounds, upkeep, cleaning, and inspection visits up to the income received, depending on choices about permanent residence. If the property has fallen in value and is sold after being a rental, even the fall in value is a deduction against the capital gain.

Further areas might be possible where a low-income but asset-rich partner rents assets needed for the business of an income-rich partner, creating a deduction for the latter and transfer of income. Again, such transactions should be undertaken only on the advice of a tax professional—preferably a tax attorney with whom client-attorney privilege over confidential information applies.

▶ Dependent Determinations and Medical Expense Deductions

Taxes can also help couples facing disabling illness when every tax dollar saved counts. Because partners aren't usually recognized by public authorities, the sick partner can get public assistance, food stamps, Medicaid, or programs that pay for pharmaceuticals and medical insurance premiums regardless of the other partner's income.

When its numerous requirements can be met, it may be worth it for one partner to claim the other as a dependent. Even if the dependent partner receives disability income, it's still possible for the wealthier partner to pay for nonreimbursed medical expenses—and to claim them as deductions (as long as they're in excess of 7.5% of income.) The healthy partner can even pay a small stipend of less than $200 a month to a disabled partner without its resulting in a loss of benefits. If a higher amount is paid as a *charitable* income, this will both create a deduction and transfer income to a lower tax bracket that will not impact Social Security Disability Income (SSDI).

In addition to income, asset, and tax status differences, we can play age differences in our coupleships to tax advantage, especially if life-threatening illness is in the picture. An example of where this works is in the use of the charitable remainder trust in May-December relationships. If the younger partner has AIDS, the IRS will use life expectancy tables that ignore the foreshortened life, permitting great tax savings. See tax counsel if this is a possibility.

In general, none of these tax maneuvers is a sure thing for do-it-yourselfers. These are just examples to show that even with disability and seeming impoverishment, there are deductions and public entitlements to be gained because the government refuses to recognize us as couples. Get help, and get to work.

▼ ▼ ▼ ▼ ▼ ▼ ▼

Unmarried with Children: Financing Parenthood

▲ ▲ ▲ ▲ ▲ ▲ ▲

Few investments compare with our growing opportunity to parent children—and virtually none tax our finances more. Let's see what our special financial requirements are, and how we can meet them.

Legalities

From a legal point of view it is never a simple process for a same-sex couple to get a child; whether the child comes from a previous marriage, artificial insemination, a sperm donor, a surrogate mother, or adoption, legalities alone can amount to a five-figure expense.

For this reason, the so-called gay baby boom of the 1980s and 90s has involved only about ten thousand gays by current estimates. However, our rights are increasing in this area, and we can probably expect to see far more parenting in the future. Keep in mind, however, that most gay parenting is being done by lesbians by an estimated seven-to-one margin.

Single-Parenting

The biggest legal drawback to gay parenting has been the rarity of joint or second-parent adoptions for gay couples. This has meant that one parent in a couple was often without rights in case of breakup, sickness, or death. The exception had been California, where joint adoptions had become almost routine until the

1995 reversal of the Department of Social Services policy that allowed them. Now unmarried Californians have to go to court to achieve the same thing—a costly, lengthy process.

Under the terms of standard single-parenting, the breakup of a gay couple can permit the biological mother to remove the child—no matter what agreements have been written or how many years a gay partner has spent parenting and paying for a child. There simply is no established way for the courts to recognize the rights of parents other than through divorce or proof of fatherhood.

Second-parent adoptions, on the other hand, offer the major practical benefit of qualifying the second parent's insurance to apply to the child.

Prospective parents should refer to the NOLO legal guides for gays, referred to in the chapter on gay couples which have extensive, updated model documents for all kinds of situations—and background information.

Alternatives

The most difficult situations are faced by gay men, who must rely on surrogate mothers who can refuse to relinquish their child up to the very last minute, no matter how much money has changed hands.

A common theme in adoption is that of complication, cost, and delays. Healthy white children are virtually impossible to adopt. Many agencies are reluctant to allow adoption across racial lines. Adoption in foreign countries is full of risk, with handicapped babies switched at the last minute for the babies chosen.

Children from previous marriages raised in an openly gay relationship are still the object of lawsuits and court barriers.

Estimates

Raising a child represents a six-figure investment that authorities agree probably costs the middle class about $450,000—according to a spate of studies that appeared late in 1996. This is little different financially from launching a new business, since you don't know how the business will turn out in twenty years.

This is why it's wise to set ourselves up as a board of governors of this joint enterprise. Our first task—legal safeguards or not—is to assure child support for those twenty years. Our agreements will be tested by circumstances hard to imagine and impossible to predict. All we know is what any parents know: that we will have no claim on that child once he or she has grown up, and that one day we'll be simply the founders, with truly intangible gains to show for our efforts. Such an enterprise deserves a business plan; not the simplistic structure of marriage-and-divorce and not just a partnership agreement or child-support agreement.

Costs

The first thing to do is to get support with other parents, if only as a cost measure. The most vulnerable shopper in marketing-savvy America is a new parent who's afraid to do anything wrong. By virtue of our relative inexperience, we fit that bill in spades—and it's hard to break the pattern by which the first child gets top-of-the-line merchandise from day one.

It's a given that the child will run most of your financial decisions for the next two decades, from what kind of investments you can make to where you can live. The yearly bill for children is fairly stable—from a minimum of $10,000 per year to a more likely figure of $20,000 per year. The lost-opportunity costs are almost never included in these figures. Figure in either not working or paying for custodial care. Baby nurses can run $100 per day, and child care averages a minimum of $4,000 per year to nearly twice that in San Francisco. A nanny in New York for a fifty-hour week runs $25,000 per year alone. Nonreimbursed medical expenses are the terror up to school age.

School-district quality becomes a determining factor for where you live, no matter what the level of taxes. The cost of houses in good districts may be double those where school statistics are poor. Suddenly you have to become an expert on school quality. It may be cheaper to keep kids in private school, especially if moving is difficult. This is the kind of decision that requires up to five years of advance planning.

During school years medical expenses often drop but discretionary expenses more than replace them. And you've just acquired another full-time job: family chauffeur. The 1990s have added a new category—computers and cyberspace—to traditional ways to keep kids busy after school. Summer camps can easily run in the four figures up to about $6,000 for eight weeks of bliss. Then comes dental work and another four-figure expense, braces.

About this time tuition costs start to loom even larger. Clothing, feeding, and special events top the list in the meantime, with Sweet sixteen parties and bar/bat mitzvahs approaching the cost of weddings. This assumes that your kid has stayed out of trouble, hasn't required a child psychiatrist, and hasn't run afoul of the law. As college gets close, special tutors and SAT prep courses keep costs right up there.

College claims about one fourth of the total investment. Manipulating finances to qualify for some financial aid will be worth it. Another bit of good news is that after years of 7, 8, and even 16% increases, tuitions have now "moderated" to increases of 5 to 6% per year.

Security

Child support between parents whose union is unrecognized in civil marriage is simply too uncertain. Agreements for support should definitely be reviewed by attorneys.

It's tempting to save money in the child's name. First examine the financial-aid policies of schools the child may be applying to. If you're in a very high tax bracket, you probably won't qualify for financial aid—and you'll realize significant tax-savings by shifting income to a child under fourteen. If you're in an average tax situation, the school will absorb most of the child's savings, and you may miss significant opportunities for child aid unless you keep the funds in your name. This situation is complicated by the fact that elite schools now give financial aid to high-income families. And all this may change again in 5–10 years. This example illustrates the financial complexities you'll face as a parent.

Timing

Personal finance is all about uncertainty and time frames. Gay parenting can't do anything about the uncertainty, but gay parents can plan when to have children. The worst thing gays can do for themselves and the child alike is to have children too early. Finances need to be in shape well before having children. This means being able to save through the 20s and build careers through the 30s. Financially, the ideal time for children is as late as possible.

We're all getting older, and our health in later years is rapidly improving. There already is a trend toward older parenting. For the financially savvy gay parent, it's the smartest approach to take.

▼ ▼ ▼ ▼ ▼ ▼ ▼

Gay Careers: Fine–Tuning Your Money Machine

▲ ▲ ▲ ▲ ▲ ▲ ▲

We get money through jobs; we manufacture it through careers. Jobs enslave; careers empower. Jobs hire out our time, skill, brawn, or brain; careers reward our choice of interests and values. We're vulnerable with jobs; we're independent with careers. Jobs are spent time; careers are invested time.

The most successful careers are those that get the farthest away from mere jobs—brains or brawn for hire. The name of the career game is to generate value; to get those we serve to pay us for the value we can generate. When we start out, that value is merely our time and effort; when we finish it's evolved into something so unique, so valuable, that our time and effort have little to do with it. This vision of what a career can be is our gay money machine.

Our Only Money Tree

In the gay garden we have to work, because we have few other traditional ways to get money.

• We can't count on family money to bail us out. Older generations may still look on us as "that peculiar one without children." We're sometimes disinherited or often get the short end when it comes to legacies. We often walk out of an insufferable family—and we don't often walk into a family business.

• Few of us are nonworking spouses, or alimony-supported ex-spouses.

• Even our AIDS and cancer survivors end up with bills, not an inheritance. It was commonplace to say up to 1990 that we were the ones who didn't need life insurance; then when it was needed, it was hard to get. And most HIV positive/negative couples in my practice see life insurance as an invaluable asset to be used while the positive partner is alive, rather than as launch money for the survivor.

So work is it: *the* cornerstone of gay finance. Putting it in place means clearing many hurdles.

Our Timing

If our life's work remains at the jobs level, all we face is a jumble of jobs that never gel into a career. Without families to support, and with street skills to fall back on, we can handle this for a decade or two. But after a while age catches up with us, and we realize that job jumping is a game of youth—about the same time that the world notices, too, and demands we choose between just-a-job and a career.

A career is a living thing that changes with us through our decades.

• In our 20s it pays for us to explore, to push the envelope, to spend time abroad, to see what we and the world are capable of.

• Many like to settle down in the 30s, sink roots, and build—invest, refine, and boost the horsepower of the money machine we discovered or created in the 20s.

• Our 40s find many of us taking a longer-term look—and often changing course. For gays this may be our best time to get out from under a single authority, and to depend on many clients rather than a single (possibly homoignorant) boss.

• Our 50s can bring together health, experience, endurance, and direction in a powerful production decade, generating cash and value in virtually all that we do. The question in this decade is, are we doing it for ourselves—or for someone else? While we may have landed on our feet if dropped from organizations earlier, a fall now can destroy our delicately wrought money machines.

• In our 60s we get another chance to turn our lives in a chosen direction, with the choice of our life's work unfettered by demands of income—probably the freest of our gay lives.

• Our 70s may see us again hard at work, but this time it may no longer be for money, for others, or even for ourselves, but for something bigger than ourselves that we've come to love and value.

Does it always work like this? Of course not—but these are the elements we have to play with, the raw material and the fundamental formulae of our careers. Now let's look at those hurdles we must clear to get our careers off the ground, and make them soar.

▶ Gay Career Hurdle #1: *Job Discrimination*

What's stunning is how rarely career is mentioned as a personal financial tool in personal finance books. Yet career manufactures not just money but cheap insurance benefits, tax-deferred income possibilities, paid perks, and retirement protection. For us it's also as or more powerful a socialization process for the 90% as the teens, providing contacts, information, and values.

For this reason it's important for us to be able not only to anticipate discriminatory situations, but to assess the strength of our opportunities or our opposition so we can make work work in the short run and maximize it in the long run.

Careers, corporations, and heterosexuality have been intertwined for centuries. The family was the unit of work until the industrial age. The family farm is part and parcel of family-values myths. The post–World War II era, in which the corporation, marriage, nonworking spouses, and kids seemed a seamless combination, became the American Dream—after the war's nightmare.

And where were we in all this? Until Stonewall gay men survived in America either by denying gayness or by taking non-straight jobs. A four-year survey done for the National Institute of Mental Health just before Stonewall showed that more than 85% of the public felt that gay men should be allowed to be artists, musicians, and florists—and 70% beauticians. Fewer than a third felt that gays should be government officials or doctors, and fewer than a quarter felt that we should be ministers, teachers, or judges. Lesbians, like all women, have to deal with the fact that until World War II it was not felt proper for women to do "men's work" at all. Although feminist strides have been strengthened by equal-opportunity legislation and women's rising salaries, corporate America's governing ranks are still virtually free of women, much less open lesbians.

The Forms of Discrimination

Some of us don't know when we're hit with discrimination, much less how to respond. Some common forms, and successful defense strategies, include:

• We're not hired. Response: Identify gay-friendly companies, mobilizing every contact available.

• We're isolated. Response: Consider the feminist career literature and its exploration of the kind of subtle career blocks we face, and be prepared to move on if it's clear the time has come.

• We're badly managed. Response: Network the possibilities for transfer, and avoid sharing our emotional baggage with bad bosses.

• We're not promoted, left to hang, or paid with promises. Response: Insist on a transfer, get training, and have another job ready.

• We're assigned to bad jobs in bad units. Response: See if we can make lemonade out of the lemon and make ourselves a star—or assess how bad it is and get out fast.

• We're evaluated poorly. Response: Avoid wishful thinking and read the writing on the wall, for few superiors will take the risk of going against an appraisal once it's in writing.

• We're laid off, fired, or downsized. Response: Assess options from day one of any job; amass a war chest or knit a safety net; negotiate as much as you can as your price for leaving; and get the hell out of there.

Career Coping Strategies

We work around discrimination in several ways—some successful in the short run, others in the long run. See which of these you've already tried, and which hold promise for the future.

• We stay in safe gay occupations. This is a time-honored tradition—except you'd better take into account the fact that many of them aren't as gay anymore. They're now also among the toughest occupations to practice as employees—and no picnic as the self-employed.

• We stay in the ghetto. It's jumping in the same place—and it's a dead end. Remember: our early years are critical. The majority of ghetto jobs are usually poorly paid, offer few benefits, and have little future. The best time to go gay careerwise is in the 50s, when we have something to offer, have security, and are entrepreneurial.

• We freelance. This works best in the 20s, and it's usually downhill from there. However, some professions, such as writing, are organized on a freelance basis, offering considerable upsides to those who master their opportunities. When this works it's really a variant on being an entrepreneur.

• We jump jobs. This is another great 20s technique that wears thin with time. This is what freelancing can become when we shy away from making it a real business. Consider regularly changing careers instead. Properly planned, each career can synergize with the others, setting you apart. You'll end up with many money machines, in case one breaks down.

• We seek staff jobs. This is a great 30s technique, especially if it can be parlayed into a consulting job. There's no better way to build skills, contacts, and knowledge. Beyond the 30s this risks sidelining us, unless we convert it into an entrepreneurial consulting practice or become part of senior management in a Merlin-type role.

• We seek war-zone jobs. This is a risky but rewarding 40s way to show our stuff—and blast through any kind of ceiling on a corporate career. When it doesn't work, the downside isn't terrible; it was war, after all. But plan it as well as Patton would, and don't underestimate your enemies within.

• We work extra hard. This time-honored tradition works well all through our 50s, but we may end up with great careers and lousy lives. In olden days it may have been the only way; but today it's a choice we need to consider very carefully. The problem is similar to other addictions: we constantly have to increase the dosage, and we may overdose.

• We specialize. Now we're getting sophisticated in our strategies. The crucial mistake is painting ourselves into a corner that's made technologically obsolete. This happens when we focus on the technology instead of the skill. And remember: employers have come to distrust irreplaceable people—but they love service.

• We invent. Who cares if we have creative genes—we come from situations with all the makings for creative outlooks. Let's not ignore that a large number of us innovate in very significant ways. If we take this path, we need all the hired help we can get—and we may not be very happy or effective managers of the enterprises we spawn.

• We get many bosses. The most reliable solution for work dead-ends is diversifying our risk by making our bosses our clients—and getting a lot of them. P.S.: This is called "entrepreneurship," as discussed in the 40s chapter. By taking this route we keep the risks and costs of transition as low as possible. This is where we get to choose our own professional extended family—of clients, employees, suppliers, advisors, and funders. These smaller corporate families are being replaced in the 1990s by the corporate clan. If we play our cards right we get to sell our own corporate family to one of them.

• We get paid for capital. Ah! Don't forget to recognize that investing is our second career—as laid out in the 30s chapter. All that savings has been multiplying so fast that managing it becomes our primary concern. After all, that's what money is: value distilled from work—our ultimate job.

▶ Gay Career Hurdle #2: *Income Discrimination*

The bottom line of discrimination is that we simply earn less money. This is almost totally obscured by the fact that the discretionary part of our incomes is much larger because many of us have no children. As producers of total income we're poorer; as consumers with greater discretionary incomes we look rich.

Lesbians seem to earn slightly more than most women, but share the gross income discrimination against women in general. Gay men seem to be paid somewhat less than most men, but share the gross income advantage of men in general.

Our Discretionary Income Advantage/Handicap

So we're rich in discretionary income. And our magazines have promoted that image to sell advertising. But that doesn't help our personal finances one bit—for the world now thinks we're filthy rich, period.

Conservatives have been quick to pounce on these partial truths to demolish our protections against—among other things—income discrimination. Even Supreme Court Judge Scalia justified Colorado's Amendment 2's removal of our protections because he said we are a group with "disproportionate political power," "enormous influence in American media politics," and "high disposable income." Does this not recall justifications for past attempts at genocide? The implications are chilling.

While this image can make it more difficult to reach out to other disadvantaged minorities, who now see us as affluent and upscale, even our own politicians have been known to promote us as a rich and powerful group.

The political wisdom of this strategy is less relevant here than the individual financial repercussions. The bottom line is that we probably have no higher than average incomes as men and as women—and most importantly that we face discrimination, period. If few in our community acknowledge this, it's not very likely we're going to try to solve it. But as individuals we can, through the career measures outlined above, through the career actions outlined below, and through the saving and investment of our temporary surplus of discretionary dollars.

► Gay Career Hurdle #3: *Privacy versus Politics*

Workplace discrimination is real, and many of us need protection. Keep this in mind when you're asked to consider coming out at the workplace as a political act.

As individuals our career priorities may take precedence over our political goals, and many if not all of us do camouflage all kinds of personal information at the workplace. Not one of the gay men and lesbians I've advised considers the closet or coming out to be a workplace or financial issue. They want their sexual orientation to be irrelevant at work; they prize their privacy. Let's look at how to weigh the career impacts of privacy and coming out at the workplace.

Clients

What ultimately counts with careers is not employers but clients, the customers who ultimately pay our bills. This is one reason why it makes strategic sense in our work to have as direct a relationship as possible with our clients, and eliminate any barrier to that relationship.

We present a corporate image to anyone who pays us—not a personal one. Business values not who we are or even what we have, but what they want from us, and the degree to which we provide it.

It is in this context that we may want to decide whether or not to be privately or publicly gay; that is, if our clients don't want us to be gay, we have to stay private; if they don't care, we choose to stay private because it's extraneous to the sale; if they want us to be gay, no problem.

Employers

Employers are clients too. Our job is to find out what they value—and to give it to them. The same conclusions for how we treat other clients apply here, although we may have to change jobs or play politics if our employer/client explicitly wants us straight.

Privacy

With clients and employers we're paid to do specific things. Most of us leave huge parts of our personalities out of the job. At work we're paid to perform narrowly.

Most heterosexuals don't think about sexual orientation—not so much because it's assumed but because it's not relevant. They don't ask us to come out; usually they're homouninterested, rather than homoignorant or homophobic. Educating them isn't in our job description.

Privacy means managing information about ourselves so we have our best chance to get the work done. Everyone does that at work, by keeping some parts of private life private there. Few at work reveal more private information than they have to, wisely choosing to reveal only what keeps clients buying and employers employing.

Work has an important social dimension, though it's based on highly selected information. Consider work a *public* social life not to be confused with private social life. What employers and employees really want from the social dimension at work is for things to go along smoothly without personal glitches.

Sometimes employees or an employer explicitly wants us to be straight. If we pretend to be, we're on thin ice; if we keep silent, we're still on thin ice; and if we come out, we may fall through the ice and out of a job. This extreme case is fairly rare. For most employers it's not part of the job description and for most clients it's not part of the product specs.

Whether we come out or stay private, we can never be relieved of the task of managing information about ourselves. That's a one-on-one never-ending job. It's in our interests to manage our own careers and keep them under our control.

In most companies and professions we're not asked to act straight, the personal is truly irrelevant, and privacy works. If the company respects privacy, we've got a workable situation at work.

Coming Out

Work is about profitable action. Coming out, like any other action at work, is only worth it if it returns more value than it costs.

Costs

• Planning: We need to assess what we want and how much it's worth to get. By no means should we do this alone or with just a book. Too much is at stake. We should seek out the support of those who've done it—if possible in our profession, in our industry, and in our company.

• Uncertainty: We can never know what kind of reactions we unleash, or how long we'll have to work the process.

• Messiness: We never come out all the way—just as we're never truly private. We will always have private information we feel others have no right to; we will always have to manage the daily process of protecting or using that information in public situations of all types. Define that beforehand.

• Loss of privacy: Others may interpret our coming out to mean that we can be asked all manner of private questions.

Anyone considering coming out at work should be able to answer the following questions:

Are the company, the job, and our future prospects worth it?

What's our purpose: as a person, as a professional, as an organizational representative, as a gay, as a public person?

Is personal life an issue at work, an essential element in getting ahead? Are there strong pressures toward self-revelation? toward being heterosexual?

Does the company value diversity, especially sexual diversity, because of its policies, personalities, politics, or markets?

Do you have a champion? allies?

What are the follow-up actions, their sequence, timing, cost, and value?

Are enemies known? provided for?

Are there contingency plans for all possible reactions?

And we must consider the possible consequences, recognizing the large element of chance inherent in releasing this information. I've seen my clients become stuck with a new, unintended job of changing their company or profession, educating people at the expense of enormous amounts of time. Reactions can range from either end of the spectrum; all that can be safely expected is the unexpected. Plan accordingly.

Benefits

Properly planned in the right environment, coming out can help a career, on top of its political or personal pluses.

- Our visibility may skyrocket. This calling card may give us temporary access to many more levels in the hierarchy, in our industry, and in our profession. We'll also be able to exploit the increasing network of others who are public gays.

- Low raises, missed promotions, lousy assignments, and poor performance appraisals may now be seen as discriminatory.

- Management may protect us from insults, attacks, and mistreatment.

- We may use management's backing in being more aggressive in competing for raises, promotions, assignments, and titles.

Although some corners of our community insist on coming out at work, it only makes sense at companies and with clients that encourage gays and lesbians to come out, in both policy and in practice. In this context it can actually give us some temporary advantages, while in other situations it simply adds an extraneous element to the economic proposition at hand—the exchange of money for value. Keeping that exchange as clear of interference as possible is key to our career success.

► Gay Career Advantages

The gay experience produces five by-products that can be useful at the workplace: our diversity, networking, specialization, service, and entrepreneurial characteristics or experience.

► Gay Career Advantage #1: *Diversity*

Today's corporate climate is no longer all white and all male. Today's successful corporations have come to realize that diversity is a key to their future marketing effectiveness and product design savvy. Projections show that by the millennium even straight white males will become a minority as well.

To companies that reward diversity—those same environments where we might be encouraged to come out—we represent "diversity squared," in that we tithe our 10% evenly from every population niche. Today's divested and demanding businesses act more like gay extended families of choice than yesterday's conformist pressure-cooker corporate families. We may find that we are more than welcome.

▶ Gay Career Advantage #2: *Networking*

If the gay 1970s were all about sex and the 1980s all about survival, perhaps the 1990s are all about success. One skill is key to all three: networking, a direct by-product of growing up gay. Gays don't need to take courses in networking; we can teach them. Not only do our far-flung personal networks typically transcend barriers of class, age, race, and language, our bonding together in the face of crisis and discrimination has instilled a sometimes strong sense of tribal loyalty. As a result, the line between personal and professional often becomes very thin indeed for many of us.

New gay business, professional, and employee groups are formalizing this impulse to network with each other. As a movement this promises far more to us professionally than individually coming out ever could. We benefit from seeking out these groups if only to use them as models for forming our own. They make networking extremely efficient—although they are still weighted toward lower-level employees.

We still don't have a gay answer to the country club, golf course, and private club, all those places where the 90% make money. But these powerful patriarchal institutions are coming under fire, and the Internet has further democratized networking and may undermine traditional heterosexual inside tracks to employers and clients. Becoming proficient in the Internet is a critical gay career skill.

We can learn from the women who are a generation ahead of us in challenging the straight male hold in the business world. Many clues to successful networking can be found in emerging feminist business magazines such as *Executive Female* and *Ms.* Any gay serious about career should consider subscribing to them regardless of gender.

► Gay Career Advantage #3: *Specialization*

Faced with discrimination, many gays have chosen wisely to specialize. Being highly skilled makes being gay even more of a big "so what?" As work has become increasingly skilled, technocratic leadership has come to replace straight men who held their positions simply by tradition or social position.

To the extent a job is unskilled at the bottom or vaguely skilled at the top, discrimination is much more likely. The more a job is defined by a skill, the better our shot at getting and keeping it. This is nothing new. Gay lore is full of examples where gays pursued skills valued by the dominant society, from the medieval roles of court jester, court advisor, and priest to the practitioners of the male arts of our midcentury—teachers, actors, and the military—to the technocrats of the millennium in computers, communications, and design.

With our discretionary income, the flexibility in our relationships, and our motivation to avoid discrimination, we can often afford to pursue skill building. We can pay for the training; we can take time off for it; and we know that without it we remain subject to the whim of the majority.

► Gay Career Advantage #4: *Service*

We have a long tradition of serving—a safe occupation when you're persecuted. For centuries we've served well behind the scenes, using our invisible networks, our outsider status, and our diverse backgrounds. When you're only 10% or less of the population, and utterly spread out, it pays to study cooperation and collaboration instead of aggression and competition. We've accumulated years of experience in our exile from corporate America in traditional service occupations.

With the advent of the service economy, our time has finally come. We can turn our experience to good advantage. Service is now an essential element in the value added by American business, and it's an element that's glaringly absent or rare.

Now we can serve by choice, not just to survive, and can demand a premium for doing it better. If the world expects that from us, all the better; in business there's nothing wrong with capitalizing on stereotype as long as we do it by choice and it gives us an edge.

▶ Gay Career Advantage #5: *Entrepreneurship*

We live lives on the fringes of social groups, network at all levels, are experienced in running risks, and generally see life at an angle. As is spelled out in the chapter on the 40s, this enables us to perform well in functional, advisory, and consulting roles—and to make excellent entrepreneurs, both as employees and as owners.

Inside companies we can pursue this role as "intrapreneurs" well positioned to survive corporate cutbacks, downsizing, and outsourcing. We're used to the higher risk. Financially we have the cushion of extra discretionary income. Emotionally we have flexible relationships.

Outside companies we can take advantage of the movement to outsource entire departments by spinning them off as independent entities. Nothing should please us more than to have our ex-employer as a first client, among many more to come.

▶ The Gay Career Advantage: A Summary

We have the potential to build truly great careers if we put an early priority on career, avoid being sidetracked into stereotypical occupations, face up to the twin handicaps of potential job and income discrimination, keep politics out of our careers, and adapt our advantages to today's corporate climate. Doing this will have more financial impact on our lives than any traditional technique covered by mainstream financial media.

► Gay Groups

Workplace issues present a task that's much larger than any one individual could handle. Luckily, we have teammates. Three types of gay groups have cropped up to help an individual create a career that respects identity and gives social support in what is otherwise a very lonely workplace. Specifically we'll look at:

- Business groups that gather together employees and entrepreneurs with overall interests

- Employee groups that band together employees in a specific company or worksite

- Professional groups that tie together employees across industries and professions.

► Gay Group #1: *Business Groups*

The first gay guilds, in the 1970s, banded together mostly gay-owned traditionally gay retail businesses such as bars, baths, and the publications that served them. They reflected that era's much narrower definition of what it was to be gay. When AIDS quickly broadened that definition, the bars and baths that provided much of the fund-raising for the community came under attack, and the guilds floundered. Workplace issues understandably took a back-seat to needs imposed by HIV.

In the 1990s new gay business groups have risen from the ashes. They're much more diverse, reflecting an expansion of products and services in the community, and the inclusion of a high proportion of gay employees and professionals along with gay entrepreneurs.

The largest seem to be the groups in New York, Boston, Chicago, Los Angeles, San Francisco, Philadelphia, and Dallas, with no key national or regional grouping of gay business groups as yet. At last count there are approximately twenty-five local groups across the country—probably an undercount, since most groups are happy to stay local. They're worth your looking into; as their mission evolves from charity to self-help, their networking and education opportunities can be powerful career builders.

▶ Gay Group #2: *Employee Groups*

Within today's often widely dispersed corporations, it's increasingly important to network for assignments, promotions, salary information, recognition, and information needed to do a good job. Yet gays have long described feeling like the odd person out at the water cooler, the Friday-afternoon beer fest, the employee picnic, the Christmas party, and other formal and informal social functions—not to mention the country club, private club, golf course, and racquetball court.

Informal employee groups have gradually begun to come out, often meeting anonymously off-premises to share information, compare notes, build trust, and eventually create an agenda of common interests. Reactions have differed widely. But because of the typical baby-step, feeling-our-way approach taken, success has been widespread and gay employee groups are now rapidly forming across the country.

If you know of such a group, make every effort to become a part of it. If there are other special interest groups in your organization, a gay group may be possible. These other groups usually welcome a gay group if only as the canary in the mine—i.e., if management tolerates or welcomes a gay group, the prospects for the other groups are secure indeed.

Such groups create opportunities for gay employees to connect and change as a corporate subculture and to connect with management to change corporate policy. This "intracultural" networking cannot help but enhance performance, promote careers, unearth opportunities, and accelerate progress.

The greatest benefits from gay groups are yet to come. We need benefits to be redesigned; we have special needs and wants. Gays need the redesign of policies that inadvertently discriminate not only against gays but against those with HIV. We need help in navigating corporate life as kin—promoting our careers, sharing life experiences, and making it better for those yet to come.

With the Internet we can truly overcome geographic limitations to our banding together, forming gay subgroups of virtually any other group that exists in America. This is how we will get to know America one-on-one. And each grouping adds resources in terms of people, information, and yet further introductions to our careers. This may be the future of gay organizations: true grassroots groups organized around our concrete concerns of practical value.

► Gay Group #3: *Professional Groups*

Building on the success of the gay business groups across the country, some larger cities such as New York are seeing the rise of special-interest groups among the professions.

New York's concentration of professionals may offer a window on future developments elsewhere. Its Network of Lesbian and Gay Professional Organizations acts a nonprofit fund-raising arm for over fifteen specialized groups—bankers, accountants, nurses, architects, et cetera. Just one of those groups, the New York Advertising and Communications Network, Inc., has over eight hundred members, who use its services for job leads, professional news, educational forums, and an oft-used directory.

Gay groups should also expand by industry, mirroring that mainstay of American business, the industry association. There are thousands of associations in any of the national directories, though none have gay subgroups—yet. It is well known that gay-friendly benefits and policies tend to progress industry by industry. They've started in industries where high-talent and high-tech labor are key: electronics and entertainment. The pattern is to have a pacesetter—and a mechanism for others to learn and follow.

One of the best models for how this can happen fast and efficiently is Hollywood Supports, which started as a single-issue organization offering model policy documents for domestic-partner health benefits. Quickly the entertainment industry aligned themselves with this change: MCA/Univeral, Viacom International, Warner Bros. Studios, Time Inc., Home Box Office, Paramount Pictures. Then HS became a group of employee groups—a cross-industry group with a focus on other personnel policy and benefit issues.

The future lies in some amalgam of the business, employee, professional, and industry groups. This is true networking of the most powerful kind. Indeed, with such close links gays may have access to much more inside information at a far greater variety of levels in a wider assortment of ways than any clubby old-boys' network ever thought imaginable.

► The Gay Career Agenda

At some point gays need to decide, with careers and with our lives, if we want what we think heterosexuals have, or would prefer something new tailored to our different needs and wants. Are we shooting for pacification by a steady stream of improvements that still keep us on the other side of the tracks? Do we want assimilation, to be treated just the same? Or do we dare ask our employers to design jobs and benefits specific to our different needs and wants?

There's no better bellwether for deciding this than with employee benefits—and no better immediate example than domestic partnership benefits. While domestic-partnership benefits are a breakthrough, they're not equal and often aren't ever needed. In our rush for crumbs, we're perhaps forgetting the banquet—and our very different tastes, appetites, and desires. Employees are voting with their feet; in the first company where they were introduced, only ten employees opted for them.

Why are these benefits not a Big or Good Deal?

- Our partners are usually already working and often have their own coverage.

- The benefit allows the corporation to set standards as to what constitutes domestic partnership, without appeal and without standardization.

- Unmarried partners must pay tax on the benefit.

Our Greater Opportunity

Standardized, homogenized, monolithic- and heterosexual-benefit packages are the problem. For years corporate benefits have treated all employees the same way, for both practical and philosophical reasons. Practically speaking, there was no economical, administratively feasible way to treat people differently. Philosophically, many companies—and American culture—felt that "equal" meant "same."

What's missing are the benefits, the motivators, that will attract employees as diverse as we are. Heterosexual benefits don't apply to homosexual people. Yet we have talents that can be tapped, motivated, and developed through special benefits.

As we gain collective strength and individual corporate clout, we'll have many opportunities to negotiate benefits explicitly designed for gays—and unmarried, varied, independent people like us—that will mobilize loyalty, energy, and creativity. Since we have higher discretionary incomes, the best way to motivate us may not be through more *money-based benefits,* but something we can never get enough of: *time-based benefits.* We travel considerably more than marrieds with children. Might we give our employers the 110% they seem to want if they give us more discretionary time? Corporations are already working the time vein through features like flextime. Perhaps we will have the chance to mine this area more deeply; when they really want us, we may well be able to define the terms by which they get us.

Consider structuring yourself a reprieve from the "24/7" workweek that communication technology seems to have in store for us. Financially free gays may respond better to well-paid core positions that cover minimal basic expenses and benefits and guarantee time-insulation—leaving us more opportunity to travel, enjoy vacation homes, and express ourselves in teaching, writing, research, entrepreneurship, and community service. Why else have gays with low fixed expenses traditionally flocked to such seemingly low-paying professions as teaching, the theater, and the ministry? Because the benefits were full-time, and because of their time flexibility and freedom.

If gay employees have suffered past discrimination, we may be able to get companies to consider redressing the balance through programs that build identity, positive image, and social support. This can range from recognition of employee groups, allowing them to meet on company time and on company premises, and giving time off and corporate resources to gay pride events. Companies like AT&T gather their gay employees together from across the country regularly. If asked, we'll let companies know where the snubs come from and where invisibility hurts. As the slogan says, Use fights abuse—so when we take the initiative, we can at times prevent the subtler forms of informal discrimination that sometimes emerge in response to a formal change in company policy. Policy changes alone won't do the trick.

Recognition, already a powerful motivator, is doubly so when it has been blatantly absent. Companies can let it be known that spouses will be included in phone lists when requested, with whatever title they have chosen. The welcome, accommodation, and reimbursement of expenses for spouses for new hires will add "walking the walk" to talking the talk—at company functions, in moving expenses, and in relocation allowances. Companies can offer sabbaticals to work in local service organizations of the employee's choice and matching funds to gay charities or their inclusion if we are excluded from community fund efforts.

► Gay Careers—*Your Plan for Action*

The foundation of your financial life, your gay career faces significant hurdles, but can also benefit from your unique advantages. Take all of these possibilities into account as you ponder your career path. Some questions to get you started:

• What financial needs and wants do I have now—and will have in the future? What kind of company environment do I want to work in? What criteria of gay-friendliness are important to me? What industries, professions, locations, and specific companies meet those criteria?

• What hurdles do I face in my present career and job? Can I keep my gayness private? Do I want to?

• What special advantages have come out of my gay experience? How networked am I? Have I focused my career in an area of specialization? What part does service play in my career? How committed am I to my career? Would I be interested in intra- or entrepreneurship? How good would I be in those roles?

• How can I best invest my discretionary income in terms of my career? What kinds of career investments can I make if I have the money, the need, the desire, and the flexibility?

• What kind of job, career, and company do I want in each decade ahead? How do I see my career evolving over the decades of my life?

• How does a relationship and friendship fit into my career? Do I want and/or would I get the kind of recognition of the person I love through my career or my company? If so, how? If not, how do I compensate for that?

▼ ▼ ▼ ▼ ▼ ▼ ▼

Notes and Resources

▲ ▲ ▲ ▲ ▲ ▲ ▲

Life Stages and Life Planning

Since the changes wrought by age are largely ignored in financial planning—perhaps because everyone assumes a heterosexual family with 2.5 children—going back to the sources can be invaluable:

- Erikson, Erik. *Childhood and Society,* New York: W. W. Norton, 1963 ed., Chapter 7, and Erik Erikson, ed. *Adulthood,* New York: W. W. Norton, 1978.
- Levinson, Daniel J., et al. *The Seasons of a Man's Life.* New York: Alfred A. Knopf, 1978.

For a journalistic overview and speculation about later decades see:

- Sheehy, Gail. *Passages.* New York: E. P. Dutton, 1976.
- Sheehy, Gail. *New Passages: Mapping Your Life Across Time.* New York: Random House, 1995.

Spending and Simplicity

Because getting a handle on spending is a crucial skill for gays, it's useful to survey the literature on voluntary simplicity. One organization in particular has directly laid out an approach for translating saving into freedom from having to work for pay, The New Road Map Foundation. See their audiotape course and workbook entitled *Transforming Your Relationship with Money and*

Achieving Financial Independence, available from P.O. Box 15981, Seattle, WA 98115, or their founders' book, *Your Money or Your Life,* by Joe Dominguez and Vicki Robin (New York: Viking, 1992).

Health

What happens healthwise in adolescence impacts money issues through all of our subsequent decades. An excellent summary can be found in: Smith, S., and L. McClaugherty, "Adolescent Homosexuality: A Primary Care Perspective," *American Family Physician,* Vol. 48, no. 1 (July 1993), p. 33(4).

Most of the figures in the text come from these excellent overviews of gay health issues:

- "Health Care Needs of Gay Men and Lesbians in the United States." (American Medical Association Council on Scientific Affairs.) *JAMA, Journal of the American Medical Association,* Vol. 275, no. 17 (May 1, 1996), p. 1354(6).

- Cotton, Paul, "Gay, Lesbian Physicians Meet, March, Tell Shalala Bigotry Is Health Hazard," *JAMA, Journal of the American Medical Association,* Vol. 269, no. 20 (May 26, 1993), p. 2611(2).

- Schatz, B. and K. O'Hanlan. "Anti-Gay Discrimination in Medicine: Results of a National Survey of Lesbian, Gay and Bisexual Physicians" (San Francisco: American Association of Physicians for Human Rights, 1994).

Since alcoholism is both dangerous and ignored, these articles give solid figures:

- Herbert, J., B. Hunt, and G. Dell, "Counseling Gay Men and Lesbians with Alcohol Problems," *Journal of Rehabilitation,* Vol. 60, no. 2 (April–June 1994), p. 52(6).

- MacEwan, Ian, M. A., "Sexual Orientation Not Considered in Treatment Planning." (Adapted from *Drug and Alcohol Review,*

Vol. 13 [1994], pp. 57–62), the Brown University *Digest of Addiction Theory and Application,* Vol. 13, no. 10 (Oct 1994), p. 2.

Because lesbian health issues do not get proper attention, simply getting studies about it published is a step forward:

• Denenberg, R., "Health and Homophobia: Perspectives for the Treating Obstetrician/Gynecologist." *Current Problems in Obstetric Gynecological Fertility,* Vol. 18 (1995), pp. 93–136.

Career

Once we've identified what we want to do, our next priority is to identify best companies, available employee groups, useful organizations, and the relevant issues that can make a gay career successful.

Companies

Books continually come out that rank companies for gay employees, investors, and consumers. The first, by Ed Mickens, *The One Hundred Best Companies for Gay Men and Lesbians,* ranked companies by criteria of safety, acceptance, and equality. The second attempt, titled *Cracking the Corporate Closet,* by Daniel B. Baker and Sean O. Strub, was sponsored by the National Lesbian and Gay Task Force. It analyzes companies by twenty industries and presents tables for easy comparisons.

The key is basing the judgment of what's gay friendly on corporate practice, not just policy or opinion. The Wall Street Project (WSP), spawned by CLGRI (Community Lesbian and Gay Resource Institute), the gay incubator of nonprofits in New York City, has as its mission the tracking of gay-friendly companies in the *Fortune* 1,000 and in the NASDAQ 100. A copy of the *Wall Street Project Census of Sexual Orientation Policies of the* Fortune *500 Service and Industrial Corporations* costs $25 for individuals and $125 for organizations. (Make checks out to CLGRI.)

Write for that or for the free census questionnaire from the WSP; 185 East Eighty-fifth Street, Suite 25A, New York, NY 10028; (212) 289-1741; http://www.nycnet.com/wallstproj.

Employee Groups

Although no national association exists, one is bound to emerge. Employees or company groups may wish to contact one of the several regional and statewide associations, including the **Colorado Workplace Coalition;** the **Minnesota Workplace Alliance** (Gay and Lesbian Community Action Council, Sabathani Center, Suite 204, 310 East 38th Street, Minneapolis, MN 55409); **Out at Work or Not** in Chicago (P.O. Box 359, Chicago, IL 60690-0359); San Francisco's **AGOG: A Group of Groups** (P.O. Box 14513, San Francisco, CA 94114); **Progress** (a group of California groups; 10061 Riverside Drive #288, Toluca Lake, CA 91602).

Organizations

Grassroots groups offer little opportunity to get your head above the grass. And local news often can't substitute for national analysis.

The NGLTF has a Policy Institute whose focus is workplace issues, sponsoring an annual conference, and useful surveys. This kind of context-setting is invaluable. You can contact the Policy Institute at the National Gay and Lesbian Task Force (2320 Seventeenth Street, NW, Washington, D.C. 20009, [202] 332-6483 ext. 3302 or 3215). NGLTF publications on-line are at megngtf@aol.com.

The Human Rights Campaign has a Workplace Project (1101 Fourteenth Street, NW, Suite 200, Washington, D.C. 20005; voice: [202] 628-4160, fax: [202] 347-5323). They're particularly good at tracking legislative developments such as ENDA (the Employment Non-Discrimination Act) that may impact gays at the workplace. ENDA proposes to extend federal employment-discrimination protections to sexual orientation.

The ACLU has a National Gay and Lesbian Rights Project (132 West Forty-third Street, New York, NY 10036; voice: [212] 944-9800, fax: [212] 869-9061; Contact: Matt Coles).

Lambda Legal Defense and Education Fund (120 Wall Street, Suite 1500, New York, NY 10005, [212] 995-8585) offers in certain cases to sponsor "impact litigation" and has some literature on issues regarding discrimination at the workplace.

Academically, the Institute for Gay and Lesbian Strategic Studies at the University of Southern California generates research funding to gather the hard data needed to answer such questions as: How much do domestic partner benefits really cost employers? How much discrimination is there? Contact Lee Badgett, voice: (301) 405-6348, fax: (301) 403-4675 or Walter Williams, voice: (213) 764-2508.

Employees wishing to explore policies and benefits for their employers may contact the major benefit consulting firms that track them, such as William M. Mercer (301 Tresser Boulevard, Stamford, CT 06901, [203] 973-2000), The Segal Company (116 Huntington Avenue, 8th floor, Boston, MA 02116, [617] 424-7337), and Hewitt Associates (100 Half Day Road, Lincolnshire IL 60069, [847] 295-5000).

Issues

Workplace strategies for gays can be found in *Straight Jobs, Gay Lives,* by Annette Friskopp and Sharon Silverstein (New York: Scribner's, 1995), *A Manager's Guide to Sexual Orientation in the Workplace,* by Bob Powers and Alan Ellis (New York: Routledge, 1995), and *Straight Talk About Gays in the Workplace,* by Liz Winfeld and Susan Spielman (New York: AMACOM, 1995).

Few national gay publications track gay workplace issues or news. An exception is *Victory!* the gay business magazine ([800] 429-2874 or [800] GAY-BUSI). Write editors to encourage coverage of gay business groups—and gay business issues.

The more accessible, more influential, and more accurate coverage is local and can be found in the regional gay press: *Philadelphia Gay News, Bay Windows* (Boston), *Frontiers* (Los Angeles),

The Texas Triangle (Austin), *Out Front* (Denver), *In the LIFE* (Hudson Valley), *Metroline* (Hartford), and *Southern Voice* (Atlanta).

The best future networking opportunities will be electronic— on local gay bulletin boards as well as America On-Line, CompuServe, and now Planet Out on Microsoft Network. This is where local action and national perspective join.

What's astonishing is that workplace issues have only recently been of interest to national organizations, to academia, to consultants, to writers—and to employees. Like other areas of gay money these issues were just givens in our financial equations— part of the woodwork. Moving them from being assumptions to being issues subject to change is a key to generating more gay money at the workplace.

▼ ▼ ▼ ▼ ▼ ▼ ▼

Acknowledgments

▲ ▲ ▲ ▲ ▲ ▲ ▲

Yes, nothing is new under the sun. But oh those wondrously different combinations we give birth to. Here are the ingredients, fellow chefs, and those who stirred the pot—but remember I carry all responsibility for how this came out of the kitchen.

Lilly Lorenzen who taught me by example the power of ideas, teaching, one-on-one coaching, writing, and the discipline of writing a book.

Jim Gaynor for hounding me to call Suzanne as only a best friend could.

Suzanne Gluck, my agent, who took me in tow with no wasted effort and made it all happen.

Tom Spain, the editor who became a soul mate who became an editor who came to love the book as much as I did, for total trust combined with to-the-edge editing.

Nancy Swenson of The Cornwall Library who leaves Manhattan libraries in the dust and who could get articles from Moscow if necessary.

Mike Stone for being one of the good guys who really understands this stuff, Horst Stipp for seeing through gay market issues, and Dennis Mack for endless hours of rapturous discussion of financial strategy through years of friendship.

David Petersen, guru, cofounder of Affording Care, passionate perfectionist about the financial issues of serious illness, for ruthless training and wonderful arguments.

Tom McCormack, author of the masterful *AIDS Benefits Handbook,* for loving ideas as much as I do and for being willing to work those systems to help our brothers and sisters in deep doo-doo.

Lee Badgett, Mark Kaplan, Joe McCormack, Andy Sherman, and fellow gay writers and thinkers in business for attempting to get research done in this parched field.

Wendy Frank, Bruce Mendelson, Michael Brazin, and Beth Caton for understandings of insurance and disability issues.

Jacques Chambers of AIDS Project Los Angeles, Marty Ball of AIDS Benefits Counselors, Eric Stamm at the Actor's Fund, Body Positive for two years of seminar-making, too many fine people at GMHC, and the exquisitely wrought Friends Indeed.

Kim Calder of American Cancer Society and Karrie Zampini of Memorial Sloan Kettering's Post-Treatment Program for sponsoring pioneering workshops.

Joe Baker for demystifying Medicare and for being there for the long haul.

Mark Scherzer for being the ultimate source on HIV, insurance, and the law; Paul Schupack for patient tutoring; Diane Morrison on landlord-tenant law; and Paul Crockett for seeing the law as financial technique.

Ken Klein of National, Alan Perper of Dignity, Scott Page of Page, Jeff Zadoff of Dedicated, Rhonda Bacci of Viaticus, and the many survivors of the wonderful and terrible viatical industry for getting them to be tax-free, for marveling at creating a truly new financial vehicle, and for keeping the rascals at bay.

Valerie Heller for understanding abuse issues, Larry Harmon for generational issues, Joseph Minola for disability issues, and Jack Amelah for HIV issues in psychology.

The extraordinary AIDS physicians of Manhattan, Miami, San Francisco, Los Angeles, and all in between, including but not limited to Drs. Braun, McMeeking, Montana, Piperato, and Seitzman.

Tax input from Phil Benoit, Jim Krause, Joe Pumphrey, John Schumacher, and Artie Unger.

Ed Mickens, Grant Leukenbill, and Sean Strub, role models and trailblazers, authors, researchers, and Rolodexers from hell.

Tom Smith who backs his love of ideas and our community with grass-roots philanthropy and organization.

Shelley Alpern, Nick Curto, and all the architects of the Equality Principles—may we triumph!

MJ and Thomas McKean-Reich for launching *Victory!*—the gay business magazine—and for giving me total freedom and support.

Laurette Giardino, creator of *In the LIFE,* for encouragement, for my monthly column, and for being an example of courage.

Steve McGuire and Brett Grodeck of *Positively Aware* for giving me as much space as it took to map out the new terrain of the personal finance of serious illness.

Paul Schindler of LGNY for on-the-spot coverage of current HIV issues.

Bruce Wright and the *Advocate* for use of the business column platform there.

And especially those whom I serve who are, of course, our ultimate teachers.